CONVERSATIONS WITH *Adele*

Business Owners' Fundamentals for Success

ADELE RYAN MALLEY

*Former CEO and voice of Malley's Chocolates...
the sweetest spot in town*

SMART BUSINESS® BOOKS
An Imprint of Smart Business® Network Inc.

Conversations with Adele
COPYRIGHT ©2022 Adele Malley

All rights are reserved.

No part of this publication may be reproduced, distributed or transmitted in any form or by any means, including photocopying, recording or other digital or mechanical methods, without the prior written permission of the author, except in the cases of fair use as permitted by U.S. and international copyright laws. For permission requests, please submit in writing to the publisher at the address below:

Published by:
Smart Business Network
835 Sharon Drive, Suite 200
Westlake, OH 44145

Printed in the United States of America
Editor: Dustin Klein
Cover design: Wendy Armon

ISBN: 978-1-945389-01-6
Library of Congress Control Number: 2022911760

My Heartfelt Dedication

My dearest husband Bill stopped breathing on October 19, 2016. Up to that time, we lived a life of riding a bicycle built for two. Knowing our destination, we both pedaled and were as happy as kids in our chocolate and ice cream shop. We developed a keen alliance and a solid partnership; our most passionate collaboration was raising four boys and two girls. Our business was an exciting adventure and our hobby. Bill was my dedicated cheerleader, except when I beat him in Gin Rummy!

We had happiness. Bill made life grand!

XOXO Bill,
Forever grateful,
Adele

Special Thanks and Acknowledgments

For my Adult children and their Spouse and children: Michael (Angela), Hannah and Bill; Bill Jr. (Bee) (Rachel) Madison, Casey, Abbey, Bill (B3); Dan (Melissa) Maggie, Max, and Samantha; Patrick (Packy); Adele (Sis) (Jared); Megan (Tom), Martin, Declan, and Adele; thank you for your affection, good times, and laughter! You are all 100% amazing!

My best friend and trusted sounding Board is my sister Laurie Mooney is thoughtful, generous, and fun.

Our supportive and enjoyable Customers and Advocates have made this book possible.

William (Bill) Schalders was the first person to read my writing. His opinion gave me a heavy dose of confidence.

Dr. John W. Newstrom has written over 47 books in various editions. He lectured all across America and taught at the University of Minnesota Duluth, specializing in organizational behavior. Written with Mary L. Broad, Ph, D, Transfer of Training became my spur to write this book. Dr. John Newstrom is an individual I have never personally met. In answer to an Email from me, our correspondence grew to where he gave me his time, instructing, correcting, inspiring, and critiquing my writing, plus his valued friendship. John, you are so giving, understanding, fun, and such a gentleman! I hope your new Pickle Ball book is making converts to the game. In Cleveland, every age is playing it. (Readers can check it out at Amazon.com)

Keith Ashmus and John Roshon pointed out needed improvements in my storyline.

To Peter Chudyk for quietly supporting me over and over again.

My relatives, friends, Advocates, especially our controller, Irene Bray, my family, interested and enthusiastic, spurred me on.

Dustin Klein, an extraordinarily patient publisher. A+ for being so charitable.

Peter Osenar

Feet on the ground but inspiration up with the STARS.

☆ ☆ ☆ ☆ ☆ ☆ ☆ ☆ ☆ ☆ ☆ ☆ ☆ ☆ ☆ ☆ ☆ ☆

"While aimed primarily at chocolatiers, this is chock full of morsels useful for every small business owner. It reminds us of the importance of forethought, presentation, customer service, and follow-through. Importantly for many of us who may be bashful about claiming the value of our services, it highlights how vital it is that we charge for our products and services--and charge their actual value. An engaging work to which you may well want to return as your business grows."

Keith Ashmus, Attorney, Past Chair of the National Small Business Association

"What you have written is a perfect roadmap for business! I enjoyed that it has the human element of coaching your "Advocates" and the professional."

Ingrid Balunek, Aerial Adventures Advertising

"It's an excellent reference manual for small and medium-sized companies. I would refer to it as a cookbook for starting, building, and maintaining a very successful retail business."

Peter J. Chudyk, CPA, JD, Shareholder Maloney, and Novotny LLC

"Adele starts with her passion for the values and the culture she has created and then tells the reader exactly how to build the structure to deliver "The Malley Experience," using stories to illustrate and reinforce her points. Her advice transcends Malley's Chocolates and Ice Cream Concoctions, which any entrepreneur can follow with her dedication."

Jonathan M. Green, CPA

"It is better than the esteemed Ronald McDonald's Hamburger University. I don't think that even their famed training programs can rival yours for comprehensiveness, detail, and practicality."

John W. Newstrom, Ph.D., Distinguished Teaching Professor of Management, specializing in Organizational Behavior, Emeritus, University of Minnesota Duluth, Duluth, MN.

"A fun read and a great tutorial of a customer-focused enterprise building trust with staff and customers. This book is all about a woman's grit and determination, a woman who saw every obstacle as a challenge and worked unceasingly to resolve it. Wisely, she was never afraid to ask for help when needed. A wife, the mother of six high-energy children, always prioritized - placing family first while partnering with husband Bill in building THE MALLEY'S CHOCOLATE enterprise of greater Cleveland. The company's total preoccupation with the need to satisfy the customer with delight from entry into a store to the final purchase is well detailed - every step of the way. The author explains how to hire, train, and develop staff and coach for success. Her love of family and CHOCOLATE made Malley's a Cleveland icon, and now the next generation is following in her footsteps. In today's harsh competitive environment, all six of Adele's children happily work at Malley's, bringing delight to chocolate lovers near and far. Their blessing is the challenge of continuing to build upon a great foundation."

Peter Osenar is a current member of Malley's corporate board, former CEO of Emerald Health, and former Executive Of AmeriTrust Bank.

"How does a family business thrive for generations in this day and age? Everything from location to lighting lands on the pages of this book with a window into Malley's Manners and the Malley's School of Merchandising. It minds the details, develops employee advocates, and builds lasting relationships with its customers. Success doesn't happen by accident; a strong business plan and the determination of a family like the Malleys, who, for over eight decades, have been bringing smiles to the faces of their customers at more than 20 Malley's stores. The story of Malley's Chocolates is the story of the American Dream – a story that began at a small shop in 1935 and an all-in family effort that grew with the generations. Their recipe for success is like a recipe passed through a family for generations. And now, Adele Malley passes the Malley family business success story at Malley's Chocolates on to you so that you can design your business blueprint and develop and build your business step by step for years in the future. Like a great chocolate bar, savor this book and enjoy every bite of it."

Chris Ronayne, Cuyahoga County Executive & Former President, University Circle, Inc.

"I loved the 'Skillshops.' I especially liked that you went into explicit detail. I loved the history and the background. I would love to hear some stories behind specific rules or tips. Love the numbered lists with the Job Description tips. It is hard to read when a list becomes a paragraph. Lots of takeaways."

Mark Roshon, Tornado Software, owner

"Best I've seen written for *any* company."

William Schalders, Consultant to Business

"You don't have to be a chocoholic to find Adele Malley's helpful book to aspiring entrepreneurs or those who are struggling to grow their businesses. The book is loaded with tips, suggestions, detailed checklists, processes, and procedures developed through several decades of her experience in growing Malley's Chocolates into a dominant confectionary brand in Northeast Ohio. The examples are taken from the candy retail industry but are applicable to any business."

Jeffrey C. Susbauer, Ph.D. Associate Professor Emeritus Ahuja College of Business Cleveland State University

"Adele expertly translates essential leadership skills and core business practices into easy-to-understand principles. Her style and personal insights create memorable references that will stay long after reading the book. Although this is geared towards small business owners, it is a great resource for any leader in any organization. In the first chapter, Adele says she hopes this book provides readers '…with ideas about new ways to improve how you work. 'Whether you are a student, aspiring entrepreneur, or experienced leader, you will find information and practical tools that will help you improve.'"

Donna VanRooy, MBA, ABD

"Growing up, Malley's candies were 'special occasion treats' at my grandparents' home, boxes of Gold Cup mix often stowed-away on a top-shelf in the dining room china cabinet near the good silver for when the company visited. Going to a Malley's, with its family aura of gazebo charm and chocolate festivities, was like seeing Santa's workshop. And anyone who has met or known Adele Malley - even if only through her radio voice as the queen of confectionery and ambassador of delicious aesthetics – has likewise experienced that same warmth and friendliness, a neighborly air welcoming all. It is something that has radiated from every Malley's store for generations and something nearly impossible to replicate. Thus, her new book, articulating her thoughts and strategies on atmosphere and etiquette in an accessible, gently tutorial way, passing along her recipe of how to aspire toward the premium standard of retail presentation, is nothing short of a monumental achievement."

Matthew K. Weiland, Writer/Producer

Get "Malley Manners" now!

Increase your Customer count today!

After completing "Conversations with Adele," I felt compelled to tell you about our System of educating and training employees to become Advocates to help us reach our goals. **Malley Manners** is the place to start for success.

Malley Manners is an Education and Training System that prepares a new hire to be an Advocate, grasp your company values, understand, and be motivated to give the finest of services for their customer's delight. It has been continually used for over 45 years.

Now, you can establish Malley Manners in your company. It works this way:

1. Detailed instructions are all enclosed with the System.

2. Each new hire will receive your company Orientation.

3. Preplanning, Planning, Presentation, and Follow-up is a 45-year-old proven system. Every new hire will receive the same information, and the Retention Review will spot any employee needing retail attention.

4. Acquire the information by tapping on your computer at **www.Malleys.com**. Then, Adele Malley, for further details.

I put the entire "Malley Manners System" in a PDF so information, posters, and more can be quickly and easily copied.

There is so much more to Retail than saying and doing: "Welcome, (smile), get what the person asks for, will there be anything else? (Smile) Good-bye (Smile)."

Increase your Retail awareness!
Find out all about it right now at
www.Malleys.com

Content List:

A Taste of What's to Come 17
Chapter 1 - Beginnings: Pluck & Determination 21
Chapter 2 - Decisions: Belief in Yourself..35
Chapter 3 - Investigation & Considerations 43
Chapter 4 - Determination: Can do, Will do......................................53
Chapter 5 - Job Descriptions: Standards 69
Chapter 6 - Connections: Relationships 81
Chapter 7 - Discipline: Control 85
Chapter 8 - The Basics 101
Chapter 9 - Display Presentations, Creating, and Refilling 145
Chapter 10 - Compliance: Accountant 161
Chapter 11 - Financial Decisions..169
Chapter 12 - Assistance: Board of Advisors 193
Chapter 13 - Adjustments/Achievements: Consequences..................209
Chapter 14 - Retention Review Practices 219
Chapter 15 - Hierarchy of Responsibilities for a
              Beginning Business 225
Chapter 16 - The Power of Skillshops..245
Chapter 17 - Why Bother with Small Talk? 251
Chapter 18 - How to keep your best Advocates................................257
Chapter 19 - Make it lively...Make it cheerful...Make it exciting...
              Use LED Lighting 267
Chapter 20 - Plans and Opportunities: Thinking about the future......277
Chapter 21 - Retirement Preparation 283
Chapter 22 - Surprise, Surprise!..297

A Taste of What's to Come

   Hi! My name is Adele Ryan Malley, Chairman emeritus of Malley's Chocolates and Ice Cream Concoctions, Owner and Director of Malley School of Merchandising, in Cleveland, Ohio.

   Beginning Retail entrepreneurs, or those who entertain the dream of owning a Retail store will benefit from reading this book. It is also a catalyst for those who are driving growth or a spur to get back on track. You will read about our systems that can excite you to new possibilities or help you open your first store. These pages will explain to you why Malley's Chocolates has won many trophies and awards. "Candy and Snack TODAY" magazine inducted me to be their first retailer to join their Hall of Fame. How exciting is that! With my late husband, William (Bill) Malley, (6-6-31/10-16-06) "Cleveland Magazine" added our names into their Business Hall of Fame. Indeed, an honor.

   You will be introduced to a slice of retailing, telling how to manage a near spotless store, how to create product displays that attract and produce sales, how to create a store that is the chosen store for visiting and buying. You will learn the most critical job of a Store Manager. Learn how to get the help you need for harmony, growth, and steps to retirement. Write a practical job description and know its full use; be familiar with how to discipline correctly and get results; understand why you must have two files for every member of your company. Get financial matters in shape so you can be more relaxed. Learn of how my husband Bill and I developed Malley's Chocolates into exceptional Retail Stores.

Right now, create effective, friendly advertising and recognition for your store. Commit to two known functions for retail success: 1. Work with your Manager to hire individuals that smile, are able, and flexible with a desire to represent you by understanding and following instructions. 2. Further store distinction because of these same individuals developing friendships with customers which quite naturally leads to bonding, being the result of practicing exceptional customer care. Friends will hear directly from their friends praising their experience in your store. There is no better form of advertising, recognition and valuable recommendation; you can't buy it, but you can earn it. With your personal, permanent commitment focusing on communication (the key to all things successful), use an uncomplicated, different, more thorough concept to training, we call Malley Manners.

This responsibility cannot be handed off to another, the entire company has to know just how fully committed you are. You do not necessarily have to be the instructor but you must show evident interest, ask questions and follow up in some personal way that you are comfortable doing. It can be visits, a hand-written note, an email, your signature in Advocates Progress or maybe popsicles for everyone because of a comment heard; leave your signed business card telling of a good something seen in the store.

It has been proven time and again that if the Leader does not stay involved it becomes evident to your Managers and other Direct Reports. Soon the entire effort goes down the proverbial drain. Why should they stay involved if the Leader dosen't care? They have other things to do. Finish what you start, your future depends on it.

John W. Newstrom, Ph.D., has written over 45 books, lectured all across America, specializing in organizational behavior, considers my training and education approach as, "It is better than the esteemed Ronald McDonald's Hamburger University. I don't think that even their famed training programs can rival yours for comprehensiveness, detail, and practically."

Keep this book nearby, consider it a Buddy Book. Make notes in the margins; use a highlighter or Post It notes to call attention to a page that has an idea you want to refer to again. It will be easy to find when you want it. Reap your investment. Don't let this book sit on a bookshelf or on a pile of papers in an unused chair. Out of sight, out of mind. Decide to use at least one suggestion and make a commitment to develop it.

After all it's for your future.

This book has the potential to excite you with real-world, can-do ideas to assist you now, and as you grow your business. Are you up for it?

Adele Malley
July 2022

Chapter 1
Beginnings...Pluck and Determination

In 1934, my dad, William John Ryan (who was called Will), explored the risk and then bought a wholesale meat business. My mother, Adele (Daisy) Ryan Spittler, was an educated homemaker. She was plunged into becoming a business person in-charge after my father died in 1949 at age 44, just 15 years after the two of them said "I do." It left Mom, who had celebrated 35 birthdays with four children ages 10 to 14, an outstanding bank loan and $7,000 in the bank.

My mother decided to operate dad's wholesale meat enterprise, and how to care for the four of us. This sudden change was right after World War II. It had to be difficult for my mother. It was at a time when most women hadn't thought of continuing or even starting to work outside their home, let alone be thrown into operating a meat business in an all-male rough-and-tough wholesale meat environment with little knowledge about how it worked.

With her calm nature and determined courage, Mom took charge of dad's business—and she accomplished what she set out to do. In retrospect, this God-depending mother came to a new life. After adjusting to her initial shock, we four kids saw her stake out her place as an energetic businessperson while very much staying a fun, loving, and organized mother. She calmly took complete control of us and the business (although that took a little time.)

At dinnertime, having no one else to share these conversations, Mom told the four of us descriptions of her business day. Those stories were fascinating. While telling us what she was experiencing—new associations, bottom line cares, and simply how she was doing day-to-day—another dimension of my mother was blossoming. After Mom became somewhat comfortable at operating the business, she taught the four of us the very basic responsibilities and discipline associated with operating a business and a home.

Starting in the 6th and 7th grades, we girls had to contend with the laundry, clean the house, change the beds, and have dinner on the table every night when Mom returned from work. In the beginning, it wasn't always a Martha Stewart experience, but my mother made sure we practiced, practiced, and practiced some more. The boys had all the outside duties, and they soon were working every night after school. We lived on the west side of Cleveland, Ohio, and the boys delivered the west side restaurant meat orders each late afternoon. When they were finished, they washed the station-wagon—inside and out.

Mom showed us how to be creative with business growth. During her leadership, she added retail sales to the original wholesale transactions, got involved with the stock market, more business activities and decision-making. For a while, we were all interested in how pork-bellies were doing.

One day, years later, when my brothers were about 25 and 26 years old and working with my mother, she told me as close as Bill and Rich (Dick) were, they had very strong opinions as to the direction of corporate growth. She had been looking at a new business opportunity and realized purchasing the business might just be the cure for her sons' peer competition. The acquisition was made, and after a while the boys made their decision: Bill stayed with the meat business; Rich opted for the new enterprise. This new operation was interesting as it catered to the steamships that supplied ore to the steel industry in Cleveland. My sister Laurie, one year younger than I, spent her time between two hospitals, working with patients and their families. This position accompanied an active political life supporting her husband, who for many years was an Ohio State Representative. He was also mayor of Fairview Park, Ohio.

As for me, I worked with Rich and did the bookkeeping. Office Manager was my first official title in the business world. I "managed" me. After training, two nights a week and all-day Saturday, I taught at John Robert Power's School of Self Improvement. We taught women to become more confident and comfortable with themselves.

Mom put all four of us through private high schools and colleges. We were very close to her. This God-depending, thoughtful lady metamorphosed to a new life. God asked mom for more, and in response, she did her unmitigated best.

What a woman!

What desire!

What pluck!

From Mom's example, I saw and experienced the personal drive it required to reach a goal. More than once, in the beginning, we saw mom crying at the kitchen sink. Other times, she was so tired she hardly wanted to talk. Still, my mother found the energy every night to call us together and say the family rosary. We felt close and knew we needed to look out for one another. The simple fact is that we were comfortable being together.

I watched Mom's graciousness and enthusiasm with everyone. I often saw her help a homeless person by giving him a job, like sweeping the long main entrance to the meat cooler, and then being able to get a dinner next door at the food counter. She made everyday things enjoyable, and I never heard her speak ill of another.

Mom depended on God to see her through life's woes. We all knew she kept a 50 cent coin tucked beneath the robes of her Sacred Heart statue. She kept His statue on top of the file in her little ancillary cashier's office in the frigid meat cooler to meet her customers and be more aware of the activity.

All these years later, I can still see her after work, locking up and walking to her car in the beam of the street and car headlights, braving the cold whiplashing winds down East 4th Street. What was she thinking about as she walked along?

I remember her telling me of her disappointment in not receiving what she thought was going to be a slam dunk order from a particular organization. She told me to "Never depend on anyone to back you. Everyone lives in their own world with their own mindsets, and they don't think of the situation you may be experiencing."

Even so, she was very disappointed; it was a sad learning experience.

Beginnings...Pluck and Determination

Every business and salesperson experiences ups and downs. "Up" days are easy to handle. It's when everything you try to do either gets no customer reaction or a different kind of problem develops that is even more challenging. Mom showed us that going for your goal isn't all fun, being full of energy, or good times. Sometimes merely finding the determination to try again is a chore. Every day is not going to be a sunshiny day.

Instead, we learned the main mind set must be "WIN": What's Important Now? Coach Lou Holtz, once the coach for the University of Notre Dame football team drilled these words into his players. When a problem presented itself, they were taught to think, "WIN. What's Important Now?" After a while, it became second nature for the players to not hesitate to think about what just happened, but rather to jump to what needs to be done.

Understand, if you are following the creative thinking process, this very day may be the 'important' day to rest your mind and take it easy. Tell your subconscious mind you need to find an answer for this challenge. Name it. Remind yourself of it again before bedtime. Let your subconscious continue to work on the answer. Tonight, do something entertaining, like take a walk. Go out for ice cream or play cards. Simply let your subconscious begin to work.

You know you have it in you. Why? Because you are reading this book. So, grab the energy you are showing and do something with it. Relieve yourself of the scared feeling and take a different approach. Go over your list of customers, read about how to be a salesperson, and then call a few customers utilizing your new knowledge. Meanwhile, call for an appointment with your banker, accountant or a University/college business department Dean. Explain why you need help and ask for assistance to review your figures, and then set up a calendar of goals. Attend a business affair presenting a topic you are interested in and want to improve. Re-read your business plan and choose one item to investigate further. Then choose another. Soon you will be ready to take your next step on your way to business success. You realize your situation. Get help when you need it. That's your job. Do it.

In the 1930s, my in-laws, Albert Martin and Josephine Haley Malley (known affectionately as Mike and Jo) were loving, intelligent, generous and enjoyable parents. They were good company, too! During the Great Depression, they moved to Cleveland from their hometown of Meadville, Pennsylvania. They had two children, William Michael (Bill), and Helen Ann (Helen).

Once settled in Cleveland, they hoped Mike would be able to sell more insurance policies. However, that idea was not successful, and he became a flavor salesman. While traveling one day, he spotted a small store with a "For Rent" sign in the window. With Jo's enthusiasm, Mike rented the store and followed his dream of becoming a chocolatier.

They were thrilled to receive a $500 bank loan, which was used to move from their apartment and also add ice cream to their chocolate offerings. Not being able to manage two rent checks, their apartment and the store, they decided to move into the store's stockroom. Downstairs, they put in a shower, and for Mike, fashioned a little kitchen. In the store they installed a soda fountain, five swivel stools and three small tables with chairs—all bought second-hand.

Mike had four things going for him: an agreeable and enthusiastic wife, a decision to use only the finest quality ingredients, a new hot plate, and passion.

He made his chocolates in the basement on that hot plate while helping to keep an eye on Bill and Helen. Upstairs, Jo was busy with "house" keeping and waiting on customers who either wanted chocolates or one of Mike's ice cream concoctions. Jo's business sense helped the pair build their reputation by paying invoices on time and making all the different vendors happy. Jo's personality endeared her to customers. Many became friends; all loved Mike's chocolates, and the business grew steadily. Bill once recalled a time when he was seven years old and stood on a wooden crate to wash dishes when they were busy.

Both sets of Mike and Jo's parents made it known they worried about their lifestyle. As it was, they lived in the store's stockroom. The two hung clothes lines to demark "rooms," and then hung sheets. I have no idea how they summoned the patience to live in such close quarters with two small children. Four years later, they rented a house. Not long after, they purchased their own home.

Bill's college years at Miami University in Oxford, Ohio, were interrupted by being called to serve in the Korean War. He returned home to operate his family's business, which had continued to grow. After his father retired, Bill and his brother-in-law, Bill McConville, who was married to Helen, shared the company's reins. Bill McConville was an assistant to dad before he was called to the duties of war. He was very patient and was a natural in the kitchen with dad. They really enjoyed working together. Bill Malley enjoyed people, marketing, and

Beginnings...Pluck and Determination

organizing, and he was blessed with an inherent ability to work with numbers. His hobbies were his family, the business, the stock market, baseball, and reading business and autobiographical books. He also liked Sudoku and statistics. Bill was a master for remembering dates, numbers, people's names, and places. He liked silly things, too, which helped with the kids.

Bill had a very creative mind for advertising and how to use assets well. He enjoyed mind puzzles and figuring out new ways to do things that helped the company grow. Bill used his strengths wisely, and his stock portfolio usually outperformed the S&P 500. His stockbrokers told me he was one of about five people in his age group who still figured out what stocks to buy. Most others used a financial consultant to help and guide decision making. Bill did an excellent job, and every morning I awakened to the sound of the whirling adding machine and to see my husband Bill's happy face.

Bill and I welcomed four boys in five years. After nine more years, we welcomed two girls. It was like the girls had five fathers with all the love and attention they received.

If you are a part of a family business, you do whatever needs to be done. Bill and I were no different. During our early years together, we worked many holidays, assisted with production, decorated the store, merchandised our chocolates, and did all the things you probably do, wish you were doing, or can't seem to get to "doing." I made large decorations from home during the children's nap-time and in the evenings once the children were in bed, or during the weekends when I could hire extra helpers. Christmas, Valentines and Easter time were our big holidays, and we worked with eagerness to make them as successful as possible. There was no second chance. What small business retail store doesn't have a need or a want around the holidays?

Some years later, Bill and I created our Design Center. It led to Malley's not only becoming known for the finest chocolates, but for truly delicious chocolates gift-wrapped with creativity for presentation. That idea took off, and created new work, new helpers, and new thoughts.

In addition to a regular week, Helen and Bill McConville worked in the kitchen on Saturdays and Sundays, preparing for the holidays. Their children helped, too. Their daughter, Mary, later joined the company. She became my assistant and her organizational skills, and hard work, became apparent. Soon, she oversaw all the retail stores. Outgoing and social, Jim was an outside salesman and helped grow fundraising endeavors; while composed and dedicated Patrick was our Controller. Their other children, Tom and Ann, elected to pursue careers as adults outside the business.

Back in those days, we still waited until Thanksgiving to decorate the store for Christmas. We had a great Thanksgiving holiday trade selling handmade mints, roasted nuts, and chocolate hostess packages.

I would decorate the store for Christmas on Thanksgiving morning. Afterward, I'd arrive home and relieve our dear babysitter, Mary Ellen Brown Cozad. I'd awaken one or two of the boys from naps, dress the boys in their party clothes, get them in the car with Bill, and we were off to visit my mother. Then, it was "over the river and through the woods," a favorite drive along Lake Erie that brought us to Thanksgiving dinner at Bill's parent's home.

After a delicious meal, Helen and I made the kitchen spic and span and enjoyed some quality time with the folks. Soon, I started dressing the four boys in their pajamas for more playtime, then got them into their winter coats, and off to home we'd go.

We had been preparing for the holiday season for weeks, so we naturally greeted the joy of the Christmas season personally . . . and for the business! We were officially into our customers' Christmas rush as well as our children's views of what might be terrific for Christmas: lots of presents from Santa and mom and dad!

Despite having similar ambitions, Bill and I were never in each other's way; we preferred to control our own areas. Having mutual goals also made parenting six children flow well. As a result, four boys in five years were greeted with love and happiness: Michael (Mike), William (Bee), Dan, and Patrick (Packy). Almost nine years later, we all celebrated the arrival of a precious baby girl, Adele (Sis). Twelve months later, we positively celebrated the birth of her treasured sister, Megan. We were so happy—four boys and two girls.

All six of our children grew up knowing what they had to do every day. At dinner, however, it was not the time to check up on their responsibilities. Bill and I wanted to relax and enjoy being with the kids. When we were especially angry about one of their shenanigans, this restraint was very difficult to do. It's hard to keep steam in a bubbling kettle.

I soon became interested in creating a program for Malley's Chocolates that allowed customer Advocates to experience more insightful education and training in the care of our customers and each other. My first program to complement what we were already using developed into an audio cassette package accompanied by a workbook with its own information. To further refine our customer care, with my Managers we developed Skillshops, which taught 52 short-but-effective lessons I felt everyone should know. A plan was developed on how these lessons could be accomplished which required no additional funds, no extra-special time set aside for full staff education, and that used, in-house educators. This book is going to share some of those lessons with you.

Although we enjoyed working together, Bill and I promised each other that at the end of our respective 65th birthday year that we would retire, which is exactly what we did after working together for almost 45 years. Bill was a gracious, loving, high-spirited, true gentleman. Against his will, he broke the cadence of day-to-day life. We were married for 58 years before the guy I always got a big kick out of died on October 19, 2016. How fortunate is it that we had so many blessings—health, example-setting parents who were wonderful and generous, loving childhoods, siblings, each other, six healthy children, truly lovable sons- and daughters-in-law, the freedom to practice our religion, and lots of friends. And, all of it was topped off by being citizens of the United States.

Like most people, we enjoyed helping others. I still do. We met many good friends by donating time to various Boards of Directors and being active in school and community affairs. Our adult children have similar interests.

Some of our community board activities were LifeBanc (which educates the public on the need for donor organs and procurement); First Federal of Lakewood; The United Way; The Greater Cleveland Growth Association (now Greater Cleveland Partnership); Council of Smaller Enterprises (COSE); the Edward M. Muldoon Center for Entrepreneurs at John Carroll University; the Notre Dame College of Cleveland; and alumnae and alumni concerns.

At the Retail Confectioners International (our chocolate industry association), Bill and I both became president of the organization—but 10 years apart. I followed Bill and was voted in as the first woman to manage the lead in more than 60 years.

The KeyBank advisory board, Emerald Civic Society, Fairview Park Recreation League, and the Lakewood Chamber of Commerce were among other worthy organizations that gave us more than we gave them.

I have always kept my eyes and mind alert to learn something new. I wanted to learn from others. I never went to meetings without a question needing conversation. I figured out who would be attending that I thought could help me. The time away from my desk was just as important as being at my desk but in a different way, there is so much to learn, not just in verbal information but by watching and attentive listening. To attend a meeting unprepared is something I tried to never do.

Our family became ardent supporters of LifeBanc in response to receiving the gold standard of spectacular gifts—a donated tibia bone. This marvelous gift was used to replace the tibia in our oldest son Mike's right leg after a car accident. The doctor who cared for him was the renowned Dr. Arthur Stefee, who at that time worked at St. Vincent Charity Hospital in Cleveland. Dr. Stefee is known for his advances in orthopedic surgery and aftercare. Through his expertise, he saved Mike's leg by inserting a donor's tibia bone into his leg, which allows Mike to walk today. The tibia bone came to Michael from an unknown deceased individual. It was harvested by the "Bone Bank" supported by Lifebank. It's essential to know of them because, if necessary, they might be able to help you someday. www.lifebankusa.com   .

Eventually, Mike became an invited speaker on their behalf and later was asked to join their Board of Directors. Bee (Bill Jr., our second son) and I have educated and spoken about LifeBanc to countless groups through the years. LifeBanc personnel presented us with their first Crystal Award for our efforts in innovation to raise funds for their important endeavors. Before accepting a request to speak about Malley's, we always asked for permission to speak about LifeBanc and a donation to further their cause. Our family is forever indebted to the unknown individual who so enriched Mike's life and ours.

Our boys joined the Big Brothers Organization and developed friendships with their assigned "little brothers." They included the boys in activities, took them to Mass, out to dinner, and straightened out some of their shenanigans. The boys enrolled five boys and one girl in Pennsylvania's famous Milton Hershey School. The boys are now adults, and they have all remained friends. One son gathered contributions from generous individuals to install an in-ground pool at the Christian School on the west side of Cleveland. A group of Dominican Nuns answered a big, "Yes!" when asked to knit each boy residing at the Christian Home their own afghan when the home had but three to share. The boys received a baseball mitt and ball. Did you know baseball mitts designed for players who use their left hand to catch a ball than those who use their right hand are more expensive? The boys now know how to wrap a mitt with rubber bands and sleep on it to help "break it in." They each received a suitcase, so they did not have to transport their clothing in black plastic bags when invited to visit someone's home.

The "little brothers" depended on our boys for many things besides "activities." As the boys became adults, friendships continued. The oldest of the four brothers, who graduated from Milton Hershey School, manages 12 stores; others were introduced "about" and hired for business. One joined the security team at the House of Blues and The Rock and Roll Hall of Fame. Another has joined the Air Force. The boys gave them their time, always a listening ear, a second-hand car to supply transportation, money when needed, and lunches were not uncommon. The four boys enjoyed a "reunion" at our house. They had not been together in two years.

Another little fellow grew to be a big fellow (six-foot, nine inches) has stayed in contact, has a fine job, is married, and has a daughter and a son. Our second son, Bill Jr., known as Bee, presently has a new young "brother." He is an appealing young fellow, as were all the boys we met through the Big Brothers Program.

In 2002, Bill and I purchased Bill and Helen's share of the business. A 60,000-square-foot kitchen and manufacturing/assembling plant on six-and-one half acres supplies our delicious chocolates for 19 retail stores, Corporate, fundraising, and Internet businesses. They are all owned and efficiently operated by our six adult children.

Today, Malley's Chocolates is a third-generation operation. According to the Family Business Institute (www.familybusinessinstitute.com), only about 30 percent of family businesses survive into the second generation, and 12 percent are still viable into the third generation. Malley's continues the march forward, improving established systems or producing new ones.

Michael is Chairman; Bill and Patrick (Packy) serve as Vice Presidents of Corporate and Fundraising; Dan is Vice President of Marketing; Sis (Adele) Malley Johnson is Vice-President of Food Safety and Quality Assurance FSQA; and Megan Malley Cannon is Vice President of Retail Sales. News: I'm coming back into my writing to tell you of two new adjustments: Megan Malley Cannon decided to return to her previous career of twenty years and spend more time with her family. Patrick Malley (Packy) retired and is going to join the Peace Corps.

As a business grows, it demands more. They need to continue to create and develop their visions and advancements. It's the continuing repeated effort or attention and care in the right amount that create the successes of systems.

   I am retired, and my husband of 58 years, Bill, died on October 19, 2016. We had fun years together. I would do almost anything for him and it was definitely a two-way street. I loved him dearly. Another tag for us is that we are both Chairman Emeritus of Malley's Chocolates and Ice Cream Concoctions. Jack Malley, Bill and Helen's cousin, should receive a special thank you for dispensing smiles, encouragement and concoctions for more than 40 years at our Lakewood, Ohio, chocolate and soda-fountain store. Jack trained and educated countless "Soda Jerks". The term "Soda Jerk" has an interesting background. The term came from the action the fountain attendant made when pulling the soda draft arm. This jerking motion led to reversing the phrase "jerking the soda" and became "Soda Jerk". While the date of its origin is unknown, popularity of using the term began in the 1920s. A Malley's Soda Jerk is usually a youth who serves at one of our fountain stores for the purpose of preparing and serving our famous Hot Fudge Sundaes and other flavorful concoctions. A soda is made by putting flavored syrup into a specially designed tall glass, adding carbonated water and, finally, one or two scoops of ice cream. It is served with a long-handled spoon most commonly known as a soda spoon and straws for sipping. A Soda Jerk is a time-honored title. Dad Malley trained and educated his first Soda Jerks by telling them, "Make it like you are making it for yourself. Then you know it will be good." It is still honored today.

   Before Bill died, after decades of work and dreams, we shared one final profound joy in the summer of 2016. Our five adult children who were operating Malley's Chocolates announced their plans to welcome their youngest sister, Megan, into the company. Megan had worked in the television industry in California as the head set decorator for CSI Miami and Bones, two successful television series. As much as she loved her work, Megan wanted better hours so she could spend more time with her young family. She was always passionate about our company, so with her husband Tom in agreement, they and their three children drove to Cleveland.

   Why do I tell you all this backstory as a preamble to explaining how we built ever-evolving systems that served as the underpinning to a successful family business? Because only 12 percent of U.S. families in business survive into the third generation.

   And so, it was a heartfelt thrill for Bill and me to think how our five children were about to welcome their sibling into the company and truly make it a third-generation family business. Having them all working together is a testament to Bill's legacy.

Today, I am retired. My guy, who supported and collaborated with me as I did for him, is deceased but lives in every aspect of the business we all nurtured and expanded together. However, if my writing this book provides some of you with ideas about new ways to improve how you work, I've succeeded in my goals. Keep in mind that your most important asset is your people. If you don't attract and retain good people and build relationships with those Advocates who will champion your business, even the best systems will not allow you to succeed.

Chapter 2
Decisions: Belief in Yourself

It's understood if you are going to be or are a business Owner, you will put effort in making educated decisions about your financial structure and how you will continue to improve it. These decisions require dedicated work and often are a tough row to hoe.

If you are figuring on being an Owner and the Leader, it may be the undoing of your finances.

Realize that being an Owner does not automatically make you a Leader. If you believe you are a Leader, be careful; take stock of your ability. If you have led a business group before, it may be very different than leading a retail business. Now you will have to teach and educate everyone you hire how you want things said and done and thought about. You will be responsible for your financials, having a management style that produces fruitful results, be able to retain customers and grow the base, your advertising, inventory and everything else about your growing company. If you're in the confectionery business, add your ingredients, and how your chocolates or other confections are created. Be determined to study everything about what leadership means to you and those individuals you hire, as well as those customers with whom you do business. Manufacturing and Retailing is a very diverse business."

A truly fine Leader never stops learning. It's all about what you do, not what you know. Remember that ownership does not give you a degree in leadership. That degree is only earned by how well you understand and lead creating meaningful responses to you. The Intranet and the library have plenty of books, tapes, and videos, so you have no reason not to have the information.

Talk with your Small Business Association for direction to leading a business and people. If your day is full of frustration by not getting active responses to your direction, you may not be a Leader. Do a SWOT matrix about your dilemma. Promise yourself you will be open-minded to what surfaces from the exercise. If you continue to say, "That just isn't so!" step aside and let someone else lead. You can direct from the background.

Remember a Leader must be believable; a Leader must be able to excite followers to want to do something, not do it because they are told to do it. A Leader must let passion shine through in every encounter when being with followers, vendors, or customers. A Leader must create a "you're home" feeling in the organization, a place where they are going to be supported, guided, and bettered through examples seen and experienced, educated, and trained in what they need to know to be all they can be. All of this is necessary if you want to seek more self-assurance, poise, and inner peace.

For a successful future, your determination, enthusiasm, and trust must always be your grounding anchor. The smaller and newer your business is, the more roles that must be filled. To organize your thoughts, pre-plan and then set up a workable plan that—when completed—will be your system to tackle new projects. Keep the system simple. Don't make a big thing of it.

Plan with enthusiasm. Keep on being enthused and keep planning. Decide how you will work, divvy up the day with the different roles you will assume to get a feel for what the day holds and realize how fast time flies by, so save yourself stress, and plan with that knowledge.

Use the Creative Problem-Solving instructions elsewhere in this book. The advice if followed will direct you. Like all things the result is all about the quality of effort you put into the undertaking. If you do it right, it may save you from needing a partner.

Write or learn how to write a business plan. You can also hire a professional to plan it and write it with you. Investigate who is well versed in business and is known in the small business community. Speak with your banker for additional help. Check out your Chamber of Commerce Small Business arm or Council of Smaller Enterprises (COSE). (In fact, COSE is one of the first memberships you should secure.) You will receive very good information from knowledgeable and very friendly individuals. This should be a well thought out session. Otherwise, it's all pie-in-the-sky ideas, which are simply sketches, impressions until work is assigned to them. You will decide how to achieve your vision by figuring out what you will need to do and when. It's your strategy. If you want to develop your strategy, figure out what you need to do to get there, that becomes your business plan. This is where your idea will be broken down to tell you what you need to do every year, quarter, monthly and weekly to answer your Strategy Plans. Your Strategy and Business plans are meant to change as you follow them and learn new things you will want to employ. So many times a Leader will tell you its all "in his/her head." Would you build a house without plans? Even if you know how to do it would you proceed without written plans to follow? Before you begin, know your vision. Develop a list of what you will need to accomplish to get there. Supporting your decisions will be your Business Plan which will list your directions. Disney, with checking, told others what he wanted and they did the building. Look where that got him!

SWOTs

Are you familiar with a SWOT Matrix? It is an acronym for Strengths, Weaknesses, Opportunities, and Threats. A SWOT is a very useful planning tool. It helps with developing and examining/evaluating the goals and plans you are thinking of for your business. You can also use the same matrix when you tackle a project. To develop a SWOT matrix, start by drawing on paper a large square. In it make four equal squares using up all the space or draw a large addition sign as big as the paper will allow.

Square One: **Strengths**: A. List anything you have an advantage in, such as you are a strong, experienced Leader, well trained in management and communication. Employ trained and educated enthusiastic helpers. B. What is your company going to be good at doing? C. Will it give you an edge over other companies? D. Do you have a better location? E. Do you have a solid financial competency?

Square Two: **Weaknesses**: A. List a weak action or lack of power that makes it less than what a competitor can do. B. Include things such as being new at finances and management also lighting, indoor and outdoor decorating. C. Are you educated in merchandising your product? D. Store layout/mapping your display area for maximum visual. E. Do you have nice clerks instead of knowledgeable Advocates? F. Is your parking lot good or merely adequate? G. Notice empty store fronts, partially filled parking lots during store hours, poor lighting add up to a tired area. H. Are new roads and highways being planned for the area?

Square three: **Opportunities**: A. Keep your eyes open. B. Notice what the competitor is trending. C. Notice if your strength can overcome their singular weakness. D. Notice if they are upgrading or downsizing in store size, product, and efficiencies. E. Remember you have strong organizational backing of your industry's association. Chocolatiers have the strong support of the Retail Confectioner's International. F. Understand risk taking. G. Are you a known name in the community? H. Very versed in IT and advertising? Able to afford great in-store and window advertising besides the usual?

Square four: **Threats**: A. Anything detrimental or unfavorable to your business. B. Is the competitor part of a large chain with all its perks? C. It can be your own store full of friendly clerks instead of Educated and Trained Advocates who know, understand, and support your mission statement. D. Store hours—good or bad? E. Low competitor pricing. F. Has a bus stop or crossroads? G. Easy ingress and egress (in and out)? H. Does your competitor have a traffic light, and you don't? I. They have beautiful landscaping. J. They have access to numerous professionals.

This tool is useful to keep primed. If you have someone who understands what you are attempting to do and, hopefully, knows the retail business ask for their help. Tell them how important this SWOT matrix is to you. To have someone(s) help you through a SWOT matrix exercise, giving thoughtful, knowledgeable assistance, and then help set the decisions for action is truly a gift. Be sure to show your appreciation with Malley's chocolates and special chocolates for younger family members, and theatre tickets. Also consider using a different avenue and ask a professional to assist or do it yourself. Make sure they understand what you are going to do and that they have worked a SWOT before. Be comfortable with what the professionals charge.

Now that you know more about this company you are starting, it's time to take a good look at yourself. What are you going to do with the information? Plan, schedule it, and do it.

Invite various small business individuals who are either sole Owners or partnership Owners for lunch and ask questions about what concerns you. These types of individuals are very busy because they are wearing many hats in their roles and will have no time during business hours solely for a friendly discussion about your concerns. Perhaps, however, they can discuss the situation during lunch or dinner. It will show you understand their busy schedule. At this time, always use your lunch/dinner breaks as an opportunity to network. Be religious about keeping a journal of what was discussed and the ideas. Keep every contact's information full and correct. Further, it is nice to give your guest a small token as a thank you for their time. Keep it as a gesture not an important gift. You might try a half-pound of Malley's Chocolates famous Bordeaux. Give extra business cards for them to pass out to friends or Advocates or a business follow-up for you. Send a thank you note using as few words as possible, thanking the individual for time spent advising you and the wonderful opportunity to get to know them better.

If, after all this study for your SWOT followed by action decisions and investigation with assistants, partners, or solo business individuals, you decide with professional assistance you will need more cash or more expertise. Come to terms about sharing your passion. If you absolutely need to have a partner(s), you have a good reason to have them. If you are the one supplying the where-with-all, and your partner(s) will be supplying the intellectual expertise or vice versa, both of you must decide which of the two available roles best fit your interests and skills, then that you will assume the responsibility for the agreed-upon plans. You will either make the product or sell the product. However, no matter where you sit on the balance scale, talk with other partnerships, speak about your plans with your bank advisor, and investigate about your proposed idea.

If I were doing it, getting a partner would be my last choice. Regardless, the need must be answered. If your view of yourself is "The buck stops here!" and "I want to make the decisions," kind of person, then think over what responsibilities you want your partner to agree would be yours and theirs. Make it binding. What do you feel your partner should head up? However, your partner may have other fresh new ideas that you think are just and open-minded. Prepare to listen and then discuss. If this person is going to supply the intellectual part, perhaps it will be easier to pay a commission instead of making a partner.

Another idea used in Europe which is fair may be of interest to you and not be too costly. The UK businesses have a position they call a Senior Independent Director. It is used when a business has a Board of Directors. You can shape the idea to suit yourself. He or she can be tasked with bringing an independent third-party perspective in the decision-making process. Usually, these Senior Independent Directors are experts in the industry. They offer advice on various aspects of the business. Of course, they can do the work of anything you propose, and they agree to doing. They do not work full-time. They come in when you and your partner have a strong difference of opinion, also every 12 months to check on your work much the same as he/she will be doing with your partner. This professional will inspect your work for the year, investigate how well you have operated your area of responsibility for the company, kept your promises, and what exactly you accomplished in the last 12 months. They discuss their findings with both you and your partner. This setup can be this way or any way that fits your business. If possible, do not create a partnership with a family member or best friend. It simply creates too many problems. If history is to be believed, numerous friendships and cohesive family relationships are ruined in partnerships. Worry and unhappiness results usually from differences of opinion on how money is handled and used, how many work hours are spent developing the business, how many days off to spend the time skiing or boating or simply a strong "Do it my way!" The disagreements can be as simple as your partner regularly taking luncheons with daughters or sons or even friends at upscale restaurants, and the sales stub shows up in "expenses." Differences of opinion can very well spoil a friendship or a company, especially a family company. If you decide it is best to get a business partner, both of you should agree that your business mantra should be "Never expect what you don't inspect." You will want to give your partner a strong sense of what is right using this idea. Organization and a very watchful eye are a necessity to incorporate different types of activity to achieve your company's agreed upon goals. This must be decided upon and written into a contract. Other information such as can a spouse work with you, decide on how you will work so you both agree on the hours and find some way to substantiate the hours worked. Consider even your wardrobes. Is one of you very casual and the other more business-casual? What about background music and what volume? If you have walks, who will shovel them if needed, and what about the yard work? Oh, are you going to outsource your window washing? How about cleaning the restroom? Agree to acquire a professional experienced in creating partnerships.

There is so much to learn about business and all it entails that it might be a good idea to work for someone else already in your field but not your chosen niche before you start your business. If you decide to go ahead with your business idea, empowering a chosen experienced professional is a good idea for the obvious reasons, plus they can be the facilitator for touchy conversations and decisions that must be made.

Among these:

1. Will the spouse be able to work in the company?
2. What about children? They may be young now, but 10 years makes quite a difference.
3. When or what year will you both be willing to retire?
4. What if one wants to sell and the other doesn't?
5. What if, after you both create these working documents you both agree to, then a different slant is put upon them?
6. Who will decide what is right, what is gray, and what is wrong?
7. Ask yourself: Are you willing to give up such a good friend that you have thought about going into business with? If something turns sour, it is worth it?
8. There are always other ways to do everything: Ask a business attorney.

Chapter 3
Investigation & Considerations

As Bill and I helped grow the business, our bank suggested to us that it was time to move to a larger accounting company. It was very difficult to leave a gentleman and confidante who advised us for years. After much investigation and discussion, we decided which firm we thought was the best fit for us. When I needed to hire for a very important position, I used professionals from our new accounting firm which is a large corporation. I contacted the business department where the personnel are educated and experienced in hiring and know exactly what skills are needed for various business positions. My contact did all the interviewing and sent me three choices to decide who I thought would fit best with our culture, work well with us, and keep us on our toes.

If you decide to go this route, a firm might be able to bill you separately for this service. However, you can interview if you prepare yourselves, then have an outside background check performed on your choice.

It was gratifying to learn our new firm made many kinds of

assistance available to us. We immediately got involved with various departments and were able to bring new directions into our organization which made everything easier for us. Knowledgeable leadership will assist individuals with affirmative, inspired management.

If you are going into business with a partner, you should prepare a resume for your proposed partner to review as that person should for you. After a discussion about your resumes and you decide to get together, organize your proposed new company. I also would hire a professional that the two of you thoroughly briefed to lead a meeting where each spouse and/or personal mentor will be invited. Explain what has been decided upon and ask for their input. Decide if you want to meet once a year separately with the professional to discuss growing pains and have something concrete come from these conversations.

A fine business always has a successful Leader at the forefront.

If you believe you are best suited for executive leadership, then make sure you know how to lead and what you should know to do a good job. An Owner who usually is thought to be a trailblazer, the one who can see the opportunities does not necessarily make a Leader.

For you to do the very best job you can, you must know and understand how to lead. It is your responsibility to start good business practices, such as all management information and network organization, and check they are constantly primed. Now is the time to lay a firm and right foundation. All these steps must be meticulously done, so all the systems you will organize work smoothly. I like to use the word "systems" because in this instance, to me, it implies more strength than the word "plans." It is more organized and easily accommodates progress forms to answer agreed upon work/date decisions. The "Check-Up Forms" are to be given each other at a certain time or agreed upon consequence comes into play. This organization is important for each other's peace of mind. One should never ask the other for extensions or just ignore the agreement without serious consequence.

It's correct to organize these thoughts now before you need some of them because you will need help before much time elapses. You need to develop them as fully as possible. Consider the consequences of unkempt promises or words; will spouse or other relatives be allowed to be employed or even assist; agree on perks – time, gas, time spent away from work, sick days and vacation days etc.; get both your signatures and have your attorney witness this action. I once said in our Lakewood, Ohio store that I hoped I wouldn't forget something said in passing. One of our Assistant Managers told me her mother always said, "Paper remembers what the mind forgets." I've never forgotten those words.

The unified vision of the executives must have plans in place that create constant improvement and safeguarding who and what you are now. As you grow and often wish you had another set of hands, make a note of the need. Whenever it comes to mind in another way, add the need to your list. I'm hopeful your partner shares this wish for another set of hands. Perhaps you can find the individual who can help both of you. You might start getting the help you need by both of you employing an individual for two days a week. When it is agreed you need more help, your organizational form will easily tell you who should do the interviewing, even putting the ad on the Internet. Of course, before that time a list of duties needing attention should be listed with the top three being the most important to bring assistance to the person needing it. When you are just starting out, it's a temptation to want to hire your spouse if that individual is not already working outside your home. There are many reasons why not to work together and there are also strong reasons why to invite them. It depends on many variables so make certain the pros far outweigh the cons – even your home life will be affected. When your choice is made because of your "pros", discuss the idea with your spouse. Each of you should ask your friends who work together how their situation is evolving. Tell them you are both thinking about if it would be a good thing for both of you. Maybe ask them, what is the one thing they might do up front if they had the opportunity to start again? Bill and I had such diverse concerns; we were so busy we had no time to get in each other's path, however, we sometimes worked on projects together and that was really enjoyable; thinking out loud, discussing pros and cons, investigating and making decisions. We thoroughly enjoyed what we did and would do it all over again. We had fun and we were completely dedicated. Refrain if possible, and there are a million reasons why. Just ask some of your business friends what they think of the idea.

The Owner or partners must exert the same disciplines over themselves as they would if they had Direct Reports (someone they must directly report to). Leaders of retail functions must exert friendly but affirmative control.

Your mental companions for how to get the job done should be

Investigations & Considerations

among others Walt Disney, or J. Willard Marriott. These Stallions of Success were guided by three words, "Attention to detail." Marriott is known for having said (and proving in daily functions), "Only close attention to the fine details of any operation makes the operation first class." From studying these business icons, I know they didn't waste time on anything but thinking "What can we do to make it better today?" Walt Disney had a word called "Plussing." If something seemed to merit an A+, he still wanted to make it better, so the people in his business started calling it "Plussing" (making it even better) which is why his companies are where they are today. Dogged attention to detail. But don't be a perfectionist; you have a whole company to operate. Get whatever done as well as you can and move on.

J. Willard Marriott and Disney knew something many of us can't get our arms around. The success of your business is to simply do your job. It takes more than hard work. Success for you is equal to your grit (meaning the right kind of knowledge plus awareness and courage to put it into action). If you only use hard work and heart, you will remain pretty much where you are right now. You need time to devote to thinking and making careful decisions, not out doing your direct report's jobs (if you have one) or other time eaters. You should be thinking and envisioning what could be done to better things in your company (Plussing?). Perhaps not work in the business but on the business? These Leaders excited and inspired those people around them. They trusted and allowed their direct reports to do their work with progress checks.

From Marriott's and Disney's personalities, they came across as affirmative and assertive. Their followers knew not to deviate from their marching orders. The CEOs told how something should be done and when it should be done. The Project Leader or Managers accepted their goals, tools, and time frame. They knew it was their responsibility to know who does what the best, keep everyone rounded up to keep focusing on the given goal, keep control, and see to it that all functions were accomplished according to the working plan. Lewis Carroll (Alice in Wonderland fame) had the Cheshire cat tell us "Which way you go depends on where you want to get to," expressing the importance of having a goal. They knew what they had to do, and they got up and did it.

Don't get bogged down in research. You need to take what you know now and put it to work. You can always improve or tweak something, but by putting your energies to action, you will have something to change or tweak and you will be moving forward.

You and your partner should make up a schedule of when you will meet and what kind of information both of you will want to hear. Make sure this time is sacrosanct and be at every meeting. At the time of your business agreement, you agreed on the commitment. If you don't take these meetings seriously, your partner has every right to cease your partnership. Be sure you put these meetings in your contract and how the decision will be made if one fails in their commitment. Each of you are expected to keep to your commitment or leave. Your partner may see the inspiration and "Let's get busy attitude" as an accomplished fact. Each of you must agree on goals and be disciplined about achieving them in an agreed upon time frame. Many roads leave a town, but only one goes where you want to be. You are either on the road to your goals or off it at your personal best watering hole. Make up your mind; discipline yourself. If you are having problems, set a small goal for yourself. When you reach the goal, feel good about it, and then set a bigger goal.

At Malley's Chocolates, we hire individuals to be an Advocate rather than an employee. This kind of person has spirit, desires, is friendly and enjoys people. You can hear it in how they talk and look at you. They are not fidgeting or slumping in their chairs but answering questions with a happy tone in their voices. I always acknowledged that simply being interviewed attributed to some restraint because they were

- On unfamiliar ground answering questions they hoped were correct
- Leading to something they hoped to acquire

The inquiring individual displayed apparent initiative, looking forward to a new beginning. Also, approachability and body language tell me that our customers will decide they are friendly and will choose them to assist them. Usually these folks also have a can-do attitude that gets the job done. What would you choose?

If an Advocate needs some help in this area, a well-informed Manager can show them the way. I must admit, though, we did have one lady who started several jobs in various parts of the store, would notice a browsing customer, and immediately leave her work to attend to them. However, she never remembered to go back and finish any of her other "starts," but she was so co-operative, friendly, and just plain nice that everyone else reminded her, and she was kept on. As with most businesses, there would be certain jobs no one wanted to do, but she would see it and just do it.

"Advocate" means so much more than the word "employee" or "associate." In a dictionary, an employee is described as a worker, a wage earner. An associate is described as subordinate, an assistant. Advocate is described as a supporter, a promoter. A Malley's Chocolates Advocate believes in and promotes us by giving excellent caring service for the delight of their customers. Advocates, when possible, give assistance to other customers or each other. Through their personal strength of character, Malley Manners education and training, this person develops into a talented Malley's Spokesperson who is dedicated to our values and practices—as we are to them.

Leaders set the relationship for those whom they lead. All Advocates gain confidence if their Leader is relaxed, open to discussions, and easy to be around. This assurance starts when the Leader enriches the confidence of his/her Manager or Supervisor. When the plan for the year is explained with clear directions and goal dates, Direct Reports will know what needs to be accomplished properly finishing according to agreed-upon set time frames. (Of course, it goes without saying that the Direct Report has been checked on or help offered during the creation process.) If agreed upon set timelines are not met, the agreed upon set consequences come into play. This plan with the date and their signature and yours will be kept in office files.

When an Advocate has been educated in your Education and Training System, they should be allowed to attend to their duties, watched but unimpeded by either partner.

Employ your Advocates

Decide what kind of business you will be in your community. What will be your hours? Will you need a day and a night Manager? This person(s) is who you should try to hire first. Go over all your material for the helpers and them before starting to interview. Until you get comfortable, interview your helpers with your chosen Supervisor or Manager, letting them take the lead. This situation is their time to start influencing a possible helper and show them the confidence you have in them by sitting back and letting them lead the conversation. You hired your Manager(s)/Supervisor(s) to lead their group following your vision/directions. Let them work it out. That is the job you gave them.

Owner, your chosen job was to lead. If you keep busy elsewhere outside your office, your business will stay right where you are now.

In order to move forward, somebody must figure out how to advance, and that person should be you. You need quiet, uninterrupted time to develop planned action steps. When you give up doing what you find easy, that which you like to do most and start tackling what you need to do to become the best, you will soon see that the people working with you can lead. They will figure out the problems or challenges facing their area. They impressed you, and you hired them, and you agreed to work together. Let them do their job. Let them. Then—and only then—can you have the time to develop your job. Lead your company. Every single day that you do not is another day that your company does not move forward. Decide to be your best self. Put your doggedness in high gear. Discipline yourself, and then reward yourself.

Putting out fires may make you feel indispensable and "important," but when you are all by yourself, you admit you should have the help of knowledgeable people in the right positions. However, you haven't time to find or even develop them or even figure out how to pay them because you are busy with busy work out of your office. Maybe you were doing one of their jobs, or if you have already hired someone to take the burdens of a certain area, get out of the way and let them develop your system for heads up action! No system? Discuss the situation, tell them to produce a working copy and report back in one week.

If you are working with a new Leader you can ask for more direct reports about what bothers you the most and give them more time with your conversation. Get them outside help if needed. Now, you can make those calls and attend those meetings or seminars and have the time to think about your next important move. If you enjoy "hovering," then take over that position, and hire an experienced individual to lead, so every day you can enjoy doing the work that makes you feel fulfilled, growing the business from another angle. However, choosing this path doesn't mean you give up all leadership. You shape your leadership as you find you can work best. You make or decide the next step or long-range plan. The individual can do all the commonplace paperwork, figuring, contacting, and investigating. You can be out and about seeing new customers and making sales or inside creating a signature product. After all, it's your business! Choose wisely. Speaking of day and night work Managers made me think of my husband Bill and his brother-in-law, Bill McConville. Bill McConville worked at the kitchen with all the chocolate, production dates, helpers, and vendors. Bill Malley had his office in our flagship

Investigations & Considerations

store Malley's Chocolates and Ice Cream Concoctions seven days a week, every day from 9:30-10 until 6, then home for dinner and play with the kids until at 8 P.M. Then he went back and worked to closing at 11, getting home about 12-12:30. During the holidays, he would arrive home about 4-4:30 in the morning. Sometimes his feet would hurt so much he could hardly walk. Sundays he went in at noon. Every other weekend, his brother-in-law would work weekend nights, eight until midnight, giving Bill some free time. He, too, worked 9 – 10 hours a day during the week.

Bill enjoyed being with his group, his Advocates, and caring for all his nighttime customers. To him, nighttime was the fun part of the day. The parlor was always very busy. He was great at inspiring trust and discussing how to work together for more efficiency, so at the end of the night, they would be at goal. During the day his time was filled by attending business affairs, company accounting, creating ads, catalogs, advertising and discussing plans with his brother-in-law and all the other myriad details of operating a growing business.

Peter Drucker believed that "Leadership is not what you do—it's what others do in response to you". If Advocates do not fulfill their missions, then you are not a Leader. You are a doer. Your office person should listen to you and do what you ask. It's the why and the how. Being new, you probably have not written a system for the office helper to make sure all things are taken care of in the right time in the right way. This is an excellent opportunity to start a system by creating a way of control for every facet of work that occurs. We call ours Malley's Manners. If both of you agree to what has been written and and it's provided regular support (every week) followed with belief and conscientiously performing the tasks, you will have no weak link in the progression to a fine office up-to-date system. One that you will be very pleased with because you will have no confusion, no lost receipts, and no late collections. (Something you must keep an eye on are collections because your business is just starting and cannot shoulder even small losses.)

The environment created by all of you makes it pleasant to even think about going to work (a bond, ultimately a team or group has been established), and for a customer/vendor, it's looking forward to an atmosphere of a very enjoyable visit. Subordinates do what they have been taught to think and do. They watch and, hopefully, mimic those people they answer to... ultimately you.

Following are the key points that an Owner or Leader of a retail business needs to focus on in order to be successful. Each chapter tackles a theme and explains why each one is an important part of the process and what you, the business Owner, need to know to be effective in this area. They are presented in a logical format that takes the Owner through much of the process of building his or her business. This work is by no means the body and soul of intellectual capacity and the plain hard work needed to operate and be successful at building a business. Remember, you are reading one person's view. Use pieces or parts or turn-the -whole-thing-upside down, or take an idea at face-value. Remember, I hope you make this a workbook and write notes, highlight ideas, make this your very own. Use the margins. Make it easy to find what you think is important.

Chapter 4
Determination: Can do, Will do

Systems are a critical component to achieving success and freeing ourselves from worry. As we developed our methods, we already had a top-notch product and reputation thanks to Mom and Dad Malley. Now we wanted to continue to develop and protect our processes. We needed to be assured our Advocates could provide the backbone of our systems and build our brand in such a way that delighted customers who would want to come back again and again. So, we thought about the best way to make the connections with customers that lead to sales?

Bill and I attended a Disney seminar about Customer Care. It gave us a peek into the thoughts and sentiment shared by many executives who worked with Van France, the originator of Disney University, who used Walt Disney's core values to set it apart and make it a success. Those core values set in motion the sturdy foundation for the university. Put simply, "Disney University isn't a car wash through which employees can be sent in preparation."

Training cannot be limited to "Here's what you need to do; now go out and do it." That's not good enough. Education develops understanding, leading to an emotional connection and bond. Training needs to instill confidence through directions and imaginative coaching.

"Without a doubt," says Doug Lipp, author of Disney U. "Education reveals the roots of the Disney University: Walt's long-standing value of providing employees with a tailored, relevant training, and educational experience."

That meant an employee should feel confidant about speaking up if something appears not practical; or incorrect, or person can offer a better way of doing something, keep things simple, be flexible; if something is not understood, change the presentation, don't waste time; give more than a training program, work with them, listen to them, bond with them, continue always to educate them. Listen to employees ideas, listen to learn how to create a new approach, if you are using last year's thoughts, you're getting jaded: keep fresh and engaging by trying new approaches.

When hiring we look for individuals who smile and think well of themselves. We look for those people who will appreciate what we want them to learn and do. Before someone is hired, we make sure they understand our business plan and just what is going to be asked of them. We want them to know how we think of and treat our customers and each other. They must be aware of and understand our culture. They usually do because that is why they are asking to work with us, but they also need to understand how it is maintained. It's important for them to know how Mom and Dad Malley started and what they sacrificed in order to appreciate where we are today.

New hires are told we have certain standards in how we dress, look, and work to treat our customers to the care they deserve. If they are eager, we ask them to sign a simple statement that they want to become proficient in our instructions. Should you hire them? If you feel uneasy about something you can't put your finger on, and your gut says, "No," follow your gut.

The goal is to continuously educate and train every one of us to be able to promote our product and represent the Malley's brand in the best way possible, even though individuals may be coming to us with experience. It is essential they understand and want to participate in how we think and act and behave accordingly when interacting with potential customers and each other. We tell them they will be called an Advocate instead of an "employee" or "associate." One of our sons, Dan came back from a seminar and said he heard the word Advocates when referring to employees and what it meant. An Advocate is always for something; they support what they believe in. At Malley's, we support our Advocates to give their most satisfactory service to the delight of their customers. It also means to offer your support to another person, to do everything in your power to do what you can for another. He thought we ought to call ourselves Advocates. Bill and I were looking for the right word to describe the effort and work of our helpers, and the word Advocate fit perfectly. I thought it a wonderful idea and promised from then on, I would do just that. To us, it means so much more than employees and associates! An employee is described as a worker, a wage earner. An associate is described as subordinate, an assistant. An Advocate is a supporter, a promoter. We support and believe in Malley's Chocolates by giving our finest service for the delight of our customers.

It's easy to forget as we're taking and placing orders and managing the business side of our companies that it's people who make it all work. It's the customers who come in the door and the Advocates who help them that determine how successful a company can be. It is here where the culture is developed, and Advocates see and/or practice what we believe in. Knowledge of how to care for a customer can be the greatest accelerator of success or its biggest hindrance. It is here where loyalty is either developed or it's not. Late at night or first thing in the morning when you look over your store to give it a final check that everything is ready for customers, ask yourself if your Advocates are!

In an article about the Key to Customer Loyalty, Ken Blanchard explains that losing a customer is a costly endeavor. "It can cost six to seven times more to gain a new customer than to retain an existing one," We think of Blanchard's words when we must correct an unpleasant situation in our store or on the phone. This situation has only grown more challenging in the age of social media. Five, ten years ago, one might think "Well, Sally did not care for that upset customer very well." You might talk it over with her and discuss how to care for a customer if the situation should arise again. Nobody's perfect, and disagreements are going to happen. You deal with it the best you can and try to help your people learn from their mistakes. Unfortunately, in these times where everyone is connected, a bad experience can quickly become a PR nightmare.

As a result, we must create a system where everyone knows how to react to customers, the happy normal ones, and the unhappy unpleasant ones. It's just a part of being an effective business Owner, but it's one of the most critical components to achieving enduring success. This skill is covered in the Skillshops which you will read about later. Three very important words are "I'm sorry that..."

*New Inventions are presented to Us Nearly Every Day
Making yesterday's Excitement Old News*

One of the top marketing research firms in the country, TARP, now known as CX Solutions conducted a study for Coca-Cola and found that a median of 10 people heard about a bad experience for a small-item packaged well. Even though subsequent studies showed that the magnitude of word of mouth varied by product, price, and industry (people would tell 16 people about a negative auto repair experience, for example), a rule of thumb evolved in marketing circles that an unhappy customer will tell 10 people about the poor service he or she received. On July 6, 2009, Canadian musician David Carroll and his band, Sons of Maxwell, blew the lid off that rule by uploading a song onto YouTube that chronicled a real-life experience of how his $3,500 Taylor guitar was broken during a trip on United Airlines in 2008.

At the end of the first day the number of views totaled 150,000 and three days later, on July 9, it had amassed 500,000 hits, 5 million by mid-August, and then by April 7, 2011 it had received 10,233,487 hits!

Today, we need to adjust our thinking caps. What we believed to be "the way" for 10 years, even 5 years ago, is out of date.

As we grew in the number of stores, I became very concerned about how each of us knew how Malley's wanted our customers to be cared for, what kind of service we could provide, and how we wanted to provide it. How were we going to be sure everyone understood and knew how to take care of our customers? I decided to write a program on Malley's Customer Care and transfer it to an audio system, so our Advocates could hear right from a Malley how to give Malley service.

I worked enthusiastically on my new program. I'd get our young daughters, Sis and Megan in bed, make sure the four older boys were doing their homework, and then into my office where I worked long hours explaining our culture and practices on tape. I took my work with me on vacations and sat on the lanais or porches overlooking golf courses and work away. By the way, working by a golf course is where I found out the two most popular words on a golf course. There was a narrow creek near one of our porches and occasionally, I would hear

"Ker-plunk" meaning a golf ball was just sent for a swim. Then I would hear, "Aww, sh_ _!" This would go on all day, day after day!

Anyhow, when Bill and I took my completed work to the post office, and I thought I was finished, "Hallelujah!" I felt so free and so wonderful that I had done something wonderful for Malley's!

We used the audio program in all the stores and spoke about it in our Manager's meetings. Also, I would gather the Managers together to discuss certain points and make things even more understandable (I thought). After a while, as I visited the stores, and collected feedback from our Managers, I really did not see any real difference in our customer care level. I felt we were giving our helpers more than any other retail chocolate company and yet...

Soon after I was part of a group meeting in Cleveland from Council of Smaller Enterprises (COSE). At that time, companies were putting full-page ads in the paper about how they wanted to be "Your big brother" and help you get where you wanted to go. Someone felt they had been treated poorly at one of the places and felt their ads were, "such a sham." Everyone seemed to accept this opinion as fact, and there were even a few jokes made about the situation. The group went on to other topics. Those remarks bothered me to no end because it so linked into all the work, I had put into our Customer Care program. Considering my goal, the program was not producing. After a while, I said to the group, "Let's go back to the story again. Do we as Leaders of our companies really think the Leaders of those companies decide to spend a large amount of money and have ads made up and placed and not mean what their ads say? Some remarks were made, even some jokes, but then Sue Seidman, a COSE member, spoke up and said, "Adele, it's called "Transfer of Training." I have a book about it, and if you want you can borrow it." Bill got it for me that next night.

When my own book arrived, I continued to follow its educational ideas page by page and wrote a new program. I learned that only 10 percent of what an attendee learns from training is used, and most of it is gone within months. The authors show why the full transfer of learned skills is critical for our company's growth and survival. It requires a continual learning process and can't be accomplished in a single session or series of sessions. Transfer of Training authors are Mary L. Broad, Ph.D. and John W. Newstrom, Ph.D. of Duluth, MN.

I learned a process for getting our Managers and our learners into the transfer process so that everyone benefits. They showed me ways to manage the powerful role of "Manager of the transfer process" and the tools to get the job done. I studied that book front to back, digested it, and planned how to use the knowledge for Malley's benefit. I decided on the approach, the strategy, and the system for getting the job done. I also learned that if upper management did not support or even "own" the program, it would never be successful. "When education is offered consistently and with creativity, education is an indispensable commodity, one that is also held in high esteem in the history and culture of the Walt Disney Company," stated by Doug Lipp, author of Disney U.

"Transfer of Training" is the effective transfer to the workplace of the knowledge and skills learned in Education and Training. It is essential to support and maintain performance.

It is a sensible suggestion to work at forming an assessment of how you want to operate your company. You won't be starting with many helpers, but, shortly, it will be time to get help, and you will need to know what they should do. You most likely will be working in your store and helping customers. How do you want to do that? It is impossible to spend all your time with your customers because you have so many other business functions to attend to during working hours.

Maybe you will start with two Supervisors; a Manager has the right to hire and fire, a Supervisor does not. They also don't receive the same pay, so this plan gives you some wiggle room. Hire two more helpers. Divide the duties as you see fit but be fair in your distribution of responsibilities. Perhaps one can work with you on job descriptions, ordering of product, inventory, and putting deliveries away. Perhaps the other new helper can develop a list of everything you want your group to know such as how to explain a price increase, how to explain how your store ships to warm places, how to offer your specials to customers, how to say goodbye to a customer, history of how you started in business etc.

To that end, I developed a list of learning modules. These Skillshops offer a remarkable opportunity to teach different sets of skills to your team. How you do it is up to you and your store hours or even if you teach before you open your store to customers. It is very important you know backwards and forwards what you want your employees to know.

It is important to understand motivation, follow-up, and a pat on the back. Ken Blanchard teaches that a "Leader must keep learning and relearning what is wanted of followers." Learning cannot stop with one rotation of a cycle. It must keep rolling over and over so all in the organization can hear and see how customer service is accomplished at Malley's Chocolates. Sometimes in my Malley School of Merchandising, I used balls and wrote on them how something was learned. I rolled them to my attendees to take home to their desks to be constantly reminded how something should be done! I hoped to further impress upon them what I meant by keeping the ball rolling over and over.

Leadership support should show their interest by:
- Personal efforts in visiting and speaking with your group. Beforehand, have the Manager prime you with the sort of questions to ask them.
- Asking Advocates how their Skillshops are progressing
- Noting good displays
- Cleanliness of store
- Possibly asking an Advocate to secure a store checklist (examination of what needs to be in tip-top condition) and getting the information for it by walking through the store with the Advocate.

If you see something needing attention, point it out to the Advocate and ask their opinion. You'll be amazed what happens when you do so.

Also provide Managers with education concerning their financial goals, Internet improvements with instructions for the new improvements, fundraising innovations, and corporate care—including overseeing the importance of fortifying the foundation of long-term customer revenue.

The foundation will only remain strong by continuously innovating, staying connected to our long-term customers through email or text messaging, special offers and other fresh and fun ideas reserved for them. This coupled with our Advocates utilizing their Malley's Manners knowledge, education and enthusiasm to meet their customers will see a bounce up on the chart of Improvements which will also show the number of customers, individual sales and customer retention. You can help Managers by discussing or developing your mission statement, shipping improvements, maintenance promptness, and discuss modernization, if needed. There is so much to be done, and with you checking and your Manager managing physical presence, great inroads can be made. Don't let anyone say, "They don't know what to say." You should inform them and send them sticky notes as to what is happening with your helpers. Keep all administration in the loop. Value their feed-back. Let them see how you use their suggestions.

As you progress, you and your partner may agree to hire some needed help. The Advocate you place in charge of retail should be in administration because it is a most important responsibility and needs to be in constant communication with the CEO. It is also the obligation of this Leader to understand the responsibility to thoroughly educate and train all Direct Reports in your Education and Training System. This can be accomplished in several ways stated under your Retail Responsibilities. By delegating the responsibility is how an Owner can find time to see that all the Advocates are educated and trained and still have time for countless other concerns.

The Managers understand they are the Leaders and responsible for their stores' success. Each new Advocate receives a folder where information is stored so the Retail Leader can check progress and see that the Advocate is receiving the proper training and education.

The Store Manager will educate an Advocate or with the Owners' OK choose an Assistant Manager to take responsibility for a short time. After a Manager has educated a new hire about a certain Skill-shop and introduces the training, the Manager will introduce the new hire to the Assistant Manager, who will see that the education and training are fortified, practiced, and thoroughly understood. When the Assistant Manager and trainee agree that the Skillshops are learned and utilized, the Advocate Proficiencies Form is signed by the Assistant Manager and is placed in the Advocate's folder.

The Assistant Manager verbally informs the Manager of the Advocate's progress, so the Manager stays abreast of the work and can comment on the efforts of the new Advocate. If expectation is not met, further education is required of both the Assistant Manager and the newcomer.

So, the progression is Manager—Assistant Manager—Advocate. Then the Leader/Owner congratulates or sends a note when informed.

It is a ball that keeps rolling to teach how you want actions completed. The great thing about it is everyone in authority is involved in what you want because they are reading, teaching, performing, and checking on your training and education modules constantly. There can be no fall back into old habits when the correct way is being reviewed or taught. The Manager knows they are being watched by the Assistant Manager(s) and the Advocates in how they confer with their customers and care about our products, Advocates, and store.

Someone is always checking up on them. As Carl Sewell says in Customers for Life, "Even when people know what they are supposed to do, sometimes they forget. That's why they hold church every Sunday." All of what the Advocates are to learn is written in our notebooks and folders. This system makes sure the focus is constantly addressing our Education and Training system called Malley Manners. How often have you attended a seminar and a month later cannot repeat what you heard? Malley Manners is humming in all our stores every day. A yearly Retention Review addresses how Advocates' habits have been retained. What is the use of investing time, effort, and thought into a person and not check that they are retaining and using the information? Remember this quote, 'Never expect what you don't inspect? (W. Clement Stone) Trust, but keep checking about the follow-through.

Again, it's important to note that these training tools need to constantly evolve. The core remains in place and unchanged. Just as the core beliefs your company is founded upon need never change, but other parts of the program can become out of date, especially when new technology comes into play. These items must be flagged for updating or removed. New instructional material may need to be produced and inserted in its proper place in the program. Have the forms ready so it's easy to write additional material. This system of learning or one you devise must become your vision, your ideas, your work that you will roll out with pride and knowledge of ownership. Some Owners feel this strategy is too much work. "They will learn on the job." A blanket decision like this one immediately sweeps professionalism out the door. Yes, some things can be learned on the job. That is rote learning. Memorization by repetition is certainly not complete, and it also surely lacks warmth and understanding. This clerk does not realize the importance of "small talk," does not know how to suggest additional items the customer may find interesting thus building the sale; most likely they do not know how to create customer relationships or make a raving fan of your establishment and does not really understand why you want things done the way you want them done.

"They will learn on the job." If so, the Advocates never get to feel really connected to you or needed or important to you. This plan will make an adequate clerk, but certainly you want someone like yourself meeting your customers. Malley Manners' type of system gives the ability to choose what to teach. Each learning segment takes no more than 10-15 minutes. It is the responsibility of the new Advocate to keep moving along in their education. Soon all your helpers will have

Determination: Can do, Will do

pride of ownership and know what they need to know, so customers can feel your influence and can experience your opinions and care.

With Malley's Manners' Skillshops, you will have no need to hire someone to come in and present a seminar or to send your helpers out of town to attend a seminar. You have all the necessary information right now. You also have the instructor. To start your own system for education, you must get involved but only for a little while and only if you want to because I'm going to offer you an opportunity. You know how you want your customers cared for, so write it all out, and then break it down into segments. Be sure to write the process down in a notebook. You can discuss and teach with your chosen Manager or Supervisor what you want done. Have them write what you expressed to them, and then check it to be certain they understood your desires. Make up a form to be filled in, so every new learning segment is presented accurately and in the same way. You are now creating a system.

When assessing what made the biggest impact on transfer of learning, the authors of Transfer of Training, Mary L. Broad, Ph.D. and John Newstrom, Ph.D., looked at three different parties (the learner's Manager, the trainer/facilitator, and the learner themselves) at three stages in the process (before the meeting, during, and after).

- The greatest impact was made by the learner's Manager in setting expectations before the meeting
- The next most important was before the meeting in getting to know the needs of the learner they would be educating and training
- The third most important was the Manager's role after the education and training

This position may be the first real one a young person and sometimes an older woman/man is experiencing in retail. You need to take it as a responsibility to both them and your company and the community to educate and train them well because they will take what they learn with them as long as they live. If you're welcoming a more experienced person into your group, you will want this person to understand there are as many ways to operate a store as there are ways to go on a vacation. One is often no more correct than another. But you need to stick to your core beliefs which make up your system (we call ours Malley Manners) and make it clear that you won't waver from those bedrock principles. Remember ours are safety, integrity, and value. Everything you do in your company needs its own system.

If you approach this project calmly and very regularly, you will have created a system that can, after a short time, live on without your presence. When and how did writing a system for everything you do in your business become so important?

It happened in an operating room, and the idea of it sent Dr. Atul Gawande into many operating rooms in far flung places to those closer to home. He wrote, <u>The Checklist Manifesto How to Get Things Right</u>. It's a wonderful read, and you will be convinced upon finishing it to get your systems or things you must do correctly every time started right now. It's the road to peace of mind. Is there a greater accomplishment?

What you will learn is the importance of not being casual when it is important to be firm. Being firm to make sure everything that is important to be remembered is remembered, leading to correct accomplishment every time.

Remember my Advocate's mother who always said, "Paper remembers what people forget."? Once you set up the system of learning and follow up with interest and support, your team or group will achieve success every time without your presence allowing you to work on your waiting business. This gem is called a checklist.

An example of working without a checklist occurs when something is wrong, causing additional work, additional expense, and frustration to meet deadlines. Sometimes our Graphic Designer received certain advertisements without all the correct information: A new store would be forgotten to be added to our list of stores, telephone numbers that had been changed, hours of operation, or how we wanted a coupon to be written.

Or another issue was not making sure everything that was supposed to be sent to a specific store was packed, items like gift wrap, new scissors or ribbon, these little things that were important to the person waiting but did not create a ripple in the warehouse because the person who needed to know sometimes did not know or else might have forgotten.

Obviously, we needed some kind of remedy to give better service to our "inside Advocate customers."

Read on to see how this important information can be carried over into a good job description. Your thinking is put right into actions that will be performed without you being there.

Adele's Bonus Tip on Determination—Being Prepared!

Whenever you are preparing to deliver customer care, success often comes down to providing the right information to the right people, and then practicing until it hurts. When you own a business—especially in the early days—you have the luxury of trial and error but more often than not, lack the time and/or capital to make too many mistakes. Here's a quick primer on how you may want to consider working with your team in the early days.

Preparation for Customer Care - information and practice
Beginning days: Giving directions, leading, and inspiring are among your most important duties, especially when you are a person owning a beginning business. After you have hired the people to represent you, gather them together and tell them:

1. Your vision for the year. A vision does not have to be lofty, but it must be true, otherwise it is pie-in-the-sky thinking and will take you nowhere. It could be:

My vision for the next twelve months is to continue our development in training and education, so we all understand our version of what is efficient and effective for Customer Care in our store. I want each of you to look forward to coming to work, and our statement's bottom line will be in the "black".

2. Tell them your mission statement. Don't have one yet? It can always be changed so for now make a quick statement. Write about something that is filling your mind. Maybe it could be:

Every customer will be given service from our hearts and minds. Our Customers are our number one priority.

What to do next: Create a method that will inform all employees how you want your customers treated and your store presented. Give them the training and education they need. Tell your employees what your pet peeves are. Make your training appropriate to what each is experiencing right now. You do not want to hear, "I'm new and I don't quite understand how to work this register," or "I don't know how to page someone. I'm sorry." That is aggravating! When you first open your business, be content that you probably have employees that are not Salespeople but happy, smiling efficient clerks. It is more important that everyone does their best to treat everyone as good as good can be. That means waiting on them, giving good service and asking them to come back. All that is accomplished through thorough training and ensuring your helpers (Advocates, Salespeople, team etc.) have happy attitudes.

Value: Every shift, go over your basic instruction. No one can remember everything the first time it is heard. Now, to keep you happy, make a list of what you want accomplished every day and your pet peeves.

Number one on that pet peeve list is you don't want to ever see your helpers grouped about chatting and not watching for when a customer comes in the store or someone who wants some attention.

Number two might be what do you first notice when you come in the store? Is the stockroom door hanging open, are there boxes on the floor, is the back counter filled with paperwork or half-finished jobs?

Write it down, otherwise you are going to continue to be annoyed. Why start your day that way? Remind them of your pet peeves. All the fine tuning will come as you grow.

Purpose: You must convince your helpers that the subject material is what must be practiced with care. Make your mantra be:
a. Education to understand;
b. Training to do; and
c. Motivation to give of ourselves for the delight of our customers.

WHY: If you have chosen a Manager impress upon him/her the immense influence they have over the other helpers, even if it is two or three. The Manager will always be watched for cues on how to handle sales, waiting on customers and how they greet them and say goodbye to them.

Good communication skills are a must in order to effectively teach and convey information. It's probably the top skill needed to succeed because it will be the Manager's coaching and support for their employees which will lead to a successful store. Everyone reacts to the energy and enthusiasm of their Manager. Trust in you will be developed by always giving your support, continuous teaching, and educating in a very pleasant or fun manner; following up on their understanding and use with lots of appreciation and thank-you's. Your Manager must be one they can come to with problems, decisions to be made, or to understand something.

It's the Manager's job to fulfill your goals, to be fair but firm in fulfilling them and be good at them themselves so as to motivate their helpers to fulfill your wishes, which are your company goals.

Determination: Can do, Will do

A Manager must take on any task handed to them, fill in whenever necessary and work when the store is busiest, unless the assistants are fully capable and well educated to take part of the hours. If you haven't a Manager than all this is for you to consider for yourself.

HOW: Would you agree with me that you cannot possibly do everything yourself?

After careful deliberation choose a helper to act as the Manager. Give this person a 60-to 90-day probationary period. With his or her help begin to write a system to train and educate your helpers to be motivated in wanting to give of themselves to meet every customer need. There will have to be many discussions about every facet of store operation. You will be building a system for Customer Care that will carry you forward for years to come. Just keep it tweaked so it is modern and answers your wants and needs.

Chapter 5
Job Descriptions: Standards

At Malley's we call ourselves Advocates. The word itself means to back or promote a person or a cause. It means so much more than the word employee or associates! An employee is described as a worker, a wage earner. An associate is described as subordinate, an assistant. Advocate is described as a supporter, a promoter. A Malley's Advocate supports and believes in Malley's Chocolates, we enjoy working together, and by delighting our customers, we hope they become fans of Malley's Chocolates.

Every company wants thinking, helpful, pleasant employees. However, for them to be this way, you, as the Leader, must give them the opportunity for know-how, growth, and leadership. Your employees must know what you expect from them and what they can offer you. Nothing the administrative group can think up, create, invest in, build, or talk about, can never be successful without your company's greatest asset—your employees. You can set the stage, but without stagehands and great players, what do you have? Disappointment. You will have continually fewer audience members.

Then comes the sign: Closed. Here is how to see that this scenario never happens to you.

Have you ever shopped for a puzzle to put together? You most likely looked at the picture first to see if it was interesting to you. Then, you looked at the size of the pieces to see if you had the patience to put it together and how much time you thought it might take to complete it. You made the decision to buy it. As you worked with the puzzle, countless times you checked the picture on the box to see if you were doing it right or how a piece fit in. With your interest, this scenario is going to give you those thinking helpful pleasant employees. It starts with what a well written job description (JD) will do for your helpers.

Job Descriptions (JD) and how they should be used

Compose clear concise job descriptions that are easy to understand and can be used as a reference.

The Advocate decided upon the position because it appeared interesting, and they thought the goals could be accomplished. They asked for instructions when hired. They are eager. Help them to be successful. Advise them, check on them, be someone they can turn to when needed. Suggest they often check their JD to make sure that they accomplish all of their all duties and performed them in the correct time frame. The JD is a contract. Therefore, you want to be certain it is written correctly.

For our JDs, at the very top of each job description, our Mission statement is written to reinforce the description Advocates were presented with when they were hired. Advocates need to understand it and know why they believe in it. A well-written job description, properly developed, will give you those thinking, helpful, pleasant employees you need because they will not only have formed a bond with you, but they will know exactly what you want them to do.

After a person has some tenure with us—three months or more—we might ask that they write their own mission statement concerning their work at Malley's Chocolates empathizing what they hope to contribute to our customer's experience. They are told their main function is caring for our customers, continue to work on their Skillshops, and keeping our store and all displays in prime condition. It is explained that this position requires them to be on their feet advising and caring for customers during their shift. One of the causes of frustration for both employees and employers is a lack of understanding of what needs to be done. This problem can be substantially diminished when job descriptions are made clear. Making sure the JD is clear is up to you.

One example is that the outer shipping carton used at Malley's can hold 30 pounds. Every Advocate needs to demonstrate that he or she can easily pick up and handle the weight. We also ask them to attend meetings if called upon and be able to handle other unlisted duties. They are told how to go about getting a grievance or other mishap resolved. Their own signature supports that their JD is up-to-date and that their responsibilities are understood. If they are experiencing a complication, they are to report to the Manager or their Assistant Manager. JDs are formally checked yearly at the Advocates' Conversation Connection and informally throughout the year.

An important consideration for good job descriptions is that in a court of law, they may be your best evidence when supporting your treatment of and expectations from your helpers and their deliberate promises to you. Top those thoughts off with the added security that the person indicated their job description was accurate and up-to-date and that you have their signature to prove it.

Your employees are now relieved of the stress of wondering what their duties are. When working with you, because of your manner and disposition, they are more relaxed and willing to suggest, to offer, to try something new, to help! Trust and fair pay together is the magic formula! Knowing that their Leader is working with them in achieving results and notices their work can renew or inspire an employee's excitement about their work.

Job descriptions:
Develop a must-do list for each position. In bullet form, write:
- Main jobs (priority)
- Tasks that should be accomplished on the way to finishing (duties)
- How it will look when finished (standards)
- Estimated time to perform (time)

Keep working with your list eliminating every word, phrase, or thought that can be removed, making sure the core of what you want done still comes through.

If you have purchased a going concern, one great boost to get everyone working to your standards of what a good business is all about is to ask your present people performing that job now to write their job description for you. This exercise is very revealing. Make certain you set the guidelines, or you will receive pages and pages from some and two lines from others.

- Ask them to list in bullet form their main responsibility and the next three in order.
- How do they perform them?
- How do they know when it is done correctly?
- What is the time frame for completion?

If you only ask them to write their job description, it will be a time of reckoning. You will come face-to face-with yourself. You will find that many employees think part of their job is not at all what you are thinking their responsibilities are in the store. It will be a great learning time for you. It will be exciting because you can easily see that here is something you must correct. As you correct it, the process will lead you into more adjustments in your policies and systems. A good job description will state what the job is about and what is expected of the person holding the position. By reading their JD, a person will know what is expected of them, such as lifting a 30 lb. outer carton full of chocolate boxes, how long they will be on their feet, what they will be expected to learn and know. Other choices are scheduling, assigning, teaching and coaching, and meeting financial goals.

When I did it, (even though they already had JDs), my Advocates' perceptions and answers that came back showed me where my work should be centered!

Some Managers mentioned how important it was to have a clean store or ordering supplies, so they are never out of something a customer may ask for and putting the order away properly. Another Manager mentioned hiring and doing the scheduling. However, very few put what I considered their top job to be. My priority is the same as your priority—take care of the customers! But our assistants often think their tasks are what is important. Important, yes, but not the responsibility. For the Managers, hiring edges out Customer Care because if the hiring is not done correctly, there will be fewer and fewer customers.

The way to correct this quandary, this vagueness, is to write a good job description, and together with Advocates, discuss it and tell them to often refer to it so they know they are on track. The most difficult part for all of us entrepreneurs is to take the time to plan and not jump to the action part of the task.

To get any job done according to your satisfaction is to write down what you want to have happen. Writing your expectations is your priority.

1. Picture in your mind how you want to get it done (duties).
2. How will they know when they have done it according to your satisfaction? You will have explained or shown them earlier the results you want to see.
3. What percent of their time should a person spend doing the different parts of the job?

The first thing to do is a study of the situation. Think about the job as a whole to determine the parts. Do a complete work-up of what you want to accomplish; never go straight to the objectives (results), or there will be an inaccurate spin to your facts. Think the task through. What is the job all about?

Now, after thoughtful conversation and maybe observation of your priority, you can prepare your objectives for the job.

1. Priority: What you want accomplished first.
2. Objective (Duties): What must be done to finish correctly.
3. Standard (Result): How it's to look when completed.
4. Percentage of time dedicated for your duties. Your Manager will do the planning. It is not the duty for a helper. However, you don't want the Manager spending the whole day planning. They have other priorities to be performed or developed as well.

At Malley's Chocolates, we use words that are almost regular for Job Descriptions: Priority, Duties, Standards, and Time to do it.

1. We call what needs to be done: *Priority:* Ex. Wash a window.
2. We call the process of the task: *Duties.*
    - Shine inside and out, if possible.
    - If very dirty, use a dry cloth and brush off and down; sills and window hardware wiped or cleaned.
    - Use cleaner, dry, and shine.
    - If possible, work in the shade. It helps keep windows cooler, so cleaner doesn't dry when it makes contact which creates streaking.
    - Rinse cloths (both sides) and hang to dry.

- Wipe cleaner bottle and put back with other cleaners. Be sure directions are readable.
- If used, put away ladder.
3. The benchmark; our *Standards:*
    - No streaking, shined inside and out, if possible.
    - Complete window fittings shiny.
    - Clean and properly put "Tools" away.
4. Time to be spent getting the results:
    - 15 minutes—windows medium size, window hardware and sills in and out
    - 7 min. to put away "Tools."

Whenever a problem presents itself, always check the job description to see that you told the Advocate how to please you and how long it should take. How can anyone possibly know how to please us unless we tell them? If we don't tell them, they may please us some of the time and irritate us at other times, completely unbeknownst to them.

To help you write good Standards (results), think about the job you want to do. When clearly defined goals are lacking, no one knows how they are to please us. It's difficult to guess when the Leader is impressed with our work, or what they want, or feels is the most important work. It's safe to think that if we don't say anything, we must be pleased. On the other hand, if the assistant is concerned and think they are not pleasing us because we don't say anything, they are constantly worried they are going to be fired.

Another good reason for clearly defined Standards (results) is it tells the Manager when the job is performed correctly. It's so important to decide what you think of as a job well done. You can at any time look at the job description and decide specifically where the person or group needs help. Then you have your problem narrowed down. My stepfather was a surgeon. I can promise you he never performed an operation before he had decided what needed to be fixed and how he was going to do it, so his patient could enjoy good health.

How to Write a Good Job Description
First phase: The Standards should be written very sharply, very clearly so both you and the Advocate can agree that you both understand what the Standards mean. Now the Advocate can decide what they should do to get where they want to go. Always remember that

a Standard describes the intended results rather than the ways to get those outcomes. A Standard is a statement; it is not a description. A description tells about the content and procedures while a Standard describes a desired outcome.

The second phase of a job description is to state enough to be sure the desired performance would be recognized by another competent person and detailed enough so another person can understand your intent as you understand it. If you find out the job description isn't understood, fix it. Don't get into a discussion of words. Reword the description until it is clearly understood. Don't waste time. A condition or process, or as at Malley's Chocolates, the Duties, will always describe what the Advocate will be doing when demonstrating achievement of a Standard.

The third phase tells how well we want someone to be able to do something. You will describe acceptable performance. You will describe your desired standards. Remember, this is your business. When you decide you are satisfied, you are satisfied. To ensure your satisfaction, you must make sure that the people trying to please you understand how to perform the job you want done.

The last phase of writing a good job description is to give them percentages so a person can tell if the work is meeting your time standards. These criteria are very important because if a person can't get the work accomplished, it should cause conversation about the results. You will find you will either move job responsibilities around, re-write instructions, decide if you want all your results met, or help the person with time management. Cluster the work and write a percentage of time to accomplish the task.

Think about this: the next time someone irritates you, maybe you should be irritated with yourself for not taking the time to work on your business instead of in it!

Instead, get your favorite pen and get busy:

Priority – what needs to be done as soon as possible. Importance.

Duties – the process of how to do the tasks to achieve the Standard.

Standards – what the job will look like when it is completed—Desired outcome.

Time Percentage – How long it will take to complete the task to Standard. Example: one hour

Job Description: Full and Part-Time Advocate

Positions report to the Store Manager or Assistants. Store schedules will be posted every three weeks; request time off one week before that time; check your store for Holiday work restrictions. Holidays and events require that "days off" be banned. Must be able to stand and move on feet during the entire shift. Lift outer carton filled with 30 one-pound boxes of Chocolates. Must wear food-handling approved gloves; no skin allergies. Able to quickly move fingers.
Must arrange for transportation to and from work.

As the most important information, every job description has our Mission statement as a first priority to understand and come to believe in.

"Malley's Chocolates is committed to making and selling the finest Chocolates, roasted nutmeats and ice cream. We generate profits for growth by providing the finest services to the delight of our customers."

Malley's Chocolates is committed to making and selling the finest Chocolates, roasted nutmeats and ice cream. We generate profits for growth by providing the finest services to the delight of our customers.

Priorities	Duties	Standards/Results	Time
During every shift welcome and smile at customers	Step forward. Look into the eye to whom you are greeting or speaking. Relax customer with some "Small Talk" to convince you are friendly. Decide if they are in a hurry, need a chair, help with packages.	They appear happy.	Every opportunity.
No cellphone, etc., use during shift.	Keep mind on customers and being helpful.	Be trustworthy, so you are alert to Customer Care and Malley's values	During entire shift
During every shift know and understand our Mission.	Add value by being helpful, considerate, and friendly. Smile with lips and eyes; listen, repeat and fulfill needs and/or wishes.	With a pleasant expression on your face, repeat their wishes and quickly service them.	Be your best self
Complete the entire Malley Manners System.	Training period for full-time – 4 months. Part-time – 13.3 months.	Be a mirror of your Skillshops education.	Desire/Study
During every shift accept jobs as given.	Agree on method, time to devote, predicted results.	As projected	Willingly
During every shift be a team player.	Be flexible when working with others, and hours to work.	Include everyone in your circle of friends. Accept jobs with a good attitude.	"Do unto others as you would have them do unto you."
During every shift offer to help with Skillshops.	Help others to understand why it's essential to understand the Skillshop and help with its practice.	Make it fun.	Be an advocate with character
Arrive 10 minutes early for shift. Notice landscape and lights upon arrival – report your observation and details to Manager (or Asst.) immediately.	Put personal possessions away. Check appearance for compliance. Use restroom. Greet Advocates. When the store is not busy, check Jobs List.	At shift time, present yourself ready for Malley time. Upbeat attitude.	During the entire shift, adhere to all stated Priorities.

Job Descriptions: Standards 77

If you should feel unsafe, report to your Manager immediately. If any other kind of situation occurs, report to your Manager. If you are not satisfied, then report to the Leader of Retail.

I understand what is expected of me. We conversed about anything I wanted discussed. All the above has been explained to me. I realize going forward, this information is my total responsibility. I understand I can always speak with my Manager or the assistants, then to the Leader of Retail. At hiring, I signed a form stating I can lift 30 lbs. I can constantly stand and move about during my entire eight-hour shift. I can wear food-handling approved gloves. I can easily move my fingers. I can multiply, add, and subtract. I hopefully can work overtime when needed. I have transportation to and from the store.

Signature of Advocate: _____ Date: _____
Signature of Manager: _____ Date: _____
Signature of Parent if under age 18: _____
If an emergency arises call _____ Relationship:_____
Phones-- Cell: _____ Landline:_____
Email address: _____
Or
If an emergency arises call _____ Relationship:_____
Phones-- Cell: _____ Landline:_____
Email address: _____
Any comments:
_____
_____
_____
_____
_____
_____
_____

Chapter 6
Connections: Relationships

Our Leaders must think or see to every detail, check or develop it, and see that it improves under their care.

Studies show a disheartened person will tell 10 others about their poor experience, and a happy person will tell two. Over time, these friends tell their friends, and numbers add up. Ultimately, our reputation, our brand is tarnished or polished by what you do!

It's your "house"; are you ready for company? We must work and accomplish jobs together to delight our customers; every action must reflect the knowledge we have gained and passed onto our employees. Responsibility (our core values of safety, quality, and value) for our customers is the very heart of our business.

Once you select your core values, it is much easier to create your mission. Ideas are not direction; they are what help you find your direction and give you a sense of purpose.

But, dear Owner, do you really know how to lead? A fine business always has a successful Leader at the forefront.

In order for you to do the very best job you can, you must know and understand how to lead. It is your responsibility that all systems are constantly primed (all management information systems and network infrastructure). The unified vision of the Leader must have plans in place that create constant improvement and safeguarding who and what you are now. All these requirements must be meticulously done, so all the systems work smoothly. Everyone must be always on guard to be extremely careful about giving attention to details everywhere and report if details need attention. Distinction is achieved in the details. This is such an important sentence: Distinction is achieved in the details. Walt Disney's legacy has certainly proved that to be true. We must be always on guard to be extremely careful about details.

We must work and accomplish jobs together to delight our customers; every action must reflect this knowledge. Responsibility for our customer is the very heart of our business.

Chapter 7
Discipline: Control

One of the most important functions you must do as an Owner or trailblazer for your operation is to protect yourself and your business. That is why one of your most important jobs is to learn how to "write someone up" and keep the former status quo.

The Wall Street Journal says firing someone is one of the three most anxious jobs of a president. The most distressing I have ever found was worrying about doing it correctly. Therefore, we always contacted our HR attorney to guide us through this situation. If you must correct an Advocate, but not fire, take into consideration their personality. Few people can take this kind of conversation without some form of brooding. Anyone pouting or angry with you is not going to be able to be the kind of salesperson you want meeting with your customers.

Take into consideration the toll your discussion is going to have on the person and choose the best time to have it when your customers (internal or external) will be the least affected. Other research has shown that when a person is threatened (which they will feel they are when being chastised), activity diminishes in certain parts of the brain. David Rock of *Your Brain at Work* says when that happens, "people's fields of view actually constrict, they can take in a narrower stream of data, and there's a restriction in creativity."

Small Business Owners usually work side by side with assistants who become business friends. It is very difficult to tell a friend they must improve in certain areas. It is even more difficult to use a "Write up Procedure" with a friend. You have heard how important it is to have a paper trail on any Advocate creating disturbances. Many a friend has become a foe over a seemingly simple exchange or difference of opinion. It is a very difficult action that requires thought because this is ever so much more important than a difference of opinion. Keep yourself well versed and your voice pleasant. Review their job descriptions, comment on the part where the offense was committed and focus on what you need to say. Then explain that it is necessary, to be fair, correct and consistent with everyone, a conversation like this must be recorded and signed. I'll fill in the information and you can sign it. If you do not agree with the information, you will still sign that we had this conversation, but you can make a note in the 'Comment Section". After the signing, say something like, ". . . now let's put that behind us because we need to discuss (choose a topic-) the next holiday etc.

Depending on your business and after discussion, you might give the responsibility to speak to someone who needs to improve in a certain area to your Manager, but most likely that would cause a hardship between them, and it would be best if you do it. However, it's an option if you don't have a backbone. The Manager or Supervisor will have to work next to this person all through a shift. If you work or ever have worked side by side with the offending person, you can understand the difficulty.

You must do it because you are in a much better position as you do not have to be by their side during the entire shift. It need not be a long drawn out affair. This is one of the most important reasons you give out bona fide job descriptions and establish clear and logical rules that your Advocates have either helped write or have agreed to. Don Paullin, Principal and President of Hiring Firing Experts, Inc. says, "A simpler way is to work off the job description in everything you do. For legal compliance, simply stay with the job description for your hiring, firing, performance appraisals, raises, and promotions." He also says, "If you wonder if it is illegal ... chances are it is. You will generally stay out of trouble if you just make sure that all your questions are job-related and consistent across the board. That is the acid test. It is also a good idea to have a witness in the room. It can be an Assistant Manager or someone from the administration office. Of course, they have to be informed what they hear will have to be in the strictest confidence and have them sign that they understand the necessary confidentiality.

It often turns out that the offender has not had guidance or support or follow-up. This is another reason to call on your Assistant Manager, who can grow in leadership through the experience. Give these responsibilities for Skillshops and general handbook knowledge to them to follow up with everyone in your store. It is a system that should be established in order to free yourself from having to go over the whole process again. It's not something anyone enjoys, but you must start what is called a "paper trail" so this Advocate's history is documented.

When there is a problem and the offender acts "put upon," it is so reassuring to open their files and go over, if they have any, their past offenses. If it's a personality problem, theft or gross incompetence, indecency, or insubordination, you will react differently. Ask the person to stop by your office. In complete privacy explain the circumstances. Let them talk. Acknowledge that you heard them. If it's a theft, fire them. If its insubordination, decide how valuable they are to you. If you want to keep them, give a very serious and direct explanation of what is expected going forward.

Of course, if other Advocates saw or heard the episode, it becomes another factor that must be considered. If this action is repeated, you will have to dismiss them. Agree on goals, agree that the Assistant Manager(s) will help them by paying special attention to them. Write this all on a warning sheet and have them sign that they agree to it and send them home without pay for two or three days to think over what they want to do. Otherwise, fire them. If it's a personality problem, ask them what they think you should do if you must speak to them again. If you are met with silence suggest they think about it and return in an hour with their answer. When they return, stand so they don't sit, and simply ask what their answer is. If you are met with silence, smile and tell them you know they are smarter than this, but if they need help, they can ask you for it.

If the person being talked to asks, give two choices (1) Work it out with the other(s) within two days, or (2) You could decide to leave our employment. Which do you prefer to do? If they choose the first, tell them when to return and bring the other person(s) with them to give you their decisions. Have them sign a warning notice. At the meeting's conclusion, smile at the offender(s) and say, "When you're hitting on all cylinders again, it will be good because we have some new material coming in, and we're going to need your help!

To keep your helpers informed and willingly and emotionally in-sync with you, try this technique:

Build a strong relationship

Because this work is addressed to small businesses, and most businesses Owners call their helpers "employees," I will address them using that title. First, we will not have to dwell on spilt milk because infractions will be dealt with on the spot, and we will have cleaned those issues up long ago.

How to handle an infraction: Either you or your Manager will speak with the offender, hearing both sides of the situation or argument. After a decision is made on how to correct the issue, you or your Manager will immediately inform those persons involved:
- Tell them what you will be expecting.
- Ask if there is a need for further discussion.
- Reach an agreement on time frame.
- Tell the parties they are to fill in the Write Up form. They will notice there is a comment section if they feel the need to use it. After signing it, kindly put it in an envelope found by/in your mailbox by (name a time).

Communication is the very crux for developing trust resulting in supportive employees. When a person knows they are performing to your wishes, because you have told them, they are relieved of the stress of wondering. When working with you, they are more relaxed and willing to suggest, to offer, to try something new, to help! Trust and fair pay are the magic formula!

How to Discipline and Fire Employees

This situation is one no entrepreneur wants to face. But when it happens, you need to know how to do it sensitively--and legally.

Termination can be just as devastating for the person doing the terminating as the person being terminated. The Wall Street Journal has reported that firing someone is one of three situations that make company presidents most anxious. It's probably safe to assume there's plenty of stress inside the person saying, "You're fired."

Aside from the emotional strain on both Owner and employee, legal ramifications are also involved in the act of termination. The following article is geared towards outlining ways of dealing with problem employees and making sure the company doesn't suffer in the long run.

Disciplinary Problems and Probationary Periods

Establishing clear and logical rules, along with an atmosphere of trust between management and labor, will minimize disciplinary confrontations with employees. Often, it's the manner in which rules are established and enforced that makes the difference between a smooth-running operation and a company plagued by employee-related disruptions.

First, any rules established by the company should be reasonable, and workers should be consulted before the rules are adopted. The rules--and consequences for breaking them--should be known and well-understood by all workers. They should be impartially enforced, with any punitive actions understood by employees beforehand. You should be flexible in the enforcement of certain rules, considering extenuating circumstances when applicable. Communications channels should also remain open so that employees feel free to question rules they feel are unreasonable.

If a circumstance arises in which an employee warrants punishment, you should develop an employee warning system which should be implemented in a predictable and logical sequence and should be easily adaptable to varying circumstances. For example, you might devise a system by which the employee is gently reminded of company policy on a certain issue the first time such a warning is warranted. The second time, a sterner warning is given, often in the form of a written reprimand outlining past performance and the prior warning(s) given; a probationary—and final—warning can be issued the third time, with a thorough accounting of employee performance and a clear understanding that violating the probation will result in dismissal. All such warnings must be done in private so as not to embarrass the employee, with counseling offered on improving performance. The warnings should also be recorded in the employee's personnel file, as mentioned in more detail below. Also, warnings must carry weight behind them, or they won't be taken seriously; if a probationary warning is given, systematic follow-through should occur the next time serious disciplinary action is needed. Probationary periods should have an established time limit. The probationary warning should make clear what you expect in the way of performance improvement and over what time frame.

Try to Salvage the Job

Terminating an employee "because that's the last straw!" or because you have been looking for a reason to fire them can cause more problems in the long run than the ones you think you're solving. In these cases, it's better to try to turn the employee around than go through the painful firing/hiring process—unless the person has committed acts that are clear grounds for immediate termination, such as impropriety, gross incompetence, or theft.

First, ask yourself who is really at fault in the situation. Perhaps the employee has had little or no control over his or her performance. Often in small companies, job assignments are poorly defined. This issue is one of the reasons writing down a job description when you are hiring is so important. Yet, it is a sad fact that lack of adequate support and communication are often the real reasons behind poor results from an employee.

If the Advocate is at fault, a Communication Conversation can allow the person a fair chance to change. Remind the employee what is expected of them and that continued failure to perform will lead to dismissal. You must lay your cards on the table and establish goals for them to achieve. Do not put off what you know you should do, but just "can't" is not keeping up to your responsibilities. What kind of a Leader are you? The first experience doing this is the most difficult, but experience will give you the confidence you need to do the right move for your company. Be accountable to your dream. You must make a paper trail so when you need it you will have it.

Document Poor Performance

You should get an agreement on these goals and deadlines in writing and have the employee sign the form, so you have complete documentation on file. This written process forces you to analyze exactly what poor performance means to you. Misunderstandings about job duties will be brought out in the interview, as well as personal problems that are affecting performance. Sometimes these problems are temporary and can be worked around.

The most important reason for fully documenting performance

reviews is to protect yourself if the employee must be fired later. You will have clear and objective information on which to base your decision. The employee can't say he recommended a Communication Conversation review policy for even the smallest of companies with only one or two employees. Basic to this procedure is a personnel file for each new employee hired. Into the file go the job description, job application (signed), resume, if any, and regular "Conversation Conversations."

Every six months, reviews or efficiency reports should be conducted for each employee after an initial probationary period. Review should be more frequent during the probationary period, perhaps monthly.

Write a dated memo for the person's file whenever performance problems arise between reviews. Disputes among employees, missed assignments, and the like should be documented in writing. This notation not only helps you do a better evaluation but serves as evidence if you need to produce evidence later.

If your employee doesn't make a comeback in performance after being put on notice, you must replace that person. The best way to approach this situation is quickly, without procrastinating. Use compassion and sensitivity when dealing with this task, avoid lecturing and, above all, do not resort to a shouting match. Limit yourself to facts supported by written documentation. Some labor attorneys counsel that a witness should be present at a firing for better protection in the event controversy arises later.

In recent years, labor boards and courts have sided with terminated employees more and more by awarding punitive damages or requiring payment of compensation in cases where termination grounds were unclear. The number of terminated employees who seek judicial relief is clearly on the rise, due in part to the impact of well-publicized sums of money awarded, job reinstatements with retroactive pay, etc.

Written evidence is the only material acceptable to labor boards and the courts. You can't afford to rely on your memory. A hazy recall of the facts or reasons for dismissal will tip the scales toward the employee in almost any case where cause for termination is questionable. It's worth your time to seek the help of a competent attorney familiar with labor laws in your state. He or she will help you understand the steps you should take to protect yourself from the nightmare that a botched firing can cause.

Other Issues to Consider Before Firing

You should consider other legal and operational problems before you fire a person. Many growing companies have employment contracts with key executives, and these contracts should be carefully checked for terms. Union employees will have collective bargaining agreements that must also be considered.

If the employee is an officer or director of the corporation, no matter how small your corporation is, firing that employee does not terminate his or her appointment as an officer or director. Get a resignation or vote as required by the corporate bylaws, recording any such actions in resolutions as required by the corporation commission(s) in your state. Remember that the applicable law is based on the jurisdiction in which your business is incorporated, not where you're located.

If you've given the person signature power at the bank, withdraw it immediately. Anyone with the power to write checks against your account may be tempted to do so. Likewise, don't forget to take back any keys, credit cards, samples, or other company property in his or her possession. The best way to keep track of these assets is a checklist of items given to the employee (and signed for) to be kept in his or her personnel file.

Be careful about benefit plans and be aware of their terms in the event of termination. The Employee Retirement Income Security Act protects the rights of terminated employees and requires strict compliance. There are penalties for failure to pay vested interest in profit-sharing plans, for example. Even health-insurance plans are covered under this act. If you fail to inform an employee of their rights under health plan, you can be held liable.

Resist the temptation to transfer the employee to another job in the company if it's done solely as a means of delaying the inevitable. However, sometimes a person can be better suited for another job in the organization, and you should consider this alternative. But in most small businesses, there's no useful place for the person to go.

Don't delay firing an employee out of kindness, and don't notify the person too far ahead of when the termination will be effective. An employee who has been notified of termination rarely has their mind on the job and can end up disrupting other employees.

An even worse mistake is allowing an employee on his way out to train his replacement, although that arrangement has been done in some instances. Train the replacement yourself so that the mistakes and attitudes of his predecessor are not continued. Another approach is to groom a replacement over time so that someone on staff is ready to step in.

At firing, get from them keys and any safe combinations. Prepare any monies owed them, such as vacation pay, and any other information they might need. Walk them to the exit door. Don't be surprised if, in their anger, they may do harm on the way out or tell others about the "injustice". We had one teenager pull the plug on our ice cream freezer; another tried to steal products.

Consequences of Firing

Consider this example: A small-business Owner who got into an argument over policy matters with his Manager dismissed the subordinate on the spot. Within two weeks, the Manager had formed his own company and attracted several major clients from his old firm as well as two key employees who felt the Manager had gotten a raw deal.

Whether you call it terminated, canned, or axed, there's no easy way to fire someone who works for you. But if it's poorly handled, it can be a disaster. In addition to loss of business as in the case above, there are legal pitfalls as well. A lawsuit, win or lose, involves legal fees and the time lost defending yourself in court or before the Department of Labor.

While there is no one "right" way to handle a dismissal, you can take certain steps to balance the rights and interests of the individual against the needs of your company. This balance is particularly vital in a small company where the severance of a key employee can be crippling.

Cushion the Blow

Shock, anger, and surprise are common reactions to getting fired, even among employees who know their performance has been slipping and have been warned in advance. The important thing to remember in dealing with such reactions is that a person who wasn't right for you can be right for someone else.

You can make an exit easier on the departing employee in several different ways. Most importantly, timely payment of all money due the person is important and will keep you from running afoul of the applicable state laws covering employment.

Allowing the terminated person to submit a letter of resignation is another means of removing the stigma of being fired and makes it easier to find other work.

A letter of recommendation that does not exaggerate abilities or cover any problems may be appropriate, as may pointing the person in the direction of job opportunities that you may know about. In some cases, companies have found it worthwhile to pay for the services of an outplacement firm that helps key individuals pick up the pieces and find another job. This assistance is done, of course, out of enlightened self-interest on the part of companies who can easily be exposed to litigation by a disgruntled ex-executive.

In the final analysis, a firing can be best for all parties concerned if it's handled properly. When problems do occur, it's often because business Owners weren't aware of the potential pitfalls and did not plan for them in advance. It's clear there are no easy ways to fire someone and no simple guidelines to follow. But a business Owner who is compassionate and sensitive can avoid nightmarish legal and operational problems that result when a firing is viewed simply as giving a person walking papers at a moment's notice.

Avoiding Discrimination Accusations

An at-will employee may be terminated by an employer at any time with or without cause and with or without advance notice if the reason for the termination is not prohibited by law. For example, federal laws prohibit discrimination in employment based on certain protected classifications, including race, color, sex (including pregnancy), religion, national origin, age (40 or over), and disability. Therefore, an employer is prohibited from terminating an employee if the basis of that termination is his or her membership in any of these protected classifications.

If an individual believes he has been discriminated against with respect to an employment decision, he must file a complaint with the Equal Employment Opportunity Commission (EEOC) or the state counterpart thereof before he can file a lawsuit alleging that an employer violated those laws.

While there is no absolute way to prevent a terminated employee from filing an EEOC charge, you can take certain steps to minimize the chances that such a complaint will be filed. Moreover, an employer can take steps to put itself in a better position to respond to the EEOC, if a charge is filed.

With respect to attempting to resolve a dispute with an employee regarding termination of employment—including any potential discrimination claims—employers sometimes offer severance packages. These packages provide some form of consideration (typically, payment of a particular amount) in exchange for a release by the employee, requiring the employee to agree to release and waive any and all claims arising out of the employment relationship between the employee and the employer. Note, however, that even if the employee signs the release and accepts the consideration, the United States Supreme Court has held that this consideration does not absolutely preclude the employee from filing a charge with the EEOC; although, it does prevent him from recovering any monetary damages. However, the EEOC is not bound by the release, and thus, under these circumstances, the EEOC can act upon the charge, assuming it believed that a discriminatory act had occurred.

If an employer offers a severance package to an employee who is over age 40, and the employee is asked to sign a release, specific requirements must be met in order to comply with the Older Worker's Benefit Protection Act (OWBPA), which amended the Age Discrimination in Employment Act of 1967 (ADEA), in order for the employee's waiver of rights to be valid. Among other requirements, the release must include a 21-day review period as well as a seven-day revocation period; the language of the release must be understandable to the average protected employee; and the employee must be advised in writing that he/she has the right to consult an attorney prior to signing the release. (Please note that this article is not intended to address all the requirements under the OWBPA. Employers should speak to their local counsel for guidance when these specific issues arise.)

Whether or not a severance agreement is offered and/or signed, you can put yourself in a better position to defend an EEOC charge in other ways, which we mentioned earlier in this article: Communicating with employees when performance and/or work-related issues arise; documenting all important communication and relevant workplace events as they occur; having witnesses present when communication is oral; and having employees sign all written communication about the issues. Additionally, an employer should enforce its policies and procedures uniformly and consistently.

None of these suggestions guarantees that an employee will not file an EEOC charge or guarantee a successful defense or favorable outcome if an EEOC charge is filed. However, if these actions are done correctly, they do provide important protection to the employer.

(This article was excerpted from The Small Business Encyclopedia, except for the discrimination section, which was written by Larry Ros-

enfeld and appeared on Entrepreneur.com as the article "Protecting Yourself When Terminating Employees.")

Keeping your Paper Trails safe - What Should You Keep in Your Employees' Personnel Files?

This topic is very important. I asked a well-known attorney in Cleveland to write this for me. He helps us with HR functions. I would never want my opinion to not give you the most complete and correct information you should have and use!

Here is his information:

Brian J. Kelly
Chair, Labor & Employment Practice Group
Frantz Ward LLP, 200 Public Square, Suite 3000, Cleveland, OH 44114
direct 216.515.1620 / fax 216.515.1650 / cell 216.403.3834 /
bkelly@frantzward.com
www.frantzward.com

The following is his advice:

Creating and Maintaining Personnel Files

Regardless of whether employees are model employees or problem employees, it is important to create and maintain personnel files regarding them. Attention should be given, however, to the contents of these personnel files, and they should not simply be places where documents are placed without a plan or purpose. When properly maintained, personnel files can be a reliable source of useful information. Importantly, if there is a legal dispute with a current or former employee, the employee's personnel file will almost always be one of the first items requested.

The following are the types of documents that you should maintain in every employee's personnel file:

- Documents relating to the hiring process, including any applications, cover letters, references, background checks, offer letters, and employment agreements;
- Signed acknowledgment forms from the employee showing that the employee received your handbook and other policies;
- Disciplinary and counseling documents, including documents gathered as part of any investigation that resulted in discipline or counseling;

- *Performance evaluations and any action plans developed to address any performance issues;*
- *A signed copy of the job descriptions for all positions the employee holds during his or her employment;*
- *Documents relating to compliments or commendations regarding the employee, as well as any complaints or negative reports regarding the employee;*
- *Records of all training completed by the employee;*
- *Emergency contact forms;*
- *For departing employees, documents relating to the employee's resignation or termination.*

You will create or gather other types of documents about employees from time to time that should not be included in the personnel files. These documents include the following:

- *Medical records, including drug and alcohol test results. Certain laws, including the Americans with Disabilities Act (ADA), require that employee medical records be kept separate from personnel files and in a secure area accessible only to persons who have a legitimate business reason to have access to the records.*
- *I-9 Forms. I-9 forms should be kept separate and apart from employee personnel files and under certain circumstances may be maintained electronically. The U.S. Citizenship and Immigration Service has the authority to inspect all an employer's I-9 forms without advance notice. As a result, it is a sound practice to maintain a separate file that contains only the I-9 forms, which can then be provided quickly without having to sort through other records.*
- *Garnishment documents and documents relating to child support or domestic relations issues.*
- *Medical insurance, life insurance and any other insurance application and claims forms.*
- *Workers' compensation documents.*

One question many employers ask is whether an employer must give employees access to their personnel files. The answer to this question, unfortunately, is not a simple one. This answer is so because the answer is controlled by state and local laws. For example, in Ohio, employers do not need to provide employees with access to their personnel files. By contrast, employers in Michigan and numerous

Discipline: Control

other states do need to provide access due to laws in those states. I recommend that you determine the law in your jurisdiction and then set a policy that complies with that law."

Chapter 8
The Basics

During our face-to-face meeting with a new Advocate (what some companies call team members), we explain the main principles or core of our operations. Responsibility for our customers' happiness is at the heart of our business.

This statement is crucial to Malley's Chocolates' continued success. We impress upon those Advocates helping us that they are as much responsible for it as our Executive Group. The words, "...the heart of our business" was chosen to express this thought because as in any living breathing thing, the most important organ is the heart. It is usually healthy, strong and powerful. It must be to pump and circulate vital oxygen and (hopefully) vitamin-enriched blood throughout our bodies giving us the energy for action. The human heart is also considered as the center for emotions and personality attributes like the character or quality of a thing. We all know the heart cannot think; that's the job of our brain. However, the heart has been given these characteristics because the heart is the center—the very core of our being.

Of course, the business itself is not alive. But by our brains, vigor, and determination, it becomes like a living thing, growing, changing, and prospering. As you progress through instructions and practices in how we need to treat a Malley's "Inside" and "Outside" customer, browser or shopper, you will see how we helped Malley's Chocolates continue to grow and improve.

Just like our heart pumps healthy, renewed blood, our Malley Chocolates Systems continually improve to flow healthy, strong and powerful throughout our company. We educate and train our Advocates in our core beliefs through our Malley Manners Systems, so when they leave personal time and check into Malley time, their mindset is on customer care at Malley's.

It is to be understood, as I am sure you will agree, that to have the power to pump healthy renewed and powerful blood, your body must have a basic structure of strength. That strength is realized from a system of proper food, liquids, and vitamins, sunshine, sleep, and other health support. In business, that support is called your businesses infrastructure, or organization, directed by a person who knows the work of a Leader. This responsibility establishes the focus of the company, realized by educating, directing, trusting and spot-checking the actions of others, and getting positive responses.

In retail, some people care for inside customers while others care for outside customers. When our customer leaves us--via phone, the Internet, a personal visit, email, the website, or through our corporate and fundraising arm, it is our determined desire that they feel and know they received knowledgeable, efficient and warm-hearted service. This service includes such things as:

- When a Manager calls the production department, they must be able to get a correct and prompt answer to their question. (An inside customer)
- When a customer's phone order is placed, that customer must know that the chocolates will be fresh and carefully arranged in their box, packaged attractively, and properly shipped to get to its destination on time. Every box or bag must look exactly like its catalog or Internet picture, described over the phone or texted. (An outside customer)
- Our Managers know that their spirit of kindness and approach of 'let's get the job done" sets the tone or atmosphere for the whole store. They are the Leaders of our Malley Manners Cus-

tomer Care Program. Because of their care, Malley Manners will be nurtured and continue to be improved. Newcomers are welcomed, trained, and educated in our Malley Manners system. The Assistant Managers practice with them until they are comfortable with the material, before they meet their customers.

When we meet with a new employee, we tell them that of course an individual employee is not responsible for the humming along of our whole business. However, the employees must realize that if they don't do their part, it creates a weakened place in our way of doing something. The order is upset until it is corrected. It may not show up at first, but each time someone, an "Inside" or "Outside" customer is not correctly cared for by you it creates a weakened place, a bottleneck, a breakdown, and if continued, our system gets weaker by the day. It's as if your heart was able to pump less blood each day until a terrible day when you may have a heart attack. You did not notice it until you started feeling weakened or had a difficult time breathing. There is a strong possibility of death. It takes work, care and an infusion of medicine to repair your heart and your weakened body. All attention must be given to it as other parts of your body may suffer. This chance of a breakdown in the system is why we give such attention to each responsibility within our company, which is why we hire certain people because they said (and we believed them when they said) they are flexible and will do as asked. We are depending on our employees to help us achieve "Delighting our customers".

Coca-Cola commissioned a study that showed a disheartened person will tell 10 others about their poor experience and a happy person will tell two. Over time, these friends tell their friends. The numbers add up; our reputation is tarnished or polished by what our employees do!

For each of us to do the very best job we can, everything must be ready for us, so we can do our work. After all, we are not superwoman or man! So, to have everything ready, we all must do our singular part well. That means to be kind to everyone and follow our job descriptions. It is the responsibility of our CEO that all our systems are constantly primed. Safety, quality, and value take care of budgets and financials, banking, marketing, item numbers, procurement, ingredients, general items, hiring, management, website upkeep, infrastructure (buildings, offices, sidewalks and parking lots smooth and clean); vans, trucks, cars checked; handbook correct, files in order; helpers educated and trained; new ways of doing business; Account executives on top of their responsibilities checking out new, better, easier, smarter methods for Corporate and Fund-Raising customers.

In short, it's all our management information systems and network infrastructure. The unified vision of our Executive Group guided by our core beliefs must have plans in place that create constant improvement and safeguarding who and what we are now. All these items must be meticulously accomplished, so all our systems work smoothly. We must be always on guard to be extremely careful about giving attention to details everywhere by either fixing or reporting if they need care. Distinction is achieved in the details. This is such an important sentence: it means by taking care of the little things, those same things taken care of enable us to have a solid foundation that can grow the big things that bring success.

After studying our stores, how we spoke to each other, how helpers came to know how we wanted our customers to know we really cared about them as individuals; how glad we were they decided to come into our store, we directed the thought that each person who comes into our store or tells us of an unhappy circumstance is giving us two gifts—their time and their opinion—and for no charge!

With our Managers, we collaborated on over 59 details which were then developed into little learning structures I call Skillshops. We studied from how to say "Hello!" to a customer, to how to complete a store checklist, to how to clean a restroom, to cleaning schedules for almost-immaculate stores. As the business grows, some Skillshops are changed, and others are created. This research is how Malley Manners evolved. I am offering you this information because it has been in use for a very long time and has proven successful.

We worked on Skillshops for some years but, oh, it is worth the effort. To make sure we covered the most important skills, we studied what information to instruct in Skillshops. Further on you will see some examples of our snappy learning modules. These are skills everyone must know and practice before meeting our customers. Every hire goes through the same education and training as the Orientation System is always ready for them, and it gives us peace of mind that everyone has been told the same information. Each Skillshop generally takes 30 -45 minutes to think through and write but only takes a Manager about 10 – 15 minutes to discuss with a new Advocate. A Manager can easily fit that amount of time in their daily schedule. Think of this, how often is an Advocate replaced? Write your Education and

Training program; I've shown you how I did it. However, if you want it now, all completed with lots of additional information, "Malleys.com" has the information connecting with **Malley Manners**. I think it's an appropriate name for the instructions. I hope you will agree! In Malley Manners, I have written the entire preparation, the welcome, and the first 16 Skillshops and Retention Reviews. You can copy all the information, and you will be organized and ready to present our Education and Training System. It will save you hours of work and time while giving you peace of mind as you journey to increasing your bottom line. Your satisfaction comes that you can cross off another line on your "to-do" list and know you have taken another step in reaching your goal. Check out Malleys.com and click on Adele Malley.

Have you ever thought about how many hats an Entrepreneur must wear?

Every impressive small retail store entrepreneur juggles and wears many hats, constantly changing them as needed. The hat a business Owner should wear the most often is the Hat of Determination.

Hat of Determination

Starting a business involves more than finding a good location, getting financed, hiring a Bookkeeper, displaying products, and hiring customer-centered people to take good care of them. We all come from different backgrounds and amounts of education. When someone says, "take good care of them," different listeners can hear the instructions differently. If you are caring for young children, you hear, "Be alert and give tender loving care." If you are a young adult and after introducing friends to your parents, you hear this phrase. At that point, "take good care of them" may mean your parents have given you the OK to use their credit card. If you work for the "Godfather", "Take good care of them" alerts you to employ the death sentence.

So, you can see if you want your customers cared for in the style and manner you prefer, it's best to create clear, detailed information for them. Do you remember when you were in school your teacher always re-capped what was taught yesterday before presenting new material? That method should remind us not to think by telling someone once how we want something done and believe that is the end of the matter. We must think again.

Football and baseball coaches know that to get their players primed each season, they must go back to the basics and practice and practice to be ready for play. If someone does not arrive for spring or summer training, they are fined or let go. There is no nonsense accepted. Follow the rules or don't play. The same idea goes for retailers—employees must know and follow the rules. A good starting place for retailers to find out how much of your information is retained and being used is to present them with a yearly Retention Review.

The success of your retail business is going to take more than hard work and heart to be successful. The triumph of reaching awareness of your brand has everything to do with your own grit as an entrepreneur. Don't be thinking, "I love the business. I'm not concerned about the work; I'm not afraid of long hours and tight budgets". It takes the right type of knowledge complemented by awareness with the courage to execute what you have absorbed. It's easy to get busy but harder to think about what you have learned and decide how to put that into action.

Good businesses are established by pre-planning, thoughtful, dogged preparation for solid planning how to establish your goals. Deciding why you want this business will help you create a Mission Statement. What should your goal be? How you are going to make it a success? Answer that question by investing in yourself and take the time to write a strategic plan. What you write can be altered, changed, blotted out, and rewritten but it gives you overall direction right now.

Also write a business plan so your thoughts about daily concerns can be properly taken care of in a timely manner. All this thinking will give you short good thoughts about why you are going to have a business and what it will do for you.

If you plan to reach success through hard work and heart, you will not advance very far. When the first serious challenge occurs is when so many entrepreneurs slam on the proverbial brakes when they should be pumping them. Pumping saves everything from locking up and perhaps airbags hitting them in the face, so they can't see and can hardly breathe.

The way to meet a bump head on is to quickly and repeatedly press your brakes and then let up; just as before, you keep going forward – that's pumping your brakes, you do not lose complete control, and your car stops. Essentially, the people in the car and the heater or air-conditioner continue to act as before.

Everything does not lock up. So, when you hit a problem or bump in the road, pull the right people aside to help you with the pumping. The others? Leave them be to keep going forward. No sense getting everyone involved. Knowledge, connections in the community and your associations can help you with this seemingly insurmountable bump.

Once you have met this challenge, why, the rest of the huge bumps will dwindle in size. They will never go away, but you will meet each challenge armed with awareness, with knowledge, desire for a right decision, and the know-how to get it! Don't get so locked up in worry by pushing hard on your brakes. By pumping you will soon stop, and if you choose you will continue to go forward.

Speaking of writing strategic and business plans, I read the most interesting article by Noah Parsons, with a great deal of help from Jeff Gish at the University of Oregon. Parson says Gish was immensely helpful in gathering and analyzing the research. The article was called, "Business Planning Makes You More Successful, and We've Got the Science to Prove It." I highly recommend you Google it.

So often, my husband Bill and I visited chocolate shops in many parts of America and some other countries. In some stores I was struck by the lack of merchandising skills. Kitchen work, warehouse interests, and office responsibilities far outweighed the enthusiasm and know-how needed in their stores. To be successful, the entrepreneur has to pay the same respect to presentation as he/she did for their actual products. It's a two-way street: Creative products and creative merchandising. That's the winning combination!

Think of how every upscale restaurateur takes hours planning the look of his/her restaurant. The frame for the future meals becomes a work of art. It may be a vase of flowers sitting on a spotless cloth, the chosen napkins may harmonize or match or accent the tablecloth, gleaming silverware and sparkling glassware topped off with easy-listening, quiet music. Perhaps artwork adorns the walls, a careful selection for tables and chairs. The background is complete. They open for business. You arrive. Educated in service, waiters and waitresses are ready, heightening your anticipation. When your order is taken and goes to the kitchen, you know something delicious is being made for you. This meal is not by casual happenstance. No, each dish becomes an innovation through the use of color, flavor, and textures complemented with decoration and garnish. When the server presents your dinner, the aromas alone make you even hungrier. You must have a taste!

That picture is how your merchandise must be presented in your business. That's what your store must do. It must create the background, the frame, to showcase your chocolates. Think: quality product, create anticipation, secure it with a presentation befitting its nobility – regal, down home, or fun! Appearance is all about the intricate details that may not seem essential but always are very important because they complete the picture our customer has in mind or surprise and please him/her very much.

Creating the edge, the excitement for your store takes a great deal of thought, attention to the details, and follow through. In the process of completing your plans, realize that information comes from reading, attending good seminars in the correct way, and joining and becoming active in chosen organizations. Talking with others whose work you admire is often answered by being active in your association. Here you will meet other folks who are living somewhat the same life as yourself. They have the same challenges and concerns. Sign up to help on committees because you will find no way quicker for making friends. If you only join but don't take an active part in the events and affairs you may as well not join. What will be the use? For those people in the chocolate retail business, we have a marvelous association called The Retail Confectioners International, which I've been a member for years. It's very worthwhile for a chocolatier to join. In Cleveland we also enjoy COSE – Council of Smaller Enterprises.

Another source for assistance is Score – "Counselors to America's Small Business." It is a 501(c) (3) nonprofit organization that provides free business mentoring services to entrepreneurs in the United States.

Find out what organizations are in your town. Once you connect, don't sit back; get active! Ask questions; be prepared to offer some information or help in return. In your business, it's up to you to build what is in your mind. You might tell others, but they will not know your whole story, all the details you think you will have in operation. After all, this is your story, your passion, your business. You must build a solid foundation that you can copy again and again. You do want more stores, don't you?

Once you have your finances in order, it's time to think about location, location, and location. After preparing your store it's customer, customer, and customer. However, before we can get to our customers, we must build, lease or rent a store

Just as you may have, I too know what it is like to have projects, tight schedules, meetings to attend, speeches to write, and still be home on time to be with your family and their requirements. The house and yard need attention too. All the while knowing what is silently nagging at you is growing like a vine with scratchy tentacles. Every day that which worries us just gets more troubling. I wrote this book to hopefully help you with ideas on how to stop the vine from growing any larger and start letting it bud. Like any athlete, we must all practice the fundamentals over and over, so they are rote when called for. We need coaches to watch and inspect the actions of our "players" and inspire them to be the best they can be. If not ourselves, we need someone to teach our coaches (Managers) and inspire them to be the kind of Leaders we want to call our own.

Here are some steps to get you started:

1. Create a system so everything can flow smoothly the same way time after time.
2. Decide what kind of person you want to hire to be your Manager because this decision is where the personality of your store starts. This person you think about will be hiring others, and we often hire people like ourselves even though it's a grand idea to have some of every type personality and ethnicities in your store, so a customer might want to gravitate to a particular someone. The way your Manager will speak with your customers will soon have all your helpers speaking somewhat the same. The personality and manners of your Manager is very important because he/she will be setting the standards, getting the work accomplished, and, hopefully, an easy friendly manner will be felt throughout your business. Be careful in your hiring!
3. A good foundation strongly supports, while a weak foundation like the first little pig had will allow a strong wind to blow the house down. Write out everything you believe you need to do to operate a fully pledged to success business as your foundation. At the beginning, you will put more time working in and developing your business, but as soon as you can get out, do so—at least for part of the time. Save your mind and time for thinking about how you are going to grow. If you must, hire extra help in so you can devote time to growing your business. It's the same as for your Manager; he or she is hired to manage; well, you're the Owner, and your main job is to grow the business. Isn't it?

Let the Manager put out the fires. Don't get so caught up in yourself that you are the only one who "knows" how to care for a customer or oversee a project in production! Every day the main objective is to be sure we are answering what our customers and community

The Basics

perceive who we are and see to it we offer them the same high-quality products, presented with flair and flushed with service, every single day so brand awareness grows!

If you haven't dedicated yourself at building your confidence about your work, you will have a much harder time reaching your dream, if you ever reach it at all. Confidence and capability must meld as one. Be flexible; give ideas a try. Support a cause. Do what you think is right. Gain confidence from the good you see from doing "right." How are you going to do all these things? You will learn confidence, and you learn to become more creative. People are not born creative. They can have a flair, but they can't take "flair" to the bank for very long. Creativity is a learned skill. If you have the interest and are willing to work, it will be yours.

First step is pre-planning. Then already you have a product you are thrilled you have made. Who did you make it for? A customer, of course! Your company must be thinking customer, customer, and customer in everything you do. You want to make your customers feel special, appreciated, and respected. Look at them as a special treat; let them get the sense you have been waiting for them; give each one of them your very best treatment. Greet them with a smile. Look them in the eye and make a friend. Remember as Walt Disney said, "It's all in the details."

Think about what you are doing. Sometimes pat yourself on the back. Other times give yourself a good kick.

Let's get started. After pre-planning, planning is the crux, the heart of success. Following is what I am going to discuss with you:

- Benchmark positions of a Leader
- Be known for your creativity
- Worthwhile job descriptions
- How to hire: One of your most important functions
- Develop the confidence of success
- Acquire the expertise to train and educate
- The difference between a clerk and a salesperson, and why that matters
- Advice and/or help
- The power of communication
- Create a journey – store presentation
- Merchandise your product
- How to begin a Custom Center
- Create imaginative packages

- Windows are so chatty
- Stipulations of discipline
- Opportunities
- The role, development and thoughts of the President
- The role, development and thoughts of the Manager
- How to create your first store
- How to present your store and products

Quick thoughts: A key element of store planning, from a merchandising point of view, is understanding why you should make sure you have enough lighting, interesting windows, signage and electrical outlets. You will need the outlets for the baseboards, up behind the counters, in display nooks, up on permanent display fixtures or on the floor beneath large display pieces, so the pieces can be moved for different occasions. It's critical to have enough power available.

For example, on your actual tables have holes drilled to accept a plug with an outlet up among where your products will be displayed. Only in the last few years have good battery-operated strings of lights become worthwhile for decorating. An outlet will support an electrical sign or a moving eye-catcher. Even consider the ceiling for moving many branched displays.

It's important to study your store, if you have one. If there is a lip or decorative board running around the wall near the ceiling, put some electrical outlets up there. I know they are expensive, but the decorative spirit in you must prevail. Always be certain children cannot harm themselves because of electrical outlets.

No matter what you opt to do, make sure electric outlets are the same color as what surrounds them. Also, and, most importantly, make certain you do not tell an electrician to put the outlets in without your approval. I learned the hard way to do this. Trust me. If you tell the electricians where to put them—if it does not go against safety regulations—they will put outlets where you want them.

I've included an entire section on lighting. My advice: Use a very well qualified lighting expert. At this point, LEDs are more expensive (for now), however they will burn 24/7 and for the average retail store should probably last 10 years. They use less heat, so there will be less air conditioning. And, for chocolatiers it's especially exciting because they now can get light right there with the chocolates. The best news? The price is coming down.

LED stands for "light emitting diode." A diode is an electrical component with two terminals which conducts electricity in only one direction. With an electrical current, the diode emits a bright light around a small bulb. Do yourself a favor and get on your computer and look up information about LEDs. Move around the different sites until you find the one that speaks very plain language, and you will come away believing in and understanding why LEDs are the way to go. It will be a whole lot easier for you to understand than for me to give you the information. Your signage and windows if they are to be effective demand you study how to make them work for you. You have them. Why let them stand around, ho humming? Your sign has to be changed regularly if it has a changeable copy area to it. You will read more about signs and windows further on. Your signs will call attention to your store and your windows will entice shoppers to become customers.

Beyond this, make a detailed list of all necessary decisions as you review your space: lockers, telephone system, computer, registers, safe, desk, chair, and if you have the room—table and chairs for lunches and dinners. Also, install a slop-sink and a sink for dirty bucket water. Make sure you have a snow shovel in the north. Brooms for outside and inside, coffee pot, vacuum, bags, extra keys to store, etc.

Another basic is to make a detailed list of businesses needing to be contacted to help with all of this.

Actually, what you will be doing is the "gathering" stage of 'How to be Creative'. You will not need to worry about copying someone else's work. You are making collections to study, get inspired and maybe be able to see how something was made, to use the process, but change it for your needs. Know what your customers are seeing and buying. Teach yourself to slow down and look for the construction of what caught your attention. If you can, take a picture of what you see. Think more and see more.

Recently, I was reading a monthly magazine. In it, a well-known interior decorator made this remark: "I enjoy looking at Pinterest and seeing how my ideas are being used." The presentations on Pinterest are not all created by one mind. They are the result of what that creator has studied and experienced. An idea begets an idea and brings something else to life. Do you remember the story of the young boy watching a famous pianist play the piano? The boy said, "Gosh, I wish I could play like you." The pianist responded, "You can if you will practice every day for two or three hours and do it for years and years." The same idea correlates to becoming good, better or the best at whatever you desire. When determining how to present your merchandise, from what you have learned you should create packaging that compels attention, recognizing what you can make available pricewise.

In addition, create an efficient and effective Custom Center. Even if it is manned by one person, the designs—and, thus, the center—will grow. Use a table in the stockroom. Locate all your special papers, ribbons, tie-ons, scissors, books, tablets, journals, scrapbooks, pens, and pencils in one place; even if it's only a basket or box. Go to an art store and buy a color wheel for package design ideas for color. Have available a small camera or use of an iPhone to snap a picture of packages that impress you or merchandising ideas. Pop them in a special scrapbook or file specifically for pictures of gift-wrapped packages or interesting textures; check out catalogs, wreaths, department store gift-wrapping sections. Be careful of reds that look red but when mixed with others you will notice how orange red it is. The look under fluorescence light will be different than under other light sources, such as daylight, incandescent, Halogens or LEDs.

Think about window designs and clever ideas. If the sun is too bright to use a camera, draw them by hand; what is important are mainly the placement, depth, width, and signage. And just as important, what are you going to do about in-store presentations of merchandise? How will you design them? And as you do so, and you think about other stores or places you've seen presentations, note what caught your attention in the first place. Look past what catches your eye and look for how it is assembled or built. You always want to be alerted to learning something new.

When determining how to present your merchandise, create imaginative packaging that compels attention. Construct exciting displays to WOW. And always look for new ways to merchandise your products—including tapping into the "I want" factor.

Just as important is learning how to develop effective team members. You should learn how to lead and inspire—and understand how to teach your senior team Managers how to do the same. This means understanding how to:
- Hire and fire people
- The difference between a fantastic clerk and a fantastic salesperson
- Educate and train your assistants
- Teach the skills needed before speaking with customers
- Develop a confidence of success

The Basics

This work is an important element, a part in the development process of making you more successful. I are not going to worry about anything other than what you need to know about basic store presentation, merchandising, and service.

Merchandising is visual, so it stands to reason we have to watch and see and become more aware of what is happening all around us. Any business will only develop as its Leaders develop, so we not only do the right things but do things right.

Planning a store is always a process, it's never an event, never fixed or stationary; it's on-going and fun. Plans will change as you learn more, experience more, think more. The planning is so important. Ideas must be written down. (The pencil remembers what the mind forgets.) However rough, draw what you see, diagram it, and write a few notes about it. Collect pictures you have taken, clip-outs from magazines, the computer, and other books. Even though we constantly change plans, we know where we are right now. Hopefully, you will gather fresh, new ideas. New creative ideas. Then you will always be changing your plans for the better.

The basic components of creativity are
- Fluency of ideas
- Flexibility (range of ideas)
- Originality (uniqueness of ideas)
- Elaboration (depth of ideas)

Long ago Henry Wadsworth Longfellow said, "We judge ourselves by what we feel capable of doing, while others judge us by what we have already done." The fact that you are reading this book says a great deal about your hopes and dreams and what you feel you want to be able to do, if you only knew how. Some readers already "know how" and merely want to brush up or polish up what they already know to be true. Perhaps, someone hopes I will be able to bring a new concept or inspiration to set a fire within them. Perhaps a new use for this item or that color, or an explosion of new thoughts will be generated because an idea begets an idea.

If you give parts of this book to a valued employee, explain to them that you have judged what they have already accomplished, and you want to help them to be even better which is why I am offering this program to you—I am making an investment in you, to assist me in furthering my vision for the future.

1. I want my store to be the only place to go if someone is

thinking about chocolate. (Focus on a special segment.)
2. My store needs to have the reputation of being the best.
3. Study what showcasing chocolates is all about.
4. I need someone who will be a—store name here—Spokesperson.
5. I need someone head up, that I can talk with and make plans.
6. If you agree, we will attempt to complete these ideas for
90 days and then get together again and discuss our thoughts.
7. Now, let's get started on your and my future!

Attending the Creative Education Foundation was exciting because it was all about creativity. This idea might surprise you, but people are not born creative. You may have a flair and that's a good beginning, but that does not make you creative. It all comes down to a simple statement. You have got to study, practice, and believe in yourself. You must have a diligence, a persistence about what you do, keep your eyes and ears open to new ideas and never stop learning. You will be fresh and prepared. You will feel and see and even hear yourself in conversation that you are getting more competent and more at ease. You will have more fun and feel better about your capabilities. Belief releases endorphins that trigger positive feelings, just as chocolate causes the release of endorphins in the brain, to feel good or happy, a can-do attitude. Feeling that you know enough and are merely keeping busy with your business put the brakes on.

> **"Compliancy delivers mediocrity."**
> *– Adele Ryan Malley*

Here is the way to develop the confidence that "this plan can happen".

- **Creativity is a process.** People are not born creative! It comes from investigation and thinking about a situation. There are four steps in the creative thinking process:
- **Saturation,**
- **Incubation,**
- **Illumination,**
- **Verification.**

To explain:

Saturation - Gathering of ideas, visiting other chocolate shops, reading other's advertisements, filling yourself with information, learning new ways of doing things. You must visit museums, read

The Basics 115

many various publications, especially ones you normally do not read, listen to the news, learn what interests the different ages of children, senior citizens, and everyone in between.

Find out how things are being sold, what are your competitors offering? Just who is buying on the Internet and what are they buying? What do your customers have to say?

Incubation - Letting it rest for a short time. This time is when your subconscious state gets to work. Our subconscious mind never sleeps which is why you hear people saying, "I'll sleep on it, and let you know in the morning."

We free our minds by thinking of other things, and this break allows the subconscious mind to surface.

Illumination - When suddenly, we may be getting out of our car, or tying our shoelaces when the answer flashes in our mind. The ah-ha! Why didn't I think of that before? Well, we could not because we hadn't put all the material in our minds to get it in motion and get it to work. Of course, it stands to reason that the more material we give our mind, the better the answer is going to be! I think it must be like meeting a mentor for the first time. The person can get to know your name and a little bit about you, and if you insisted, might offer a business suggestion or two. But, how much better the solution will be if you visit each other often, and this person learns how you think and what has shaped your thinking and how much you know about the situation and various methods have been discussed before you choose your plan of action. So, too, with our minds. A ha!

Verification - This is the next step, and always the most difficult. Verification, checking to see if we did do our Ah-ha(!) what would happen to this idea and/or that plan? If all goes well, we implement our new idea.

Remember the first part of the Creative Thinking Process. We are gatherers. We will be assembling a super abundance of store and merchandising ideas. We want the plethora of ideas to be so great that we have an overload. When we get to that stage, we will know it and then put the baby in the cradle and let it incubate. Did you know that to incubate something means to let it get to maturity? That is what we need with our ideas. We want to fill our minds, and then let it rest so it can work in our subconscious mind and reach maturity and blossom into the correct ideas for us which is the great part, (when the correct idea comes to us): The Ah-Ha Illumination stage.

Let's go over that again:

First, we are going to learn everything we can about what we want to do.

Second, when we are very tired of thinking about the whole process, we are to stop and do something else. Hopefully, something entirely different in a different place. It will give back that energy you had when you started. While you think you are doing something different, your mind is fooling you because it is working like crazy—only you are not thinking about the process because it's your subconscious mind working. So, relax, while you are out having fun, your mind is continuing to work figuring out what you need to know.

Third, you might be tying your shoelace and what you need to know erupts on your conscious mind, and you say to yourself, "Why didn't I think of that before?" The answer, of course, is that you did not give your subconscious mind enough material to work with!

Now, you feel wonderful. Of course, it's short-lived because now you must put yourself through the Fourth Step, the Test of Verification. As you consider this new idea against all your other ideas and challenges, you must make sure it will work well and improve the chosen situation.

Ask yourself if you truly want to be creative. Are you willing to go through all the steps? You must complete all four steps; otherwise, you very well can stumble and fail at what you so wanted to be successful doing.

To recap:
- Everything has to do with your grit, your determination. Are you ready to accept your own accountability, or will you continue to blame others or situations for where you are right now?
- How to create a cutting edge for your store.
- Practice the four steps of creativity in order to make good, right decisions.

Strategies for a New, Leased or Rented Store – Use what applies

Remember this information is to help a beginning entrepreneur to open a first store.

Preparation:

Know your competition before you do anything, attack this seriously. Check out similar stores and those stores within five miles, including drug stores, grocery stores, Discount operations, every business has the possibility of being your competition including

wine shops, florists and bakeries,
• Keep a log, write the name of the store being visited, time of day and weather conditions:
• Check traffic flow.

When you find competition, decide that either you will do better or possibly not carry certain products. The competition may outdo your capability in location, merchandising, space, available customers, and price.

Write down what you see and feel
Does the store make you feel welcome? Why?
Does the store feel and look clean?
Inside the store, what made you decide the direction you are taking?
How it is arranged?
What is the Special? What's on sale?
What are they selling, who manufactured it and at what retail price?
How many stores are selling the same items? How different is their approach?
How are you offered help?
How do they display the retail cost of an item?
Why does one store impress you more than another?
Is there background music?
How is the check-out line handled?
Is the restroom well lighted? Is the floor clean? Is the sink(s) clean and faucets shiny? Is there soap for hand washing and some type of drying offered? Are the commodes/urinals clean? Is there toilet tissue? How did the restroom make you feel?
Store information: Are you greeted, offered help, said good-bye to and invited back?
Visit at least three to five stores. Study your notes. Decide what you want to take from them for your store. Decide what you don't want to see happen in your store. Write it in a journal titled, Definite Decisions. (Paper remembers what people forget!)

Choose a carrying case for only this project
• Keep handy in your case, your landlords, architects and any assistants cell phone and fax numbers
• Keep a journal for every phone number, address and contact names
• After each meeting whether on the phone or in person write

down what was decided while the other person is with you or on the phone and send a follow-up email. This is important, you don't want any costly or frustrating misconceptions.

For any application: (Use what applies)
• <u>Review landlord and tenant responsibilities,</u> **(prior to lease signing)** <u>and include these in calculations of overall costs and profitability, HVAC, electrical and roof current condition.</u>
• <u>Discussion/awareness/responsibility for all future maintenance of building components, tenant needs to know responsibilities.</u> **(prior to lease signing)**
• Be positive you will have enough air conditioning. No matter your location you will use the air conditioner year around.
• Do the neighbors make noise?
• Does any business take up most of the parking spaces?
• During special times of the day or evening, does any business such as bowling alleys, theatres, night classes take up most of the parking spaces?
• Are there challenges from wind?
• Are there any plumbing challenges?
• Is pest control charge located in the rent or lease?

Mall stores:
• Before signing for a mall store check their management style, rules and handbook for information that may concern your operation. Ask other businesses about the care and concerns they are experiencing.
• Check on delivery rules or options and trash pick-up
• What kind of maintenance is available; if necessary, ask about snow removal
• If you have a sun problem in a window (s) ask for sun protection
• Be sure you will have enough air conditioning
• Where are the banking facilities? Is it well lighted?
• Try to negotiate CAM charges (Common Area Maintenance fees). These are fees added on to the base rent in addition to taxes and insurance costs. Inquire what might be a surprise add on fee.
• Are restrooms up to date, clean and working and well lighted in and around the area?

Renting?
- How old is the hot water tank?
- What condition is the air-conditioner in? How old?
- Does the furnace make noise?
- If you are responsible for landscaping know the details and decisions
- Have store professionally checked by professionals in that field
- If sun is a problem, try to negotiate awnings in the rent fee
- What kind of maintenance is available?
- Do the neighbors make noise?
- What is the parking situation? - Parking/Traffic patterns for the customers should be reviewed and analyzed, for the retailers projected needs

Leasing
- All of the above
- What are your obligations and theirs?

Every new business
Read again: For any Application:
- After you have chosen and signed for your space, immediately put up a professionally made sign announcing what is coming . . . your store!
- List everything you will have no use for that was left in your space. Advertise on "Craig's List, Etsy or similar interest. Habitat for Humanity will be interested and might be able to make a pick-up or donate to another enterprise.
- Become handy with an architect's ruler
- With your architect take measurements of your space and everything in it, including ½ walls, windows, doors, stairways, storage or planned for storage area, restrooms and planned for spaces.
- On graph paper sketch and re-sketch different ideas for working around existing challenges; pillars, ½ walls (if you keep them), doorways, or anything stationary. Your architect will offer suggestions. Remember to check your collected pictures scrapbook. Together make your final plan.
- Ask your architect to review for you the blueprints for electrical outlet locations, (Be sure to read, Some Tips for Store Planning) wiring for electronics, plumbing. While the electronics are being installed write on the list inside your fuse box what switch is for

each electrical piece. Now is the time to do it, there isn't time later to turn on and off every electrical item to see where it's connected in the fuse box.
- Be careful that you do not plan for a store with tables all along the perimeter and then something in the center. Insist upon more creativity from your architect or cabinet person. They will do the best they can, but they may not be that familiar with small retail endeavors. Before you choose an architect, ask about the firm's track record with small retail establishments. Cabinet people may take your store measurements and propose cabinets all along your walls. How interesting is that? Create display tables, counters, shelves, cabinets, fun carts, interesting shelf buildouts
- If possible, keep the Manager's desk as close to the action as possible.
- If it must be in the back of the store, consider a one-way mirror, a window (hard to do) or some quick way to have an overview of the store-or at least the registers and/or door.
- Know existing sun patterns for each season. Decide how you will handle the heat and the rays of the sun. Do this before you open, otherwise you will be scrambling for answers and not want to put the outlay for protection when you already have so many invoices to pay. Make it be one of those invoices. It will save aggravation, frustration and lost merchandise.
- Make often, unannounced visits to site
- Keep in mind your theme and color scheme.
- Now, plan the best lighting you can afford and your layers of lighting – overhead, chandeliers, sconces, cabinet interiors and direct focused lighting. This is where you should invest, it's a great payback. Know the rule of thumb in lighting: ambient, task and accent lighting.
- Decide placement of both permanent and temporary display units
- Create a natural journey through your store
- Decide where your main attraction will be presented
- Will you have a chair or chairs for persons accompanying the shopper?
- Knowledge of how to construct displays that attract and sell product
- Imaginative packaging that compels attention
- Read very informative information at end of this article
- Discuss progress and goal dates at agreed upon times.

- Continuously; check that materials are arriving on planned dates
- Be aware that some workers do not work during the start of hunting season – late November, early December. Check and then plan for it.
- Be available at inspections
- Ask your architect to explain the Health Code and what was done to meet its specifications. If you are going to install cameras, decide on placement.
- Ask your Construction lead to tell the plumbers that when faucets etc. are being installed be certain workers use rags to cover the "teeth" of their wrenches so as not to scratch the surfaces.
- Ask your architect to review blueprints with you, for that which will require gas, water, electricity, phone, a fax machine, security cameras, etc.
- One month before opening take final blueprints to County Health Department for approval before you can open
- Decide what products and spaces will go where
- The "I want" factor created by trained and educated Advocates
- While doing this gather your Tools of the Trade
- If a "Kitchen" is part of your plans: Efficient, effective and on time manufacturing is agreed upon; never assumed. If it's a chocolate shop set up a side project to provide all necessary needs and assistance to help you or in the shop when you are cooking, enrobing, assembling and packaging. Be clear at time of hiring this work is part of the job offering. Understand potential vendors manufacturing dates, delivery times and any assistance they can provide.

Opening a New Store

Pre-planning: Use a SWOT to guide you. It's a time waster if not used correctly. It can be a wake-up call if used with deep thought and honest decisions.

Home: Get support; agree on scheduling; decide to never use home equity for tight situations or emergencies; agree that the cash needed to start your business is correct; otherwise decide what needs to be accomplished to make it right and do it. Perhaps work a little longer to have more funding than recommended saved to weather an emergency and in a separate account marked; Crisis Funds.

New store, leasing or renting: **(Prior to lease Signing)** Research and then determine location. Location of store/demographics is critical to success, and cannot be overstated. Remember to review landlord and tenant responsibilities,) and include these in calculations of overall costs and profitability, HVAC, electrical, roof current condition. Also, discussion/awareness/responsibility for all future maintenance of building components, tenant needs to know responsibilities.

How to choose a licensed, professional architect and contractor

To determine the architect and construction contractor for your first store, takes some study. If you are in a new store and like it, ask who their architect was and what company constructed it. Ask the building commissioner in your area if they might suggest some names who they know have built small retail shops. When you start to feel confident about certain individuals, visit their web sites. Notice their credentials. Make an appointment to meet them. Interview at least two. Make the visits short. Tell them how you came to want to meet them because you are told they are familiar with developing or building small retail shops. Explain what you intend to do. Ask to see some of the smaller projects they have developed. Ask to speak to a few of their former "small store" clients. Tell them at the end of the meeting you are going to interview another and will choose what you think will make the best fit for you right now. Tell them you appreciate their time and that you will be in touch. Give a time frame. Tell them that you are, "excited and nervous at the same time as this is my first store."

Make your choice. Call the other and say you think you have a better fit for where you are right now. Thank them again for their time. Good-bye. If you want to be remembered put the cherry on top of the sundae. Send the one not chosen a ½ lb. box of Malley's Chocolates. You will be remembered. You may want to choose their firm for your next project.

Know investment limit. Ask accountant, then discuss ideas with architect and contractor to determine possible costs; make possible adjustments; remember finishing costs.

Keep your banker in loop for OK with proposed budgets for interior and exterior work.

Only if you have individuals supporting you:

1. If Principals are involved ask if they would like to meet your architect and contractor and maybe your attorney to hear the budget as devised by four of you and approved by banker.
2. Obtain the "go ahead" if necessary, from Principals.

Decide if there should be progress reports with your attorney's OK, sign a lease or buy.

Immediately display a professionally made sign at site announcing the opening of your store.

Make an appointment with an architect to start proceedings!

Be Aware... Be mindful that what you will read next is what I did. If you are not going to be a chocolate shop the following will give ideas on how to set up your store. Your architect will know the following, but to make the store yours they have to hear from you. Some of what you will read is for your own knowledge and reminders. Following is a grid to assist you in organizing your work. It will make the planning/receiving easier, quicker to check up on progress or insert information about something needing to be added to the list. On the far-left corner is where you can write who is responsible for that certain line item. Then the next column can be a place to check it off when completed. In the middle will be your planned work and on the far right is a place to keep notes.

Person Responsible	Check-off	Text	Notes
		For the architect; prepare all planned activity in your store; offices and/or any other requirements; will there be a kitchen/manufacturing area in the store? If possible, pictures of special display pieces. Show other requirements such as needing a work sink and slop sink to clean mops or if you will be needing special electrical outlets to handle higher power electric draws. Show a scrap book of store or fixture pictures that have impressed you. Explain the type of store you envision – period, rustic and contemporary or modern, nostalgic or out of this world. Any and everything you would like the architect to know. If you need a place to work – decide if cross-hatches and a simple board top and chair, perhaps a space heater could be arranged in the new space. Discuss possibilities at this first meeting. Plan store lay-out. Re-connect when blueprints are ready. Discuss any adjustments wanted. Talk about each part of the undertaking. Set up follow-up dates. Explain your plans for when your Construction Company is ready to turn over "possession" to you. Make sure Construction Company is aware and agrees with your plans to inspect for cleanliness and no paint splatters anywhere, in or out of the store. Tell it with a smile and very politely, in front of your architect (as a witness,) Once open, you will be so busy that there will be no time for you to get down on all fours and scrub up splatters; yet there it will sit.	
		Be mindful things will happen very quickly. Keep an orderly Project Case. In it, file every invoice slip or instructions or any kind of printed material that speaks of what you have purchased. In a separate spiral binder keep a calendar, your notes and ideas	

The Basics 125

		with dates and places. Create your own "shopping list" from suggestions offered as you read this chart and follow-up subjects.	
		Ask architect for help and guidance on all the following: **This dash mark —means to ask your architect** **I'm leaving clear spaces for you to add what is necessary for you.**	
		Begin the work: - Research Display Cases. Your architect and you can review measurements to accommodate cases to space before ordering. Read further on, "Tips for Designing" - If space is "tight" there will be a definite and natural tendency to stay behind the counters, not out with your customers. Remember that digging up floors to accommodate electrical or plumbing lines is expected, but more costly to resolve a miscalculation or change of mind.	
		Very carefully plan the placement of display units for best arrangements – for safety, no electrical cords can be crossing the ingress and egress between display cases, cabinets and counters; also in manufacturing area. - If ordering display cases, write out what you will order; be certain you order each case as if it was the only order. - Each display case must be ordered deliberatively. Tell in detail what you are imagining each case to be, even though it seems redundant. You know and can see what your mind is telling you as you place your order. However the vendor can only hear what you say. Ask to have repeated what is written for each item; and match what you hear, to what you have written about each. I learned the hard way. Set up follow up dates to assure delivery accuracy.	
		- Decide when items should be ordered. Make a preliminary plan of action for each item.	

			- 'Think 'Out of the Box'- move things around, you may surprise yourselves with a new configuration. Think of your customer's journey. What will pull them to the back of your store, to the secondary display, to a popular, wanted item? Think of your favorite grocery store set-up. - Once you have decided on your customer flow it's important to know you are not through, as customer flow is very important to your success. See my article, "Customer Flow for Optimum Purchasing" at the end of this chart.	
			- Your architect will be working with handicap codes, not only in the store but restrooms and getting into the store. Double foyer doors need special figuring as do ramps.	
			- If you want customers to enjoy more assistance or other customer/floor needs, spacious ingress and egress between register(s) and counters for service is mandatory. Round corners at end of counters and cabinets. Make it easier for your helpers to do their job. -When your cabinets are being made think about asking for a sort of ½ box cover for register cords behind the register. The top might have a grove in it so any sort of card could be slid into it not needing a display stand, or it could hold advertisements.	
			- Discuss outdoor sign possibilities with a reputable sign maker. Get guidance on font choice, design and colors. If possible, purchase a changeable sign. However, a sign is only as good as its message so if you don't change your sign often your store will appear to the public as tired and there is nothing interesting going on inside.	

The Basics

		Think headline, information and call to action for a good sign. Short and sweet. Find out from the City what the ordinances are for signage. Decide your most beneficial sign real estate. Most cities allow one sign only on a building. If you are working with a corner store you can usually place a sign indoors near the glass that can be easily read, on the less important side of the corner. Check out the new, modern approach to informing the public of your business. Your sign is your 24/7 calling card. A person has about 5 – 7 seconds to read a sign when passing by. Make those seconds count. Change it often so you train folks passing by to look for it. Be witty, be questioning, be informative but don't be boring! The inside of your store will be judged by your exterior. Read more about signs at the end of this chart.	
		- Decide final store theme/colors; work with architect and Sign person to develop a chosen font/corporate colors	
		- Form a needs list to order everything that takes months/weeks to receive. Place all orders for goods that you will sell, other than what you will make. Set-up an agreed upon date to check the order will arrive on time. Have them delivered two weeks before opening. Don't get so busy elsewhere that you can't meet the manufacturing deadline date for goods to sell if you are responsible for the "Kitchen."	
		- Ask architect about listing needs for your manufacturing: Plan for growth (electricity, storage.) Order needed equipment – check electricity availability for that store, for now and the future, written and signed by Owner	

			or if you're building, your architect and electrician company Owner.	
			- What does architect say about: Review needs for Health Code? Ask questions, learn about everything. If used, decide best locations for cameras/ monitors (Think: Registers and doors).	
			- Ask to go over the blueprints as a review (for you) for electrical outlet locations, remember candy/chocolate scales, wiring for electronics, also wiring areas for registers/ phones if you use a landline/security cameras/music and manufacturing.	
			- Be visible at site; visit often, be available at "inspections," be aware that friendly or "business" conversations with you are costing you additional fees because they are not working while you are talking	
			- Declare a date when all supplies should be complete.	
			- Plan for arrival/departure of Advocates and their parking locations	
			- How and where will you receive and send mail? What shipping company will you use? Investigate options and don't forget to negotiate.	
			Order tubs, decide on framework to display merchandise/price information, package and display stands.	
			Order chocolate/candy case trays, display trays, food tongs and small scoops along with nut scoops. Shopping baskets, display baskets, security, music conveyance, and walk-off floor mats – which can also be used for developing your Brand. Put your Company colors, store name or "Home of (the name of a favorite chocolate") or "Welcome" or "Thank you for shopping with us!"	
			Order registers and supplies, three computers; Owner, store and Manager, monitors, fax, phones, decide software program for bookkeeping	

The Basics

		-Sun exposure - order blinds or a different method for control	
		Decide when to start advertising for a Manager/Supervisor and general help according to the business market. It's either a shortage or an abundance of help available. Order or create and print applications, handbooks. Of course, use the internet.	
		Educate and Train Manager; To allow you to work on the business instead of in the business instruct your Manager/Supervisor how to hire, (with your approval) educate and train staff members. Explain all forms that will need filling in and what file folders will be named to care for newcomer's information. Go to Malleys.com and get excited! Available for you (small fee) Is a "Malley Manners" PDF with complete instructions for establishing a Customer Care educational system for new or experienced helpers. It's perfect for a busy Leader.	
		-Injury report/worker's comp booklets - secure any government posters each business is required to display including your Worker's Compensation certificate.	
		BE AWARE - Take final blueprints to County Health Department for approval - one month out - to obtain food license. - Cannot open store without it.	
		- Decide on customer contact possibilities. Set up phone area – pens, papers, advertising, directions to your store, hours of operation, journal, and your name.	
		Establish bank. Set up credit card processing. (May need assistance from Information Technology (IT). Read Credit Card article at end of this chart.	

130   Conversations with Adele : Business Owners' Fundamentals for Success

		- Put your name on all utilities accounts. Order a dumpster service. If so, do you need to build an enclosure?	
		Introduce Manager and helpers to the general rules of merchandising displays. They should practice with empty boxes, all sizes. Check out, "Merchandising," further on in this book.	
		Make sure all store staff members have proper paperwork to receive employee numbers, set up in register. Read register book for how to. . .	
		Order wrapping paper in widths to match your box widths to handle your box sizes – 1 lb. 3 lb. and 5 lb. sizes handled most everything we needed. We had a 30 in. cutter that was used for many different reasons other than box wrapping. Then consider assembling requirements: Think how many boxes you will be wrapping. Be stingy on ordering. Order various size bags, folding boxes, ribbons, and bows. Order shipping cartons to matchboxes and clear tape or tape to match outer cartons. Decide on printing or have decals prepared for the above. Also, order stock boxes, usually to hold 5 lbs. Order invoice, order, forms needed. If possible, attend your industry convention and exhibition for ideas and ordering needed items.	
		Instruct how to wrap your boxes and close your outer boxes. Teach how to fill outer mailing cartons with your products. Consider calling your industry association for guidance. Chocolatiers call Retail Confectioners International - 800-545-5381 info@retailconfectioners.org.	
		Get on the Internet and check out what you need to know.	
		Display stands for packages.	
		Laminated photos of actual products.	
		Enclosure cards, envelope & display rack.	
		Decide on uniforms with help from uniform stores, a uniform company or any one of the four companies mentioned below.	

The Basics   *131*

		Plastic tubs	
		Merchandise/Price tag displayers	
		Decide on lockers, if coats are to be outside of lockers decide where and how they are to be hung and on what type hooks. Will there be a need for locks? What kind – key or combination?	
		Price tags for all items, employee name tags, VIP Cards if you are starting a program of this sort. If planning to ask for business cards have a viewable container with a professionally made sign telling what you will do with the cards.	
		Display signs for featured items.	
		Install all electronics - we have had another company help with this and wiring in the past.	
		Order all office supplies needed. Order company stationery/personal company stationery; stamps or stamp machine, company forms: invoices, mail order and other forms to suit your work.	
		Decide who, how and when store needs will be ordered and "delivered." Decide how you want them stored in your stockroom. Decide if a five day a week person will receive deliveries, date fluctuations can cause problems. Count in the packages while the driver is present. (Note time and date.) And possibly put the delivered items away. There should be a protected folder in a box or case to store paperwork. Perhaps this person might create a workable pattern for stock box positions. Maybe at first, use post-it type notes until satisfied with placements. Store computer inventory should start at 0.	

			Initial Custom Center (CC) order (If in your plans, decide invoice forms or set it up on your computers.) Also, decide how and when and how every single item in your store will have an item number and a bar code.	
			Put together all items for initial Custom Design (CD) store order, such as what will be needed and how to display the items.	
			Set up maintenance, mail order, daily deposit sheets on Manager's computer; plan that computer will be accessible by others as needed.	
			Create (if artistic) or purchase decorations for the store. Be careful not to over-buy. A simple garland of a season can go a long way. Wrapped packages can introduce the season. Employ professional signage to give your store a look of "we are here to stay." Do not use anything hand-written if at all possible. Be sure to post your open and close hours in an easy-to-see location.	
			Decide now your advertisements for various venues. Also, in store signs made by a "Fast Signs Co." Decide what you will sample. Know and teach its features and benefits. Have selected persons practice sampling. The instructions are in this book. Decide to have a number of trays readied to be sampled so you don't lose someone – out of sight- preparing trays.	
			- Install safe. Decide if you want the Manager to have a Petty Cash amount. If so, order a Petty Cash lock box with key, pad for Petty Cash information and instructions on how to care for a Petty Cash transaction and reports. Check at a business store.	
			- Plan electricity for retail - weighing scales. Set up scales for retail. Have City check for accuracy. Order glassine liner papers, containers for the various size glassine papers. Company decals/stickers/tape.	
			Start accounts with local businesses or State Chemical and Webstaurant	

The Basics 133

		Store which are both nationwide. Cintas covers North America. Each will supply practically everything needed for a business. Contact them, study and see what fits you best. Order a pest control company to visit once a month. Initially they will make a survey to check for the absence of pests or find out what they will be exterminating. Order a window washer and if you need snow removal.	
		Check that all doors have locks and keys (that are proven to work).	
		ALERT - Schedule final health inspection to get food license - **cannot open without it**. (Contractor does all other inspections.)	
		Buy first-aid supplies	
		Decide storage for cleaning supplies. Label how holding containers are to look and be cleaned.	
		Before accepting "possession" of your store, investigate that there are no paint splatters on any part of the floor, window sashes- entrances and exit doors, no paint on cement around the doors or thresholds, no paint drips on or in sinks, commodes or urinals/floors.	
		Do a detailed search. Also ask for all paint information and how to care for anything of that type. Understand your chosen floor upkeep. After total satisfaction, accept Construction Co. turning the store over to you.	
		Complete all internal work – architect can assist, finish restrooms, mirror, liquid soap dispenser and liquid soap, paper towel or heat dispenser by hand-sink, toilet tissue, wastebasket. Screens and cakes for Urinals. Fragrance dispensers, Hand sanitizer and dispensers. If wanted a wall decoration or picture. Don't show food items in the restrooms. Tucked just above the sink place a proper hand washing technique laminated card.	

		- Establish Owner and Manager/ Supervisor's area: Manager: Desk/chair and one additional chair. Owner: Desk/chair and three guest chairs. For both: Business phone decisions, in total Four large face flashlights (One for each office, one for store and one for stockroom.), file cabinet, lamps (?), Bulletin/white boards/pins, washable ink markers for white boards, pens, pencils, yardstick and steel measuring tape.	
		- If needed, install a doorbell for deliveries.	
		- Decide on refrigerator, microwave, coffee pot, tea pot, coffee/teas, sugar and "cream", paper goods, utensils; if room - table and chairs.	
		Three and six footstep ladders. If using a changeable copy sign that must be done by hand, purchase a ladder with the correct safety height for "letter installer" and the height of your sign. Fire extinguishers (store and manufacturing) – ask for instructions, do they instruct as part of their service?	
		Once you have taken possession of store, completely clean store and restrooms. Order window washer, attend to landscaping if available. If a parking lot, have it striped and handicap zones put in. Consider pregnancy space. Sweep front walk.	
		Install IT shelves and desk /chairs and all the electronics.	
		Order change and set up, funds from bank, day and night deposit bags and deposit slips. Pick up same.	
		• Confirm registers and music conveyer are understood by Manager to operate correctly. Make sure everything works as expected: • commodes, • faucets, and • electrical outlets, • keys in locks, • phones, • registers, • safe, and • doorbell. Make sure • software is understood. Make sure you tell all the following: • Location of all exterior and interior light switches. Remember • lights for the Sign.	

The Basics

		Show • main water and • electrical shutoffs. Show where a • high-powered flashlight and • fire extinguisher are kept. Besides the • offices, consider the • stockroom and the • main register for flashlight placement. Order a • dolly – a wheeled platform to move heavy objects- to transport supplies from stockroom to store. Decide how • register keys are to be used and stored. Once again go over the • features and benefits of the Special of the Month. • Practice. Have a discussion with your helpers on what to expect; what to do if they get in a challenge, you plan to be in the store come with any questions, have fun, you're excited and hope they are.	
		First store "delivery?" • Wednesday before open	
		• Thursday/• Friday • Arrange store displays, • Keep focused on job at hand • break down boxes, etc. • Open store on a Monday.	
		God Bless You.	

Customer Flow for Optimum Purchasing.

Once open, watch how your customers move in your store. Watch when they first arrive. The entrance, or front part of your store is sort of like a landing zone. Customers are getting adjusted, both mentally and physically, and then they are prepared to shop. Most likely front displays will be walked by so don't be hesitant to display them again in another part of your store.

- Keep display tables far enough apart to make for pleasant movement of customers. Heavy coats, children, wheelchairs, friend's shopping together, all need to be given consideration. 36 inches between units is the needed space.

Consider the layout of your store. Will your customer's journey or chosen way to shop be comfortable and will it also, easily, show off your entire store?

It's *effective* if your registers are singing and you are continually restocking all your shelves.

It's *ineffective* if revenue is lagging. Here is what you do about it:

1. All employees, (we call ourselves Advocates) know your products and how to sell them. That is a lot to swallow but more help is available by checking out my book Conversations with *Adele: Business Owners' Fundamentals for Success* (Malleys.com. Click on Adele Malley.) Study our pacaging while you are there. You must make Salespeople out of very lovely happy clerks.

2. Observation by your Manager/Supervisor, Assistant Managers, helpers and you can easily tell the tale. Start watching, rearranging, and thinking about how sales are increased. Watch what sells easily. Adjust your displays.

3. Checking your purchases bought activity, through your cash registers, will tell you most of what you need to know

4. Parts of the store or lack of visits at gondolas or displays should flag a heads-up.

5. Check that your store is merchandised correctly. **See Merchandising chapter.**

6. You have had effective lighting installed. Be confident your accent lighting is focused. **See Lighting chapter.**

7. To create a successful Special of the Month:

✔ Help your team impress customers with clear, professional, and compelling signage, made with the idea of being used again. Use a quick-print shop; the sign will not be expensive; get two. (Perhaps use one in your window or a second attention-getting location or near your register.) It is usual for the salesperson to help design the sign using their experience.

✔ Order a separate smaller sign to be placed off-center in the front of the more prominent sign to display the weight and price as this may change when using it again.

✔ Prepare how the sign should be handled, cared for, and stored ahead of time. Decide on a location and watch that that customers are attracted to it. If necessary, move the Special to another spot and watch for added interest.

✔ Be sure your lighting is doing it justice.

✔ Step up product education. For example, explain what makes up the Special of the Month – our smooth signature chocolate covering just roasted crunchy Cashews. Empathize certain words everyone is to use when possible, in this instance: smooth, just roasted, and crunchy.

A salesperson might say,

1) I notice you looking at our Special of the Month. Are you familiar with Cashew Clusters? (Keep looking pleasantly into the other person's eyes.) I like them because (name a feature) they are always fresh and crunchy and (Name a benefit) they are very popular because who doesn't like crunchy Cashews!

2) If offered at check out, indicating the display near the register, quickly describe the item with a delicious sounding adjective, coupled with a statement. "Our Special this month is crunchy fresh roasted Cashews. They are so good to have at home while relaxing or to use as a gift. They are all wrapped and ready to go. Would you like a box?" If a "No, thank you is received," a new salesperson can become very embarrassed and not know what to say next. So can the customer who is responding. The friendly eye contact and developing bond between the two can become severed. Smooth that awkwardness aside by preparing for such an occurrence to help both parties. It is vital to practice to become comfortable during such a situation. Keep the conversation going. Keep eye contact and wear a friendly face. Continue smiling and perhaps say, "Check us out next month when I hope one of your favorites will be the Special! What would you like it to be? If the answer is, "Yes," say something up to the minute, such as, "You're going to love them. The Cashews are delicious for home or a gift. Most everyone enjoys eating Cashews!"

8. Take advantage of all your available "selling" real estate by reasoning out what should be where. Most of your customers are coming in to buy something. Most probability they will notice your attention-grabbing main display. Your secondary display will most likely be noticed. Another secondary display should be at the back of your store beckoning them to "come and see".

All the in-between packaging will be noticed and if not purchased, it is now in their mind that you sell that product. This is valuable knowledge.

Once a customer decides they want to checkout, you may have lost the opportunity to peak their "want to buy," thus increasing their purchase total. Outside of Advocates yourself included; and displays, your register can be the Queen or King of your additional sales. Yes, it is a "Pick-up" area and we are all used to seeing gum, breath fresheners, pens, and trinkets shown here. Do you want to pick-up an additional small sale or something more worthwhile?

a. Have a stack of your month's special, near-by so your cashier can easily reach them. Give it a modest size sign and instruct your cashier to ask the obvious question. And it's not, "Would you like a box of our special this month? It's something like this but said in their own natural style of speaking, "Fresh out of the kitchen is our special of the month, Nutmallow, and it's reduced by $4.00. Have you ever tasted it? Would you enjoy a sample? (Bring a covered tray from a drawer or below the register.) I love the chocolate and marshmallow together. Great for a gift or while watching TV. It's a bargain, want one?" Now, it stands to reason the cashier can't say the same thing to each customer, especially if there is a line of customers. Teach them how to convey the idea with the features and benefits you will have discussed with them. Compliment them when you hear them asking for the sale. It will give them confidence to keep at it. Step up your register offerings to ¼ and ½ pound boxes of a product. Celebrate through your wrapping the holidays, festivities, events, birthdays, and other days to be remembered. If your cashier is too rushed to give it enough play, a modest sign in keeping with your store colors, company colors, design and/or font can express what you want the customers to hear. As your customers are in line, they keep busy by looking around, forming opinions, and remembrances. Keep units nearby your registers filled with packaged take-home goodies, fun modest presents, your month's special and a medium sized sign, that's fun to read or see about what's coming next month!

Make your Signs Talk

Make your signs talk, sing, be funny or serious, but whatever, make them do something.

The following article is so well written and full of needed instructions that I am enclosing it as is.

It is written by John McRae, Vice President of Brilliant Electric Sign Company. They have handled our signage for years and years. They serve clients nationwide. (216-741-3800) www.brilliantsign.com

"Often one of the most overlooked and understated forms of business communication is exterior signage.

With the demand for more complex signs that demand high visibility and attract attention at a moment's notice it's important to properly plan and partner with a signage provider versed in numerous facets including, but not limited to, design, city code, site survey analysis, custom sign fabrication and qualified sign installation.

With sign design and city review averaging one week to one month, it is important to align yourself with a signage partner that has a full staff of design professionals that can interface with the client, architects and city planners on the same level, assuring design intent expectations are met. These services wrap hand in hand with city code requirements, which quite often are restrictive (by design), and can have a great impact on project schedules (size and sign type variances can extend timelines up to two months depending on the municipality).

Site survey analysis, fabrication and installation transition the signage design to reality typically in a two to three-month period. Site survey analysis helps bridge the signage design by providing a clear map of existing conditions including areas such as topography for ground and wayfinding signage and building elevation photos for wall and projecting signage. With regards to fabrication and installation, the average life expectancy of the signage typically ranges ten to twenty years so the age old saying "You Can Pay Me Now or Pay Me Later" applies to the "nth" degree. There are numerous materials with varying thickness and quality levels utilized in fabrication that make it very easy to cheat when fabricating signage and we unfortunately service many poorly constructed signs creating much angst for local institutions and business Owners.

Common sense prevails here and you are best served to partner with a full service provider that has invested in the latest technologies and materials, has a tenured staff of production craftsmen that build a high quality product in- house and has a qualified installation team with updated equipment.

Exterior signage is a large business investment encompassing branding, marketing and wayfinding. Partnering with a qualified firm is critical. Time tested due diligence practices such as references, fabrication plant visits and visual inspections of signs in the field at least three years old will insure you make an informed selection of your signage provider" (John McRae, VP Brilliant Electric Sign Co.).

How do you get the most BANG for your Credit Card Buck?

If ready to set-up Credit Card Services, you have some work to do. Follow my BANG Theory for a worthwhile credit card deal.

Make Ben Franklin's Pro and Con list about the various companies' credit card fees and what they can offer to you – make it bare bones, and easily read to help make your decision. To organize use the BANG Theory.

B/ang. Basic Comprehension

1) Use your computer fact finding opportunities to gather your understanding of Credit card fees and such before you ask your banker about it, or you may be directed to the bank's treasury department where you can learn about the credit card business. That's what the credit cards represent. Each is a business taking your direction to pay your bills, but they are also selling us something, such as fraud protection and cell phone protection and are willing to tie all your delinquent debts into one package to lessen the amount paid each month.

However, their main source of income occurs when a card user doesn't pay their monthly balance. There is a system to decide what interest rate they can charge. Usually, the average rate for interest is 14.87%. {The formula can be read on your computer.} Credit Card companies also collect a fee from each merchant who accept card payments. It's usually 1.75% of each transaction, but it can vary from each card and each retailer. It's their second largest source of income.

Banks have other expenses such as loans that are never paid back, annual fees, working with less than creditworthy borrowers, (they pay a higher fee because it is assumed they may not be able to pay it back.) There are also other types of overhead expenses.

A/nalyze

2) Each card offers somewhat the same perks and advantages, but there are differences. It's your job to figure out which card offers you the most protection, the best fit for your circumstances, the fastest service – 24-hour Customer Care. This will mean a great deal to you if a register malfunctions or a card is not accepted and there is a line of customers waiting to be waited upon and they are all looking at you.

Be sure to also consider the very large banks who own their own processing system. They can offer 24-hour Customer Care (Find out exactly what that means.) a free checking account, and if ever in a real bind they may offer same day credit on your funds and other interesting offers.

A smaller bank may be just the thing for you. Some will help you out in a pinch and be there for you to help make decisions. A very large bank can very well offer you more perks because of their buying and selling power. It's a puzzle, yes.

N/egotiate

3) Do not hesitate to try and negotiate a better merchant fee. Keep narrowing your focus. It's your job to see what fits best in your picture. Don't be afraid to negotiate. Say "no" out loud. Did you hear yourself? You knew the word was coming but you decided to listen anyway. Continue to keep this agreeable mind. Make your decision.

G/ame plan

4) Establish your company at the bank of choice. Set-up Credit Card Acceptance. Gather any information offered. Make a list of why you chose your bank and credit-cards. Explain the information to your Manager/Supervisor and Bookkeeper. Make a note on your calendar for three months out to be sure all your "Perks" are percolating. That is how you get the most BANG for your business bucks. To explain this further, read about the process flow of a credit card payment

Process Flow
1. Payment
2. Merchant (Malley's) sends all credit card details
3. The acquirer (bank or financial institution that processes transaction on behalf of Malley's) sends details to issuing bank
4. The issuing bank is the bank that issues the card the customer used to make payment
5. The rest follows back down the process flow to authenticate the payment
6. Lastly comes clearing and settling the accounts between the credit card processors, banks, and merchants.

Of course, you can go to your bank and ask to have the Credit Cards set up for you. I think it is interesting to understand how credit cards "work."

When you are just starting your business the unusual need not be a WOW factor, but the steps beyond what friendly service can be.
Get your group together and thresh it out. Keep them thinking and talking about it. Remember these will be simply ideas until you put them into action. Find out where the folks in your area shop and why. Really come to terms with how you want to be perceived and then follow through in every possible dimension. Folks in your area and your customers will grow in awareness as you grow and become better and better. Be alert to trends, stay a step ahead. Make your store a place someone really wants to visit. A question to ask yourself is to think back to when you were a kid and all the kids always ended up at one friend's house. What made you all want to go there? How can you use that idea in your store?

A good crash course in Branding can be found at Shopify Blogs on your computer. Don't throw all your energy into it but become very aware of it and keep the ideas in your mind and you will see that you will find yourself incorporating their points in your work as you progress. Mark on your calendar to reread the articles every three months or so. Choose one thought and put some action into it.

- Hiring and Dismissing
- Manager that can lead and inspire with directions, instructions and follow-up
- Learn how Malley's Educates and Trains our Advocates
- Difference between a clerk and a salesperson
- What must be acquired before speaking with a customer
- How to develop the confidence of success

Throughout my career, I studied our stores, how we spoke to each other, how helpers came to know how we wanted our customers to know we really cared about them as individuals, and how happy we are they decided to choose our store to shop for their wants and needs. I tried to drive home the thought that each person who comes into our store or tells us of an unhappy circumstance is giving us two gifts—their time and their opinion. And all for no charge!

Chapter 9
Display Presentations, Creating and Refilling

Once customers come through the door, the display presentations must draw them further into the store. If a person will view short columns of boxed selections or bagged goods lying on their backs, what is there to entice? It's all flat looking or vertical columns. Upon entering, it doesn't look appealing. Spotlights misdirected add to its demise.

Who has the time to investigate if something is worth looking at, on their lunch hour, or shopping with three children in tow? The display has to hit them in the eye and make their heart lurch, "Wow, here's something worth looking at," as soon as they see it. Displays should target our five senses as much as possible: what we see, what we smell, what we hear, what we taste, and what we touch. (I always start from the top down: seeing, smelling, hearing, tasting, and touch.) The more we work at addressing our senses, the more a customer will want to make a purchase. Experiences of treating our senses will make us understand how to do this. As we educate ourselves, we become more aware, we know more, then we want more, so we will do more.

Beginning entrepreneurs usually have a smaller store, few helpers, less expertise, and no person knowledgeable in display. I know you wish you could speak to each of your customers, but that is usually impossible, so your displays have to do it for you. That includes lighting, the first thing to think about, and to check continuously, to see that each display will be viewed at its best advantage. So many smaller companies ignore this to their loss. The more a customer can understand what they are looking at, the less you will be needed, because your display can do the talking for you. Of course, correctly done, nothing can take the place of face to face communication. Your presentation can do it all by showing different sizes, different colors of material, wrapping, containers, boxes, or the actual item, with the price and description plainly on view so a customer can easily make their own decision. If you give attention to and work at it, the following will get you an A+.

Keeping in mind that at our busiest times, when revenues can make or put a huge dent in sales, we naturally want every customer to be delighted and purchase several items. So it stands to reason how important come hither-look-at-me displays are. At this time, who is building or filling our displays? Part-time helpers or short-term holiday helpers!

We depend on our new helpers to keep our original display's winning factors going. It's not a time to require expertise because you are not going to get it. Now is the time to give them and show them and have them show you four easy to learn (but not easy to perfect—that's for later) display methods to attract. Show them the Snug and Taut—Symmetrical, the Loose and Casual—Asymmetrical, Skyline, and Breathing designs. Demonstrate how to maintain them. Use the following sketches to give them the basics. Discuss and show them each design idea and then let them try to duplicate. Be sure to compliment. Find the good. They are working, and they do want to be good at it, especially in front of you and the others.

Before I begin, set the stage so your helpers can perform to your expected needs and wants. I know your mind is full of ideas and also thinking about what you have just read. Let's move on to actual plans.

Everyone must be told or given:
1. Small spiral bound Memo pads with pens attached.

They are to carry them at all times to take down information from a customer. If they hear the customer's name or, very pleasantly, ask for it, they should write it down to be able to recall it. Write down any idea, yes, any purpose they see that needs improving, and also for those whose job it is to go about the store and see what needs filling and how to judge the amount needed.

2. When the stock is getting low (you decide how low) or when the stockroom can supply no more, how do you want to be informed; by email, text, written order on paper, or cell phone?

3. A clipboard, a whiteboard, or a corkboard with attached writing instruments are ideas that everyone can see and use to write what products are needed.

4. Who will be the GTP (Go To Person) to shoulder the responsibility for keeping the store well-stocked via a smooth operation?

5. Finally, and this doesn't have anything to do about displays. Still, I don't want to forget: Designate a specific place where a designated person will tack essential messages from you. Decide how each will acknowledge they have read your information.

6. See that each keeps their notes up to date in their Advocate's Progress Book. No one can remember everything said to them the first time. The Malley School of Merchandising was so well received because I used three of our senses: seeing, hearing, and touching. Attendees did not just sit and listen, I had them get up and try, and one of us was right there to praise and encourage and then compliment!

Display Presentations, Creating and Refilling

Put this picture in your mind because it will surely happen during a hectic holiday: Think of customer's mingling, looking at a display, perhaps have merchandise in their hands, and maybe wearing raincoats or heavy winter coats. They may have children with them. That is why, for everyone concerned, it is safer and better to carry a large amount of product to place in a display, because you can excuse yourself and get into the area to place a fresh supply for their viewing and buying pleasure. It is much safer than a moving cart.

Displays will have sell-through, and you must develop in your helper's habits and knowledge of how to replenish displays. To prepare, with their pen and memo pad, they should go about the store and make lists of what needs replacing and about how many are required. Explain that when inventory is getting low (you decide what "low" means) what to do about it. Decide how Store helpers will tell you of inventory conditions. Perhaps where all can see it, so when their stockroom has a low inventory or no inventory, you can be alerted.

Show them what to do when you are so busy, it is difficult to replenish a display. Helpers can use three display concepts. Loose and Casual (Asymmetrical), Snug and Taut (Symmetrical), and Skyline. Breathing Space is as valuable as the Skyline approach in that it too saves a display from being dull or washed out. The answer to that is to remember every presentation should not be all one kind. What if every chair in our house was the same—boring! Mix your design approaches, so your customers are kept being enticed, carrying them throughout your store. Breathing Space is a useful designing tool. Learn how to work with it and what it can do for your displays and even your bottom line.

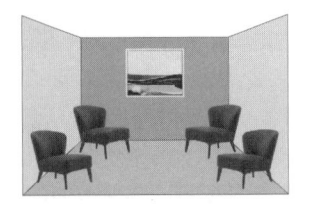

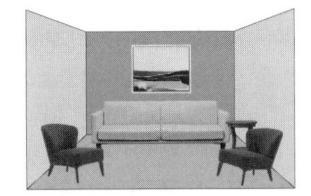

1. A display can be made more dynamic by using the Loose and Casual (Asymmetrical) design because by intentionally ignoring balance, you can usually get the eye moving. It makes a display seem to have more life to it, and customers seem to be very comfortable viewing it. You have created a pathway for their eyes to follow. You are unevenly distributing the 'elements' within the space by using, for example, larger boxes, such as our Pretzels boxes and then introducing one or two items such as bagged "Pretzel Babies, Chocolate-Covered Pretzel sticks, or any of the following; boxed Chocolate Pretzel bars,

two Pretzels in-a-bag, individual chocolates called Pretzel Domes or the "Pretzelnormous" a great big bar. Different items present us with more possibilities for arranging a space while creating attention to what you are displaying. It's also a help for our customers to see what they enjoy, in another shape and size. You could do a "Pretzel Passion" space and display all pretzel products. Be sure to show proper signage.

2. In a Loose and Casual plan of presentation, you can usually:
a. Give the eye a vacation (visual relaxation through space)
b. The display will seem it has some life in it
c. Make the viewer comfortable
d. Incorporating the use of "Breathing Space" between packages helps not to make the presentation appear relentless.
e. In creating anything, an odd number usually works better than even numbers. You can get more movement, some rhythm going, carrying the eye along. If doing a formal presentation, be careful about odd and even.
f. It's fun to look at too!

In the following sketches you will see the Loose and Casual and Snug and Taut displays are sitting upon platforms, in which all three boxes are a different size. I highly recommend that you have them made in a lightweight wood, so they can be carted around and can easily take the bumps and falls. Cut a hand indentation on one side to make them easier to carry; otherwise, they are awkward. Of course, you can change their cover whenever it pleases you, but you should have a sturdy foundation cover that you can use at any time. Choose a covering that will readily accept study pins or tacks that won't show pin holes when you want a temporary change. For your foundation, make your choice be one that will blend nicely with colors of seasonal and special events, and you may not need to change it all, dark green, black, beige, or whatever will quietly fit in with your packaging and your store colors. Remember, your decision must not ever take anything away from your Hero. Take your top five sellers, get some support stands, and decide how wide to make each step. Be mindful you will be putting a foundation box upon a foundation box. Make your first box the widest. Set your sample box near the edge and at a slight angle and measure how much space is needed. Do the same for the next box and then the top box. You'll get great use out of these for your window too. Consider if you want to make one and work with it and decide what modifications or enlargements will best fit your needs.

Another approach is more formal; it is called "Snug and Taut." (Symmetrical design.) The Snug and Taut design is usually balanced as far as the "viewing" weight is concerned; it's all lined up and is more formal. With practice, a balanced arrangement will be quite eye-catching through the use of Breathing space, Skyline, and other aspects of balance enhancers. It can also be done through the use of large displays and be quite sophisticated and beautiful. This more formal design can make attractive compositions. I find they are especially useful after I have made some Free/Loose layout of products. I think of it as the difference between a recreation room versus a library. The recreation room will be in a casual way, and it's always welcoming. On the other hand, it feels good to go into the library where everything has a feeling of calmness and is in order. It gives a balance, and that's what I want to have happened in our stores. Items are usually closer together, providing a tauter look (Sometimes even a stiffer look) to the layout. The formal design makes beautiful compositions.

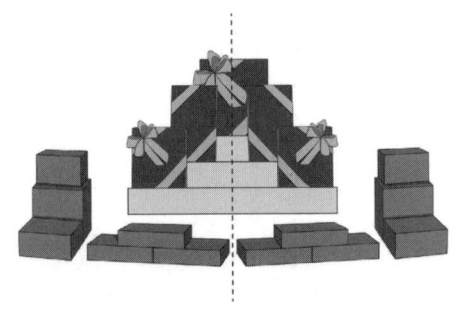

The Snug and Taut Design

a. From the center of the proposed space, there is an equal distribution of items.

b. It gives balance. Think of drawing a straight line down the middle of the display. Both sides will be identical in design. There is a sense of discipline and order.

c. Packages are proportioned evenly throughout the display

d. Breathing Room and Skyline considerations are or can be employed if duplicated throughout the presentation.

e. Snug and Taut teach another significant factor: color balance. This design forces a balance. It helps to remember to equalize the "weight" of all your displays. Think about your home. The feeling of weight your couch presents, made you most likely to arrange something on the other side of the room to give you a sense of feeling balanced. If one of your offerings is dark in color, balance the coloring, so the eye does not pull all the attention to the dark offering. No need to be fanatic about it, you can always break the dense color up by presenting another color with it. Work with the balance idea until you feel comfortable.

The "Skyline" approach stops our eyes from going right over the display, not even noticing what was in it, is often called "eye-washers." It means that the eye passes over the display washing out any meaning. Something must attract the eye. Think of a skyline you have noticed. The buildings are all different sizes and shapes. Some are close together and others slightly apart. Some are squat and flat while others are tall and slender looking (from a distance.) The eye travels from one building, bridge, or stadium to the next, and the viewer is interested in seeing it all. They are attractive to view. If they were all one height, how boring would that be? There is usually one building that is taller than all the others. It demands and takes more space, but it gives more. It anchors the space and becomes the focal point. However, it is not needed as long as there are differences in the heights or tops of the packages.

Look at this design showing a Loose and Casual approach. It is also an excellent example of Skyline Design. It's evident the height of packages are different but note the differences in size how some "buildings" are tucked in or placed in the rear or sides of "buildings," sparked by one building bestowing a further enhancement to the scene.

The saving grace for boredom. The Skyline layout.

Leaving space between boxes or bags is called Breathing Space. It happens when a space is allowed between boxes, bags or other packages. It's like being able to catch one's breath. The skyline technique is advantageous when it is not a busy gift-buying season. A "Look" of a display is usually one of two options: "Free/Loose" or "Taut/Snug." Most always, Free/Loose displays are designs most turned to when there is a lot less merchandise needed. It's a time when packages can create an illusion of more packages than there are. It, too, is fun to work with at any time because of its casualness. If appropriately arranged, the free space, when viewed, will show more exciting sights deeper into the store or might show off a Special" also making the viewer want to go see what the "Special" is all about. It might show off a product you want to further develop in Customer Satisfaction, or to introduce a new confection or combination. The Snug and Taut display choice usually show breathing space just naturally because of the type of display it is.

Think of Breathing space like casting seed upon the earth. It releases from the hand and usually lands in pleasing arrangements, always with space between the seeds or clusters depending upon how they fell. Some may be standing up with others leaning against them. Some may be lying down with others leaning against them, Use "Breathing Space" to make attractive arrangements that are appealing to the eye with space between each "seed or cluster." It is also wise to remember "Breathing Space" when there is a change in the type of merchandise. If using boxes in a column, tweaking them (slightly) gives more breathing room and a certain rhythm to the scene. It's important to remember we must make it fun for the eye to look at a display. Even in hectic seasons, it is essential "Breathing Space" is incorporated. Create it between package groupings or by arranging a product, so you create space in the display.

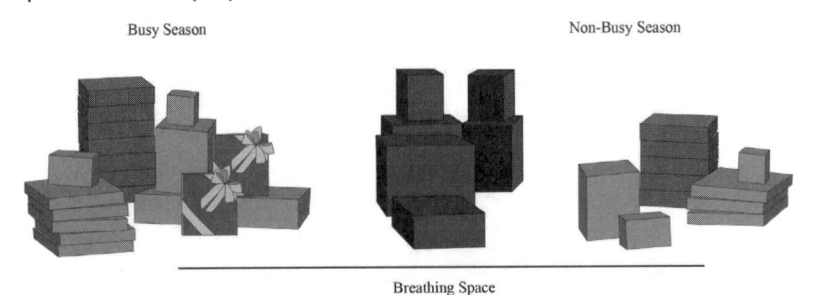

Busy Season　　　　　　　　　　Non-Busy Season

Breathing Space

Display Supports

Often during my Merchandising School, I'd hear the lament, "We have no room for displays or any decorative object, much as I'd like to use them." Especially at holiday time, we need to use every scrap of space we can find or use. I think one of the most accessible areas to discover is to go up. Make the column of boxes about 10 -12 boxes higher than you ever had before. You know the customers are going to have it leveled before you assist ten more customers, and it's different and fun to view and then to tell others, "You should see all the chocolates!" Of course, make the columns of boxes in front more natural to reach. Be sure to give each a twitch to provide a feeling of space. If that seems too time-consuming, teach your helpers to do something more interesting than to make a column. If your hand has four boxes, as you remove them from the outer case, place them catty-corner to the boxes below. Using this technique will give some pizazz to your column.

Use a seasonal enhancer attached to your price sign. Wrapped boxes with ribbons or other decorations provide a finished look and save time at the register. If you are going to use only pre-wrapped boxes and someone requests a bow on their package, have them pre-made so someone who is "all thumbs" can quickly wrap, strap and decorate the box. You will sell more "decorated" boxes if you choose unique chocolates (or add a selection into your regular assortment creating a new offering) wrapped in exceptional wrapping paper topped off with a well-made bow. Hopefully, not a ready-made bow. Explain to your helpers what a special box it is. It must have its sign. Perhaps in a frame and information professionally written or typed using a distinctive font. Mention some of the unique chocolates in it and its price. Wrap one of your special pieces in foil. Be excited about this new offering and make sure your helpers can describe it successfully. If you have never taken a risk with larger box offerings or perhaps a different assortment and wrapping, do so now. Our Hero is the chocolates. Be sure not to go overboard with the decorations. If you decide to make a few and see how they will be accepted, purchase a low amount of tie-on's. The excess will be marked down, perhaps sold at a loss, or it will sit on storage shelves adding to maintenance and their cost. You will see that more decorated boxes will please customers as it becomes closer to the holiday and "time" is shorter.

If you decide to make the addition of a new style of packaging, present it full of confidence. Make a substantial display, put a spotlight on it. Give it a descriptive sign and perhaps frame it. Do not show your helpers your lack of confidence, saying, "I hope this is going to go over with our customers." Be excited about it. Introduce it with enthusiasm. You might decide to make up some half-pound boxes too. Customers may not afford the more expensive box, but in a smaller size. They can still taste the wonderful selections. Please don't make a mistake about its presentation, do it right. For heaven's sake, don't mention anything but words that describe this exciting offering. The more often descriptive words are heard, the more your helpers will feel comfortable using them when speaking with your customers. Without thinking, your helpers may not realize how their remarks sound to a customer: "Yes, it's a new box with special pieces in it, and specially wrapped too. Everyone is wondering how it is going to sell." Really, who is going to buy a box described like that?

How about: "Yes, this is a new offering, and it's becoming a favorite gift. There are unique dark and milk chocolates in the collection, such as Red Raspberry creams swirled with dark Chocolate, Smooth Peanut Butter splashed with strawberry puree" or a box of "chocolate caramel topped off with crushed roasted Almonds." Hand them a box: "Look at how well wrapped it is. Would you say it's pretty special? " (Smile) I think a collection like this will please someone special. If you would like me to, I will put one or two aside for you and have it all ready to go when you are! Would you want me to do this for you?

"If you made a sale, be sure to thank them and tell them you know they are going to get a big thank you when they open this collection because it is exceptional and delicious!

    a. [If the answer is yes, add something unexpected]: If you would like to tell me, will it be for one person or a group, because I will want to choose just the right enclosure card and envelope. Should I do this for you?

    b. If the answer is, "No, thank you, be prepared to add to the conversation, "If you would like to choose one or two pieces as a surprise for home, they are in our chocolate display case." Smile.

Instead of the word "box," I chose "collection" to remove the word box and its shape from their mind and put in a softer picture of a gathering.

Give a fun "taste tour" and describe what they are viewing with wording like swirling, snappy, splashed, smooth, crunchy, brisk, crushed, and slivered. Language like this saved the three sentences from becoming monotonous. In this application, the mind went swirling, got smooth, splashed, and even roasted and crunched. That was a good "ride." It will also be fun to listen to you if you add voice inflections. I asked for the sale by offering them an idea and ending my question by going up the scale a few notes <u>punctuated</u> with a question.

I asked for their opinion. I offered to do some things for them, gave them an unexpected courtesy of choosing a card with an envelope, leaving them feeling cared for, and I was interested in making their gift special. Thus, leaving them and me in a right and happy mood. I delighted my customer. (Mission statement.)

How can you wait on a long line of customers, answer the phone, and take an order and keep replenishing your displays? You have to plan to do the best you can to refill your displays.

Perhaps buy a chrome fixture of five shelves on wheels. Load it with your most favored packages. Put a touch of the season colors, a sample or picture of the product, and a price sign. If hiring a helper(s) is out of the question, make a list of what to do. Don't be a penny saved and pound foolish. Customers like to get in and get out. They are busy. They want questions answered quickly, not have to go and find a person to answer their questions. (You know how frustrating THAT is!) An answering tape can handle telephone calls. Many times the information wanted is the hours you are open. Ask to have the caller's number if more information is desired. Say you will call back when you know you will be less busy. Tell a time such as between 1:30 p.m. and 3:00 p.m., and after 6 p.m. until 9 p.m. Remember, you are to be professional, not harried. A new customer will be impressed by your service and friendliness. Think of hiring an extra person or two as an investment in your future.

If you have shelves above a counter or table, place your most frequent sellers here because a lot of weight can go on the counter or table. Arrange your offerings as you will a regular three-shelf display fixture or have more fun. Mix in your half pounders and also a third different package. Include in the display more of the same so customers can easily choose an assortment. Take up the whole space with this idea.

Devote possibly three different packages to utilize a shelf situation. On the bottom shelf, divide the space as needed using the three boxes. Moving vertical, keep the same pattern as you go up the shelves. This way, every package gets a prime area. Customers do not like to bend to take a box or a bag, even if they do notice it on the bottom shelf. We all prefer to shop from our waists up.

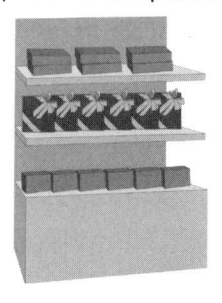

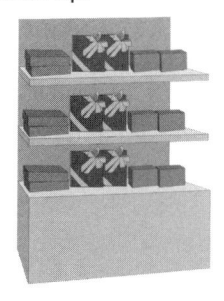

Difficult to replenish:

For additional temporary tables, use tablecloths that almost reach the floor to save the hems from being spoiled by wet boots or work boots. Full-length table coverings are better looking than a simple tablecloth showing the apparatus for legs supporting a top creating a table. Not only do they offer some softness to your scene, but also full-length tablecloths can conceal supplies in outer boxes beneath the table. Explain to your helpers that no one likes to see outer boxes but to make things more convenient for customers and you, when the display needs replenishing, and the store is full of customers, this will be quicker and heavy rolling carts won't be in the way or view of your customers. Tell them to watch when there is space around a certain display needing refilling, to quickly lift the table covering a small amount and pull forward the outer box and get needed supplies.

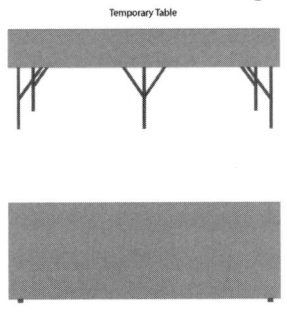

Temporary Table

To cover tables, we used heavy 45-inch wide Polyester material. We arranged the cloth to appear upholstered. We simply wrapped the fabric around the table at the height we determined was the best and laid the excess material on top of the table. There were usually 16 inches laying on the top of the table, creating 16 + 16 = 32 inches of material on the tabletop. We straight-pinned the cloth together. Tip: When you first start to dress the table, have someone hold the fabric steady on the tabletop due to the weight; otherwise, it will keep falling off. On the end, where the edges of the cloth meet, pin it in place. About seven inches in from the top edge or side of the table, turn under the material down to the "hem." From the inside of the cloth very neatly blind pin or tape it, whichever turns out to be the neatest way for you. You might try Velcro little circles that come packaged. Just make sure there is no puckering. If all sides of the table will be seen, you are finished. If the table is against a wall, make sure the dressmaker fold will be facing the wall, creating a very smooth presentation. What about the ends? There are other ways to handle the end where the cloth comes together, but this way is simple and will get you started. We used bubble wrap on the corners to protect the fabric from wear. After assembling the packages on the table, the slight rise on the corner edges was not noticeable. After the holiday, the cloths were washed at a laundromat, hung on very sturdy hangers, and covered until we needed them again. Ironing was not a factor because of the make-up of the material and its weight.

Do have some worthy decorations and one main attraction. Perhaps use a large textured tall basket, more vertical than round (to save space). Place filler in the basket bottom and then pop some garland in—some hanging over the edge, long enough to bring the eye down to your packages. Add some wrapped boxes, perhaps with a large "To and From" tag addressed to the mail-carrier, beauty-shop, baby sitter, or another we sometimes forget to thank. Operated by batteries, a string of lights could be festively tucked in the garland. Be sure to have an ample amount of batteries. If you are decorating for Hanukkah, pop some big dreidels and little ones too in the basket. Decorate the rim of the basket with totally different greenery than Christmas greenery and tuck in some dreidels or gold coins, big ones, and smaller ones. Decorating for Kwanzaa? Use the basket ideas and fill them with brightly wrapped packages. Put a big tag on each addressed to individual family names—Mom, Dad, Michael, Sam, Marie, and Kathy. Decorate the rim of the basket with flowers and greens that will be different from those used in a Christmas display. This display will not be viewed from the top, but from the floor looking up, be sure to check it from this viewpoint. Assemble displays around it. Focus your narrow beam lights. No need for anything else.

If you are wrapping as customers are buying, stop most of it and pre-wrap. Customers are just as busy as we are, and they need and want quick service. When you are just starting, choose wrappings that look well with each other. If you have lots of rolls of wrapping paper, you will not use much from all the paper, and they will go back into your storage area as inventory adding to their cost. Unless you started your business with a war chest of cash, watch for every opportunity to spend and save sensibly. Your wrapping paper can have different textures and finishes like matte or glossy. The same wrap for the particular assortment of the entire box weights: 5lb; 3lb; 2lb; 1lb and ½ lb. or however you choose to offer your product. For a box, you will display with these assortments, consider a print but it must complement or contrast with the "main" wrap. Either choose a solid for your third wrap or perhaps a stripe, again keeping your other colors in mind.

Display Presentations, Creating and Refilling

As you gain some history, you will notice that the closer it gets to the holiday, the traditional colors of the holiday prevail.

I always considered that some of our packages wrapped for Christmas would be gifts for folks not celebrating the birth of Jesus. Another important December observance is Hanukah. It is a Jewish festival commemorating the re-dedication of the Second Temple in Jerusalem. During the war with the Macabees, scant oil-maintained light for eight days. Hanukkah is also known as the Festival of Lights. Packages wrapped in a classy paper in medium blue that is not glossy or decorated but with a distinctive ribbon are well received. Another observance is Kwanzaa. It is a week-long celebration held in the United States to honor universal African heritage and culture. It is a happy time, a celebration. Bright, cheerful colors will provide ideas on how to wrap packages. Keep in mind that there will be lots of dinner parties at all these family and friend times.

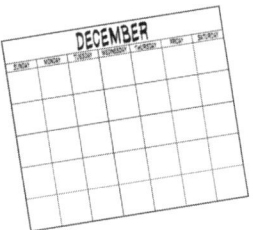

As you decide how to wrap your holiday packages, consider an assortment that will appeal to folks appreciating Vintage, Early American, Sophisticated and contemporary wraps. Which of your wrapping papers would satisfy each of those desires?

1.Use solid colors or an imaginative stripe (It is not to call attention to itself) to cover your tables. Nix decorated holiday designs! A harmonizing color or quiet scheme will give more flexibility allowing using the color at another time during the year, and not steal the attention. Your product is to be the Hero. Don't detract from it. Keep your eye on the prize.

2.In our Design Center, Donna Coyle, our Manager and I, pondered the flow of color, texture, and choice for wrappings, bows, and decorations to complement the assortments. Sometimes, when we had trouble coming to a decision, we "slept on it." We always knew the next day what to do. Be sure to read "How to be Creative" in this book. Gift wrap should also add to the ambiance of your store. Be aware of your store colors where your packages will be displayed. Our bread and butter assortments are more classic, so use a more subdued but classy and attractive paper. When a box had a variety of items, we used a more light-hearted approach. We have a Nutcracker offering, so guess

158   Conversations with Adele : Business Owners' Fundamentals for Success

what paper we always looked for to convey its contents. Consider not picking colors that do not go with your palette of colors. All your other packages will have to take a backseat to an offering that does not compliment, associate, or live happily with all your different packages and backgrounds. It will stand out like a sore thumb. Choose a selection of wrappings that compliment your store colors. I would suggest not putting a best seller or one of your top five in a paper that would not fit in with every kind of purpose: homes and individuals, and the corporate world of business. Link the wrap with the contents. Being a new business, be careful in your selections, too much of anything is too much, and what will sit on your shelves is costing you more money every day. Talk with wrapping paper vendors and ask about smaller rolls, the cost of precut for your most bought package. Ask if they have ideas on how a smaller business can save on gifting wraps, envelopes, bags,

Tie-on's, what trend is developing, and what is new this year. Do not allow a vendor to talk you into something. You must first build your network of vendors you trust. If there is a display house rather close to you, visit it and talk with the Owner and ask if they serve smaller businesses. Floral distributors often sell wholesale to the trade. Try not to buy what the big stores are selling as package decorations because you want your packages to stand out, not look like every other wrapped package. By using a primary color, you can get many miles out of it through the year. How you also decorate your box or bag will catch the eye. Have fun, explain what you are doing so others can learn, and you can eventually give them the satisfaction of the responsibility.

Chapter 10
Compliance: Accountant

Your accountant should be working very closely with you offering ideas and opinions. If he/she does not have the experience or the interest to be able to do this part of the job, get a new accountant. This requirement is too important. You might decide that after the budgets are completed for the coming year to discuss that the accountant meet with your employees about their wages. These meetings should be before the start of your fiscal year and should be commenced within the first two weeks. Have your accountant make a list of what all your company is paying the different government offices, your 401K plan, FICA, or whatever plans where you share company costs with them. Let your employees see what all is being paid for them out of the business! Also this explanation should be enclosed with their first paycheck each fiscal year.

For a real time saver, have your accountant explain that:
a. Your employees will be receiving their paycheck every two weeks. Giving this information should be done as soon as possible before the start of the fiscal year, so they can adjust their own budgets.

b. Also get their compliance on direct deposit of their check into their checking account at their chosen banks.

Your accountant should be made aware of your mission and what your growth plans are for the coming year as laid out in your business plan (every year). As with anyone representing you, explain how you want them to speak about the development of your culture, how you want it said, and what you hope to gain through their understanding of your target. The accountant should keep a short description of the conversations with employees. If unpleasant, you should be contacted immediately. Then together discuss how to resolve the conflict. Your accountant should also make contact throughout the year to discuss performance movement and bottom-line additions or lack thereof with your Direct Reports whose positions have that responsibility. The accountant should discuss what the goal is for that month which allows your Manager to know every month if they are performing to their goal or not, so they may see "the writing on the wall" and leave if they are under-performing. A "Quick Tip" from SABA (Learn more about them at www.saba.com/rethinkretention). (They can help you on your road to success.) The tip for when you speak one-on-one with your Supervisors or Manager (which I have changed for a small business) is:

- What have you planned for this coming month to increase sales? Now discuss how to coach and energize everyone to meet the goal. Perhaps set a lively competition with the store's own numbers.
- Let's review your goals and discuss the success or lack of in earlier plans.
- Tell me how you like to work with everyone.
  1. "Give me a job, and I'll do it. I like to work alone." A person is **Independent**; usually, a Leader likes to drive change, get results, be blunt, confidant, outspoken, and excite others to their cause.
  2. "I enjoy leading and working with others for their feedback in making the project (job) more successful", (**Cooperative**.) (Thrive on feedback and human interaction, diplomatic and good at communicating. Likes to influence others, enthusiastic and trusting)
  3. "I like to do my project but be part of the job." (They connect people's styles, versatile and adaptable) (**Proximity**) (Calmness, co-operation, dependable)
  4. "I like to get to know the people I work with and show interest

in them. I thrive on getting everyone to work well together to deliver accuracy and ensure quality." (**Supportive**.) Works conscientiously, a people person, calm magnetic personality.

I learned of this method from Sue Seidman and Tony Robbins. Both are interested in the DISK assessments to help you understand your working style and your employees. No one is a straight DiSK example. We are all combinations. I'm showing this here to give you ideas to think about how your employees would work best because they are most comfortable. It is not something to use in an interview. It doesn't tell a particular skill, aptitude, or something that would be good for a position. It only measures personality designed to facilitate teamwork and communication.
- How are you growing professionally, and how can I help in the process?"

The accountant should meet with your Manager enough times, so he/she have a feeling of support when they meet. The accountant should be aware of the Manager's skills and generously help anyone who needs extra time to learn what the accountant requirements are to reach the goal. The accountant should also help with new employees if the employees, for example, price anything made in the store, or need help with overtime.

You must decide that once a year your Supervisors and/or Manager will meet with your Controller or accountant to discuss wage and budgets. After preparing the company's budget, the accountant will tell each department head the amount their departments will have to divide among their helpers or to announce they will be no increase. Also, he/she will tell the Manager or Supervisor of any increase in their wages.

At this yearly meeting, a Manager or Supervisor should not be surprised by anything the accountant will tell them because they already know their efforts toward reaching the goal they agreed to the year before was not met, met, or exceeded goal.

The Manager and the accountant must come to agreement on the new goal. The Manager, if possible, should be told why the Owner believes they can reach the proposed goal due to:
- Enrichments in advertising
- Additions to your lines
- Any new catalogs

- Seminars planned for them
- Books and articles to enhance your position

Marketing and the person responsible for retail should meet to discuss what is needed and wanted—what and when—and also discuss signage for windows and in-store displays. Marketing should issue features and benefits, and describe how to sample. Beyond this:
- Role play in the stores about telling a customer about the sale.
- Construct a system for the sale and display of the monthly items.
- A general "Favorites Book" telling which customer loves a particular chocolate and offer to call the customer when it is on sale.
- Discuss fun "goings on" within the store about the special of the month. For Christmas, construct a large display in the store and another by the cash registers. Buy large jingle bells on a strap or ring or another way and have one at each register. Have your salespeople ask if they would like a great gift, "Our special of the month!" Whenever someone buys a "Special," ring the bells enthusiastically and give the purchaser another sample. It will add fun and cheer to the atmosphere. When we did this for a baseball promotion, the customers wanted to ring the old-fashioned school bell themselves! Or feature or create a "thank you for shopping with us" special for in-store customers (Make them feel special.)

This suggested plan is one way to be very aware of the numbers. The accountant will divide the yearly goal into monthly goals and discuss approaches to reaching them. The Manager will then prepare by breaking down the goal of each month into a weekly goal. Then the weekly goal should be further broken down into a daily goal which should be discussed with all the assistants.

At the store level, we even knew what we wanted in the cash drawer by noon, so if we needed to, we would increase our effort to larger add-on sales. We talked about it in the store, and we made certain all Advocates suggested that the customer get something for home, or someone's birthday that was fast approaching. We could ship our customer's number one favorite, Chocolate-covered Pretzels and remind the customer that we could even send a greeting with the gift. Also, a sale or discounted item could be given greater display space and pointed out. (Make sure your Managers know how to create these larger displays and teach the techniques to their Advocates!) While these things should happen every sale, added emphasis can get a department to or over goal by concentrating on these additional sales. When the Manager can see that they are not going to reach the goal, with the Owners or the Leader of Retail's, "OK," discuss what they can do differently to try to meet it.

- Can certain products be reduced so by selling more they will reach goal? (A note could be placed on each of their cash registers)
- Is there a special list of people to call?
- If it is a real slow day is there a volunteer to go home or shopping?
- Can someone step outside the store and pass out samples or coupons good for that day?
- If we were not reaching goal, perhaps not enough customers come in for various reasons. Use this unhurried customer care time, to spend more time, engaging your customer. Ask what they like about the store. What is their favorite chocolate? Did they know we ship? What did they wish we did differently? Ask them to please come back and see you. Suggest the fun that is in store for the next holiday, store celebration, or community festivity. Ask if they want to put their card in the box for a drawing for a box of chocolates to send to someone if they win. (These are suggestions, thought ticklers to help you have more enjoyable times with your customers.) These questions are not to be bam bam bam, but rather choose one or two suggestions and have a conversation with the customers. Ask them what one chocolate is they have never tasted. . . give them a sample. Have fun!

The Manager should be trained and educated on how to discuss new goals with the helpers and how to divide their department's goal by looking at the previous year's monthly attainments. December's goal, for instance, will be a good deal larger then a slower months goal. Impress upon them that when they are easily making goal, they should remind themselves of the days and weeks when they don't have as many customers, and that they should always practice good salesmanship and invite their customer to return.

They must learn to increase each sale by conversing with their customers. Practice, practice, practice! Also, they must be learning how to increase return visits. They must learn how to bring in new customers. They must learn how to suggest a customer refer them. All these efforts will bear fruit with customer visits in the slower months when every single visit will help you reach your goal!

These sales numbers must be watched closely by your Bookkeeper or you. They must be discussed with you, and you must discuss them with your Manager or other Leaders. If you just cannot bring yourself to do this task, speak with your Board, other business acquaintances, or if you have an outstanding Manager or Director, suggest they put together some ideas which they can use as a basis. Do what you are comfortable doing. See that it is done! Don't give away your standing. You can always invest in a speaker on this subject but tell them ahead of time you want follow-up sheets to help retain their information and any other assistance the speaker can or will donate to the cause.

The Owner/president must continue to invest in leadership development. Use your own time but do it or hire from the outside. Perhaps SCORE or your Chamber Council of Smaller Enterprises or other organizations you belong to can arrange for you to meet other entrepreneurs. You are never alone in wanting more leadership information in business. Together hire someone versed in the information you all feel you need and decide how the meetings will be attended and what specifically you want taught. Leadership is what will lift your business from small incremental advancements to great leaps forward. Simply because you had the courage to start your own business because you thought you would enjoy being able to work at something you believed in or could perform well does not mean you are or must be terrific in all parts of business. Get smart; shore up your weaknesses! Start with Strengths, Weakness, Opportunity, Threats (SWOT), and with deep thought and intensity, go on from there.

Chapter 11
Financial Decisions

As a kid, did you ever play the game, "I'm going on a trip and I'm taking…" then you would say what one item you had packed? The next player would say the same words plus what you said you were taking and add some item they were supposedly packing. Then the next would repeat the opening phrase, the next two "already packed items" and add another piece. Soon someone who didn't listen well enough or simply forgot something that a previous player had packed, that person's turn was over and sadly had to sit out the rest of the game. Now you are grown up and you have decided to take a real trip, perhaps the trip of your lifetime.

The adult version is way more complicated. You can't take a llama or your bicycle; you must discipline yourself and make complicated decisions to be a winner. In this version, to earn the victory so you won't be one of those who have to "sit out the rest of the game," it all depends on your determination and flexibility.

Here are the rules to play life's game:

Stay focused and prepare

Think again about what Lou Holtz, the only coach to take football teams from six different colleges to Bowl games, and the only coach to guide four different programs to top 20 rankings taught his football teams to think. Whenever a fast decision was called for on the field, think "W.I.N: What's Important Now?" He drilled it into them over and over and over until the repetition of it became a habit in their lives. They didn't think about what had just happened but quickly decided what was <u>going</u> to happen next, or what <u>needed</u> to happen <u>right now</u>.

Don't let a set-back make you lose confidence to keep moving forward. Think of "What's Important Now." I've included a small poster with these words that you can copy and use. Make the poster big or make it small. Put it on your bathroom mirror, on your desk, in your pocket, on your dashboard, wherever you will often see it, and be able to remind yourself three very important words, What's Important Now. I made one for you to copy to tape onto your computer frame, so intrusions don't keep you from your creation. Think about it for a moment, can you think of any other three words more important than "What's Important Now"?

W.I.N: What's Important Now?

Before you do anything to get your business underway, do your research. Set aside time to think, investigate, follow directions, take suggestions to heart and truly believe you don't have to know it all or do it all, and you should have a very enjoyable ride...because you "packed" everything you should, and if you work at it, approach your SWOTS with confidence and action, never give up on your mission, you will become what you visualize, you will be your dream. Success will be yours.

Always start with research

Find out if there really is a need for your product and can the area support another store of your kind. Do pre-planning, make a list of all the things you think you should know about. Then commence your planning for your business. Study the demographics of your proposed area. How many other stores like yours will be in the area? Are those stores being supported now? What kind of merchandise is being offered? Is the price range nearly the same for like stores in the area? What kind of stores is the general public supporting there now? What are the general spending habits? What is the medium income level?

Will your store be able to obtain most of the sales volume because of what you will be offering and its unique presentation? Or will your presentation be somewhat the same and you will just be sharing the available dollars with your competition?

Find out what is planned, if anything, for new roads, access ramps, and highways. Find out what is planned mall wise and strip wise for your proposed area. Check various kinds of stores that will be selling something like your product. Check major national chains to see if they are trending for more areas like your proposed successful, busy choice. What do they do when they move in? If your idea is unique prepare for it to be copied. What then? Know you can only stay ahead if you actually listen to your customers, preferably face-to-face, work on their suggestions if possible and keep trying to do what Walt Disney did. When Disney had a great A+ operation in force, he wanted to improve upon it. It eventually had its own nickname called "Plussing". Be very aware because your new competitor may not only copy what you have created but, using you as a reference, improve upon it.

Have faith in yourself

Don't let this scare you, it's to prepare you. Dave Thomas, founder of Wendy's said: "What do you need to start a business? Three simple things: know your product better than anyone, know your customer, and have a burning desire to succeed."

> *"Remember the only way to get there is to start!"*
> *– Mark Twain*

Hire professionals

If you can possibly afford it, hire two individuals well-informed and experienced: A Certified Public Accountant (CPA) and an attorney, both of whom are known for expertise in business start-ups. It will be money well spent.

Another person who can guide and direct you and remove a great deal of stress would be a mentor. If you know a businessperson whose business is established or a businessperson who is recently retired, and you admire them for what they have built, you may ask them out to dinner and discuss with them what you are doing. If they appear interested, you could ask them to help guide you through your start-up. If they accept and the union works well, you can always ask them to continue. In the first phase, you may ask to speak with them maybe once every four to six weeks at a time and place of their choosing.

Suggestion: From time to time give them gift certificates for fine dining in an envelope attached to your finest box of chocolates. If there is perhaps a hobby involved or any interest you know of, a gift in that realm would be appreciated. Always be sure chocolates accompany it.

Know what you are doing
- An accountant can do many things a CPA can, but a CPA can do things an accountant cannot. Most notably are:
- They are <u>more educated</u>. They must take arduous exams to get their certificates. They must take continuing education classes throughout their career in order to maintain up-to-date information on issues and changes in the accounting world.
- They are considered as most <u>trusted advisors</u>. Businesses that are required to have a financial statement audit or review—only a CPA can perform these services and issue the required reports. In addition, CPAs
- <u>Are considered fiduciaries</u>—a person with a legal duty and power to act on behalf of, and in the best interests of their clients.
- CPAs are <u>more knowledgeable in tax codes</u> and can represent us before the IRS if audit support is required.
- Besides completing a rigorous education and obtaining their license a CPA is <u>expected to follow a strict code of ethics</u> and meet <u>the high standards</u> of the profession.

What we especially desire and take comfort in and trust is the <u>highly regarded information</u> given us about many business functions. If you cannot afford to employ a CPA now, plan that you will in the future. Choose one now, and after you are set up in your business, discuss the best way for you to handle reporting duties. Perhaps you will meet every quarter or half year and maybe even once a year. You will feel a sense of protection and know this important function of your business is being reported correctly. You will also receive advice about business functions.

The backbone of this whole endeavor is you must establish more ready cash or resources for it than you have figured you will need. You must plan to be able to support your obligations for at least six months after opening before the average store begins to make money, plus your living expenses. Many outside influences can harm your cash position like poor judgment, recession, road construction, continuous rain or snow, helpers' mistakes or outright theft, and the list goes on. You also may experience an important family need. Figure out a revenue source to combat these possible emergencies before they occur. Six months is average, if you want to be more secure plan to double that amount or have definite plans in place in case you need the help.

Talk to others

Visit other small businesses and invite the Owner to be your guest for lunch or dinner for the purpose of asking him/her questions about starting a business. Will they help you? Ask about what is bothering you the most; how the business is affecting them and the family; are working partners or family involved and how is that working out? What is one of the things that surprised them the most about starting the business?

Possibly tell them you are deciding about what bookkeeping software you are thinking about using. Do they know anything about it? What do they think is the best way to go? Maybe assigning a person to do the bookkeeping or do it yourself? Will they use a CPA at the year's end? These questions are given as in a conversation, not to be pelted one after the other. Of course, create your own list of what is your "need to know." What would they (your guest) do differently?

Know how you will manage your business

Not understanding business finances, people management, and self-discipline are major obstacles to a good business. These three items have been proven time and again to cause business failure.

Give up the idea you need or can do everything necessary yourself. Jay Goltz is a Chicago entrepreneur and business author who owns five small businesses in Chicago. He is also the author of "Why do New Small Businesses Fail?" Reading it should be a very strong wake-up call. Don't think you are above it. Study each remark and see if the shoe fits.

Why Do Small Businesses Fail? by Jay Goltz

1. "The math just doesn't work. There is not enough demand for the product or service at a price that will produce a profit for the company. This, for example, would include a start-up trying to compete against Best Buy and its economies of scale".

2. "Owners who cannot get out of their own way. They may be stubborn, risk averse, conflict averse—meaning they need to be liked by everyone (even employees and vendors who can't do their jobs). They may be a perfectionist, greedy, self-righteous, paranoid, indignant or insecure. You get the idea. Sometimes, you can even tell these Owners the problem, and they will recognize that you are right—but continue to make the same mistakes over and over."

3. "Out-of-control growth. This one might be the saddest of all reasons for failure—a successful business that is ruined by over-expansion. This would include moving into markets that are not as profitable, experiencing growing pains that damage the business, or borrowing too much money in an attempt to keep growth at a particular rate. Sometimes less is more."

4. Poor accounting. You cannot be in control of a business if you don't know what is going on. With bad numbers, or no numbers, a company is flying blind, and it happens all of the time. Why? For one thing, it is a common — and disastrous—misconception that an outside accounting firm hired primarily to do the taxes will keep watch over the business. In reality, that is the job of the chief financial officer, one of the many hats an entrepreneur must wear until a real one is hired.

5. "Lack of a cash cushion. If we have learned anything from this recession (I know it's "over" but my customers don't seem to have gotten the memo), it's that business is cyclical and that bad things can and will happen over time—the loss of an important customer or critical employee, the arrival of a new competitor, the filing of a lawsuit. These things can all stress the finances of a company. If that company is already out of cash (and borrowing potential), it may not be able to recover."

6. "Operational mediocrity. I have never met a business Owner who described his or her operation as mediocre. But we can't all be above average. Repeat and referral business is critical for most businesses, as is some degree of marketing (depending on the business)."

7. "Operational inefficiencies. Paying too much for rent, labor, and materials. Now more than ever, the lean companies are at an advantage. Not having the tenacity or stomach to negotiate terms that are reflective of today's economy may leave a company uncompetitive."

8. *"Dysfunctional management. Lack of focus, vision, planning, standards and everything else that goes into good management. Throw fighting partners or unhappy relatives into the mix and you have a disaster."*

9. *"The lack of a succession plan. We're talking nepotism, power struggles, significant players being replaced by people who are in over their heads — all reasons many family businesses do not make it to the next generation."*

10. *"A declining market. Book stores, music stores, printing businesses and many others are dealing with changes in technology, consumer demand, and competition from huge companies with more buying power and advertising dollars."*

"In life, you may have forgiving friends and relatives, but entrepreneurship is rarely forgiving. Eventually, everything shows up in the soup. If people don't like the soup, employees stop working for you, and customers stop doing business with you. And that is why businesses fail."

If all the above information has given you a justification that all your "ducks are not in a row" perhaps it would be a rewarding year or two to be employed in a like business to get some experience. It may even give you an idea to look at your plans with a different perspective. If you decide to go ahead, make sure you have studied possible risks and discuss your reasoning with highly respected consultants.

Keep everything as simple as possible. Everything you do does not have to be the "be all and end all"; it's to get you started. Don't keep researching forever. Don't keep writing and rewriting your strategic or business plans. The way to get your business started is to begin. Action will move you along. You can always remove or add to it or tweak it. But do something. Get going. Begin!

Make a simple business plan. If needs be, the Internet has directions. To keep a plan simple is very necessary because the people reading it have seen hundreds before yours, and they don't want to get bogged down in a long (Heaven forbid a single spaced) treatise. Keep your writing free of excess, keep it as minimal as possible. Let your excitement show but still stay professional. Tell exactly what you want, and don't let this information get buried so they must look for it.

Ask for their signatures of confidentiality up front. They can sign, print, and date the last page of your handout and then return the paper to you or simply sign, print, and date a sheet of paper you give them.

First page: Executive Summary will contain:
- Your plan summary,
- What industry (retail),
- Income statement (is a profit and loss (P&L) (if not in business—forecast it),
- Forecast: state your financial projections to be. Tell in your forecast proposed average monthly expenses and what your revenue will be over the same period.
- Forecast further out: Gross revenue projection for one year will be: and your net will be: From start-up, our break-even point will be expected to occur in_____ and a __ percentage ROI (Return on investment) is projected for the financing period.

More can be added to make your plan be more insightful, and you can find out what they are by searching "business plans" in an Internet search engine, or your library will have the information in books on starting a business.

Once your plan is written, call your bank, and ask to speak with a business consultant. Explain to the consultant you are calling to ask for help to check the business plan you have written. Continue by saying, "When I visit the bank for funding, I would like to be able to submit a business plan that you would be expecting. I would hope you could read my plan and then give me suggestions to improve it." If the consultant agrees, before the meeting, send your plans so your time together can be more productive. At the meeting, write down the suggestions given to you. (Paper remembers what the mind forgets.) After you think them through, decide how you want to work them into your plans. Perhaps the consultant will meet you again to see that all is in order. Be sure to again send your plan on ahead. Send a letter of thanks for the consultant's time and effort on your behalf. If real detailed interest was shown you, perhaps a small gift such as a box of chocolates, a box of cookies, or an item you really enjoy would be appropriate.

Educate yourself in accounting terms and be able to use them. You will be the bookkeeper/accountant until one wonderful day when you can hire one. This task alone should remind you of the very seriousness of what you are stepping into. You must be familiar with what accounting demands, know and understand where you are positioned every single day to save yourself and your business of dire consequences. You must understand all the line items on a Profit and Loss (P&L) statement because business is more involved than rent, selling and what is entailed in caring for a customer. You must be cognizant of and keep up with this information and so much more to stay above board. If you don't care to use any small business accounting software and you just cannot afford a Bookkeeper or an accountant, get imaginative on how you are going to get the information you need to save yourself from great stress. Consider evening courses, online courses, given through high schools and colleges. You might be able to barter for help. It would save you a great deal of stress if you could talk with an accountant once a month and show them your books to check that you are doing everything correctly. Then maybe once a year, have a Certified Public Accountant (CPA) tidy everything in preparation for your income taxes. Also, you will find many kinds of software for small business on the market. Ask around and see what is favored. Ask your CPA which one they think is best for your business. May as well get them on board with something they like to work with, so everything will be that much easier when you get together. These programs have improved so much that you can use them with confidence.

Location, location, location is the mantra of every good businessperson's brain. Find out on the Internet what makes a good location for the type and size of your store. When Malley's is looking for a possible location, we discuss possible areas and decide what we want to check on or about. We meet with our Real Estate agent gaining their knowledge, but we make our decision carefully and right in our own mind. Other things to check on are:

Don't over buy/pay too much rent. If we really like a place, but the Owner is asking more than what we have budgeted, we try to negotiate. Is it a highly trafficked area? Visit location possibilities and watch what you see. Visit stores in that area and watch and listen to what you hear. Watch the foot traffic, and as long as you are there, in a store watch the customer's eyes upon entering, what do they see first, second, which way did they go, and why? Listen to see and hear what kind of greeting they received. What is check-out like? If the store has long lines, do store employees acknowledge folks in the line? Remember to always try to learn from others. If the store is not busy, ask a question or two about the maintenance in the area, or are there events or festivals or other fun crowd-pulling affairs, or ask about something that is bothering you, keep notes so you can refer to them. No matter what location you decide upon, this little research/information will help you in planning your store and the decision of how you will prepare for your customers.

We try to find a location that offers two sides for signage.

Be careful of an intersection that is too busy and makes drivers very concerned about making it through the intersection safely. If they miss your turn-off, you will have missed possible sales. A traffic light can help a stand-alone enterprise.

If you are in the chocolate business or other store concerned about the effects of sun on or in your windows, study the position of the sun, not only the time you are visiting, but its slant all year. As you think about it, you already know the sun will reduce color vivacity a great deal. Either nix the idea or plan for protection. Be very diligent because the slightest gap will lead to a slant of that size across your entire store.

Get established in a lively, busy friendly area. Do you need it to be up-scale, rustic, modern, down-home, or none of the above? How is the outdoor area lighted? Is there security? What are the taxes? How is the general sanitation and plumbing, how is the roof, rain gutters, where does the run-off go, what is the general indoor plumbing accountability, how reliable is rubbish pick-up service? If not a stand-alone store, are there Common Area Maintenance (CAM) fees? What about other tenants in the building, any back-up overload in the plumbing, odor, loud noises, and find out if there are designated parking spaces for each store or is it general parking? Do the police and firemen respond promptly to calls? Any weak city services? Are there any new roads, malls, state, or major building contemplated for this proposed area? Where is a streetlight located? What and where is the closest bank? Are there specific hours you need to be closed or open?

Write down what you are told, or see, or think about, to discuss or decide upon later—especially if you are deciding various locations.

I think on equal standing with location, location, location is understanding accounting responsibilities. It's your obligation. Perhaps some of your sources of support are not businesspeople but still want to be assured how your business is doing. Set up at the time you ask for the loan, when and or how they would like to be informed how their loan is "doing". You might suggest you both arrange with a bank that you will repay so much a month, after six months start-up period, and that they will be notified of the deposit each month. It's a more business way of handling the loan and a great deal of less pressure on your relationship. You should be able to guide them through an accounting sheet in language that a person not involved with accounting language can understand.

Recently, on my drive to an appointment, traffic was held up. Somehow a fiber optic cord was cut. Traffic crawled, four or five huge yellow trucks were doing all sorts of things, police were in attendance, and workers seemed to be everywhere. My appointment at this office was impossible to contact because everything was "down" across the whole area. It caused me to remember that years ago, construction was on a main road where one of our stores was welcoming customers. As soon as the news reached us, we spoke to the city Leaders and studied the construction company's work plan. It called for the work to be in front of our store right before Easter. We told them one of our main revenue opportunities was during the time they expected to be working near or at our store. We really needed their help to not hinder traffic on the roadway or on the sidewalks at that time. They promised they would do their best to not interfere, and true to their word, they moved their work to another area and kept the road to our store clear.

Of course, find out who makes the decisions. Pay friendly visits with them to get to know them and see how they were coming along. Remember it never hurts to ask. If you receive negative co-operation you will know where you stand and can make plans. How much better for you to know the circumstances so you can make creative alternatives. This example is also why it's important to be known in the community as a contributor to its functions.

Let them know there is an interested face behind the name; make friends! Go to them early on and tell them of your plans. Ask if they have any ideas for you. Tell them you will be looking for some good helpers. If they know a good candidate, please send them your way! And yes, you will visit them again with one of your first products (maybe boxes of chocolates?) that you create.

During my Malley School of Merchandising days, I found some Chocolate retail businesses did not charge the proper amount for their products. This lack was mostly because they believed that they just loved what they were doing and did not believe they could or even should place a charge for their expertise and time.

They simply thought their "customer would not like it; after all, I'm right there in the store with them, and they are buying my merchandise."

The same held true for a specialty shop. The Owner thought her customers bought their hobby items from her, and she felt obligated to give them instructions. Nearby, other shops of the same type offered lessons. She did not think that was right. She is a peppy, fun kind of person and had "always wanted a shop." Her husband would "keep shop" to give her a day off. Her shop is now closed.

I thought perhaps they did not understand how their actions affected their Profit and Loss statement (P&L). I conversed with them by suggesting they think about it this way: When all their other responsibilities and work was completed, and their take home pay was more than satisfactory, only then could they think about being in the store giving away free personal instructions, free basket designing for their items in a gift basket (of which they had to bring in as the shop did not sell baskets), free bows, and your "hourly rate". Also, you will be setting a precedent where this kind of service is expected.

As you grow, you will have to hire a person to offer this service so as not to disappoint or anger customers who could always depend on this "assistance" in your shop. You taught them to believe this service would continue. If you want to do this service, have you planned who will do this when you are not available? Will you offer this free service when you are jammed with holiday customers? Will you dedicate an Advocate for this service or hire another?

Do you honestly think that if this wise and wonderful customer were in your shoes, that they would think this service was a good thing to do, if they had all the responsibilities sitting on their shoulders, that you do? Customers are fair. You be. Being fair doesn't mean you cannot be out in your store conversing and servicing your customers; you should be out there making friends and letting them get to know you. However, don't start giving away value that could have gone to your bottom line! If this situation should happen to you and you really feel strongly about this free service, perhaps you could have one afternoon or night every week between 7:00 and 9:00 for a time when you will be available to assist with your customers' projects. Be sure to charge for supplies.

To make your business a success, understand just what "business" means and operate it as a business. To help you do just that, look on the Internet for an article by Jean Murray called "Bookkeeper? Accountant? CPA? "What is the difference?" She says, "If you are a start-up or very small business you might choose someone in your employ to 'Keep the books.' They are called bookkeepers." Their responsibilities are accurately recording transactions, including accounts receivable and accounts payable, inventory, and sometimes payroll. They are to supply monthly, quarterly, and annual reports. Most bookkeepers use accounting software like QuickBooks. Don't ask for or expect advice on your business from bookkeepers. They have not been trained for that type of work.

Accountants don't usually do bookkeeping, but they can. They prepare detailed financial statements and can prepare reports for tax purposes.

Accountants have no standing with the IRS in the matter of signing tax returns or representing clients during tax audits and other matters before the IRS.

A CPA is an accountant who has passed certain examinations and met all other statutory and licensing requirements of a state to be certified by that state. In addition to preparing and reviewing financial statements, CPAs also prepare tax returns for businesses and individuals, sign tax returns, and represent taxpayers before the IRS for audits and other matters. The American Institute of Certified Public Accountants (AICPA) is the national professional association for CPAs.

If you cannot afford a CPA, use a bookkeeper or an accountant but get a CPA to help you review your financial reports and help you make decisions on finances and taxes. A CPA will help you review your books and who can give you tax advice, as well as preparing and submitting your business and personal tax returns online.

If you give it some serious thought, I think you will agree money will be well spent to hire an experienced CPA who is known to have the experience of guiding other start-ups. They should be working very closely with you offering ideas and opinions. This is money well spent during your start-up period. The more information you can provide your CPA about your business functions, the more they can help you meet your goals and grow. If they are only a numbers person, or if they do not have the experience or the initiative to be able to explain or suggest ideas for you, get a new CPA, maybe with some business acumen and ingenuity! This aspect of your business is too important. However, if you evaluate your company's financial performance against your goal and you are not successful, they should be able to give you ideas for corrective or innovative action. You must consider your chosen financial advisor as your mentor, your sidekick as one of your most treasured confidants. After you have had your start-up guidance you may choose to meet with your CPA quarterly, half year, or yearly.

As with anyone representing you, explain how you want them to think about, and speak about the development of your culture, suggest for them the words of how you want remarks said and what you hope to gain through their understanding of your target. They should be a part of your growth plans as seen in your strategic plan and assist you in the incremental growth to get you to goal. They should certainly be a part of the planning for the upcoming fiscal year. Make them aware of your mission. Explain what it means to you and how you are educating your Advocates (employees) to understand their work in the greater context of the whole company. Do the same with whomever you employ to assist you in your financial responsibilities.

Another person to hire is a known attorney who has experience helping start-up companies. They know what the government is expecting from you. They will keep you from unnecessary tax liability, keep you from violating laws, and make sure you pay all your tax responsibilities. Very importantly, they will keep you from personal liability by establishing a business entity like a Limited Liability Company (LLC) or corporation. If you have several founders, it's important to establish company ownership and just and impartial rights of the company. The attorney will help with all kinds of answers you didn't know you were going to need to ask. Be sure you choose an attorney whom you like and enjoy working with, and one you feel is genuinely interested in you. Remember a newer lawyer has not had the experience an older lawyer has had and can give or guide you in wiser ways than a newer lawyer can. A good place to start is ask around and get referrals from other business friends. A newer attorney can easily get you set up for business and other straight forward business interests.

In this instance, we are only thinking about retail. This effort is about the retail financial track to your yearly business goal. Of course, if you expand them, the ideas can be used in the overall company. Perhaps you decide you want to study the numbers that reflect your efforts during a particular season. Always choose a specified length of time where, as always, accurate information is necessary. To get a true picture of your chosen time period, be especially certain you are working with actual numbers. If the numbers are not actual, when you find out, you will be afraid to trust your system or the Advocates behind them, creating confusion, stress, and lack of belief in anything going forward.

In the following example, the chosen time period is the Christmas/holiday season because it is the largest revenue spike for most retailers. Our Christmas catalog was and is the largest revenue producing effort in our fiscal year. We pay a huge amount of attention and funds to this endeavor. As our company grew, so did our Christmas/Holiday offering. Sixty-six years ago, we started sending out:

a. One page black and white Christmas information in letter form.

b. Our second effort was black and white drawings with package information.

c. Next, we presented one-page full color presentations. Glossy sheet.

d. We developed larger full color catalogs incrementally through the years. As an example, in 2016, we sent a glossy, full color 22-page Christmas/Holiday edition.

e. In 2017, we put our entire catalog on our website supported by four large postcards advertising that our catalog was as near as their smartphone or computer. We had mixed feelings about this because for a good length of time we always had very interesting catalog covers and fun goings-on inside. Explaining to those interested folks just where they could find their catalog that year, there were, of course, dissenters. One interested party wrote me that "of all the catalogs one receives, there was only one that people would leave out on the dining room table and that would be Malley's." However, our customers and new friends enjoyed this move as very convenient for themselves, being able to work with us from anywhere, while our mouth-watering photos were with them as were other improvements made for their convenience. They do not have to have our catalog before them because it is right there in front of them at the touch of a few buttons wherever they happen to be. We want to delight our customers! Our entire Executive Group supported marketing's calculated risk.

Our marketing department studies every item in our Christmas/Holiday presentations. Analyzing previous year's numbers, studying this year's proposed pricing, figuring out how it fits with this year's price structure, deciding if the package idea answers the needs and wants of our customers, are the prerequisites to pass, to get the golden tag and be in our offerings.

Overhead should be a central part in your business concerns. It is a very important figure in what you should charge for an item. You need to become very familiar with three groupings to get correct information for pricing. They all come under the heading of Overhead: Business Activity, Business Services, and Business Finance.

1. <u>Business Activity</u>: Anything done in good faith to make a profit, such as buying, selling, renting, or efforts used in developing a product.

2. <u>Business Services</u>: are those actions that support the business but not produce a real product. Information Technology (IT) is one that has far reaching implications: support for procurement, such as finding a product, shipping, developing plans or ideas to make it easier for a company to make a profit. Charges for creating business presentations of our products (BC) are stored under the Business Services (BS) column and usually tell where a file or database entity is located (articles, units, people information). Consulting services, Plumbing Services, Pest Control Services, and Lawn Care Services, Copywriting and Proof Services, and many more expenses that do not produce a product but enable the business to operate.

3. <u>Business Finance</u>: costs done for us by economic services provided by the finance industry. It covers a broad range such as credit-card companies, insurance companies, banks, and assistance with other finance solutions.

These costs become columns of figures under the word "Overhead" found in the General Ledger. They are the costs required to run any company. Overhead gives a stable home and the infrastructure needed for all the profit-making departments such as the Kitchen, Production/Assembling, Call Center, Design Center, Warehouse, Corporate Attentions, and Fundraising.

When we think about making a list of all things involved in preparing a Christmas package, we already have a huge time-saver. The CPA/accountants have studied our numbers and accurately analyze fixed costs like rent, taxes, utilities, salaries for our Administrative group, insurance, and more. The accountants also work up the figures from what we give them concerning the time required to create chocolates or roasted nuts, as in our case, time needed on certain machines or in copper pots, floor space needed, and so on. If a package is going into our Design Center for striking/ handsome overwrap and beautiful or pretty bows, we add on labor costs and materials used costs, to the costs needed to get the box made (in house or purchased) and certainly readied, packed, stocked, chosen to fulfill orders for shipping, or delivered to our stores. Often these prices come in under what it would cost to prepare the same in a home setting.

As a package is being developed in the various departments incremental checks can be made as to how timely it is keeping to our plan. If a challenge is evident, make any necessary changes to try to keep it to the time plan for costing and product availability. Certain changes such as the actual product recipe or design are <u>never</u> touched because our reputation is based on quality and value of purpose. Changes can be made in how work is done, such as using an ad, using more helpers or a larger machine, how a decoration is placed on the chocolate or how bows are tied on a package. Other possibilities include working longer, coming in earlier, putting new goals in place, or even holding production off on another item to get up to schedule.

Our various leaders know daily numbers to keep on schedule. They know they must inspect processes to get what they expect. Our Production Manager, for example, must watch the daily yield to know if adjustments must be made to keep to the Production Schedule. Of course other problems can come into play: weather, sickness, machine breakdowns, which is why a cushion of days is always figured in for the overall time allotment. Your other departments must be aware of the same time and cost allotment.

Also, become familiar with the U.S. Small Business Administration (SBA). They offer important information for the Small Business Retailer through a program called SCORE. It offers you templates and offers a library of financial statement guides. Your financials are the most important impact on your business success. Use the Internet to learn, think and start acting on what you have become excited about.

Learn why inflow and outflow are important for you to understand. It tells you the financial health of your company at a particular time.

Earlier in the book, I mentioned SWOTs. Here's how we used SWOTs to analyze a proposed package for retail:

<u>Strengths:</u> The following suggestions pertain to store needs:
- The leader has a trailblazing attitude with restraint
- Knows strength of communication and practices it
- Acknowledges others contribution
- Strengthens psychological perception of presentation to grow value
- Price points checked for good fit
- Advocates educated about customer expectations and care
- Advocates educated and trained concerning features and bene-

fits of chocolate presentations
- Advocates educated on how to ask for a sale
- Our known quality
- Marketing advantages created now and by our history
- Salespeople know the anticipation of receiving a Malley Chocolates gift and the genuine delight of the recipient.
- Actual owners are easy to talk with and often visit.

Weaknesses
- Anything a competitor can do better than us
- Not enough awareness of the market's offerings and pricing
- Not constantly educating and training revenue producers
- production inefficiencies
- educate departments how to reduce costs,
- a new paradigm for packaging
- display presentations have no spark and interest
- lack of exciting signage
- Better staffing deployment
- Under-provided telephone coverage
- Not a fully qualified and contributing Administration
- Increase support of ownership
- Secure upkeep of infrastructure
- Motivation needs fresh infusion.

Opportunities

This category is a wonderful demand on your time because it is not something that can be put on the shelf for later, when you have more time. This is a very special period because it allows/forces you to take stock of business so you can be financially ready for the next and future revenue spikes.
- Take stock of department pros and cons and make decisions
- Be aware of new technologies or software for a fit advantage
- Be specific that departments have correct figures before any reconciliation
- Check every package or service for its expected margin to a goal
- If the item did not reach its expectations, study possible reasons:
    a. Did the name given the package lessen sales? (At times, we have changed some names. In fact, by changing one name, it became a bestseller and has been offered for years and years, even going on to other holiday celebrations.)

b. How about the wrap? Was it too pretty? Should it have been more handsome or more formal? More "down home"?
c. If the package was taken up a size or brought down a size what would happen?
d. If the offering in the package had somewhat the same in different boxes did one of the offerings spoil the sale? Cut it or completely revise its presentation – checking costs all along the way.
e. How about the placement in the catalog? Consider the eye flow, what it was next to, etc.
f. What about the description of the contents?
g. Sometimes it just came down to the fact of a gut feeling about the package and to decide to give it another opportunity to delight.
- Check employees for concerns, needs, and ideas
- Develop infusion of motivations
- We pour over the numbers and discuss them thoroughly.

Threats
- Not able to dismiss a process, a favored history that is allowed to generate their voracious costs that bring down your margins
- Supply costs are increasing/and not able to deliver by promised dates
- Costs of doing business increasing
- Labor and material costs fluctuate frequently
- Not all parts of the company receive proper attention
- Are all Advocates in the right place, doing the right thing, and in the correct department
- Department "necessities" checked for indispensable versus nice to have
- Be a step ahead of the competition in creating more ways to delight customers and more concern for your Advocates
- Check your timing schedule of Administration and Store Avocates to meet your expectations; adjust if necessary.

Even if you opt to use a SWOT analysis, you should still work closely with your CPA/accountant. And hopefully, you have chosen a mentor to discuss growth opportunities and different ways to solve your challenges. Finally, make certain your accountant, your CPA, and, hopefully, your mentor acknowledge you are giving exceptional

Financial Decisions   187

attention to his/her concerns. Business failure results from improper financial attention, especially with a beginning business. It is crucial they are carefully watched every day, decisions made accordingly and without fail. Other reasons for not staying on track to your dream is a lack of business control, accountable systems and shouldering your responsibilities.

> *"If you want something you've never had,*
> *You've got to do something you've never done."*
> *– Thomas Jefferson*

Pricing your product (The Key)

The most obvious intention is to make a profit on your products or services that are sold. In our case, it is chocolate. But determining the actual cost of each piece is a bit more challenging. You have the obvious costs like the ingredients that go into the chocolate, but there are other costs as well.

When beginning, you might be the only one making the chocolates, and you will most likely do it during the slow times while your store is open. In this case, you might choose to exclude labor in the costs as you have decided your remuneration will be in the form of the profits generated by the operation. However, if paying someone else to make it, then the labor costs (wages, payroll taxes, costs of benefits) also need to be considered. To be efficient, employees should be occupied with appropriate tasks the entire time they are on the clock.

The rent, utilities, real estate taxes, and cost of the equipment might need to be included as well. It depends upon the situation. Is the candy being made in the retail space, or in a separate facility? If in the store, a portion of these overhead costs could be added to the cost of the candy. If in a separate facility, then these entire costs would be allocated as overhead.

A simplified calculation is that all the costs are added together and then divided into a manageable time frame. In this example, let's use a single day. How much of each ingredient was used for the Bill of Materials? Dividing all the other costs to a daily cost (wages, rent, utilities, taxes, and employee benefits) provides a baseline. Divide the total of the day's costs with how many perfect chocolates were produced in that day—either by weight or by piece. This calculation gives you the cost per unit for that day.

You will have good days and not-so-good days. One day, everything flows well, and candy is being made efficiently. Other days, the weather (heat, humidity), machine malfunctions, and many other circumstances such as people not showing up for work can create production challenges. Decide what is normal and set a standard. It should be a reasonable standard and one that can be achieved. If it is too high and can only be met once in a great while, not only will this standard artificially lower the calculated cost of the candy, but it will impact scheduling as well. In other words, on a terrific day, 1000 pieces can be made, but the norm is more like 750. When preparing to deliver a special order for a particular date, if five days are scheduled to make the 5000 pieces immediately prior, but the equipment is slower on just one of the five days due to excess humidity, it may not be possible to deliver this special order in a timely manner. On the other hand, setting the standards too low permits unjustified inefficiencies to go unnoticed such as poor work habits, poor warehouse support, bottlenecks in the supply chain, and not enough attention to the established systems and follow up.

Calculating the standard cost for each kind of chocolate can be done by using the information for that one day. Divide the 750 pieces by the total daily cost of the ingredients used, the labor, payroll taxes, and benefits plus the daily overhead (total rent, taxes, and utilities divided by the number of days of active manufacturing).

Ingredients	$50
Labor, taxes and benefits	$150
Rent, utilities, taxes, equipment	$100
Total	$300
Candy made for the day	$750
Cost per piece	$0.40

Final thoughts

There are limitations to how high a product can be priced. Once all the costs have been added together, will you still be able to sell it at a profit? Discuss Economies of Scale. Is the demand for your chocolate higher than a competitor's, so that you can charge more and still sell it? How long can you afford a loss (and how much loss) before the business becomes established and generates a profit (small profit, hopefully growing)? Make yourself know this number.

From the very beginning, create reports using language all that will be reading them can understand so more informed decision-making can be made. Periodically take a small gift to those who have loaned you start-up money to show you are alive and very aware of the fine things they have done for you. Thank them again. Chocolate releases endorphins from the brain and makes us feel good, so don't forget some Malley's Chocolates!

You are still in the game, "I'm going on a trip." Good! You've packed both a sharp CPA and a wise attorney known for expertise in guiding start-ups. A real cue would be a mentor, topped off with how you will train and educate those people you have chosen to surround yourself. If all of these points have been considered properly, your start-up obligations are completed. You can stay in the game. Have fun, work smart, and remember Lou Holtz's, "W.I.N."

Chapter 12
Assistance: Board of Advisors

    Whether you own a start-up, or your business is more mature, you've had situations where you would have valued discussions with respected businesspeople. If you are concerned about the lack of upward momentum, have become less energized, or last year's Profit and Loss has been flat, shake off the doldrums and do something about it. You, hopefully, won't have to go through this issue again. One way to get through the situation is to put together an Advisory Board. They will help you make decisions that puts your company at less risk, give you the support you need to make decisions that are very difficult, get your business working with a plan, help with strategic planning and even when it's best to retire; if you will listen. They all know it can be mighty lonesome at the top!

> *"A businessperson's heart cannot be a valentine*
> *Full of good will and sweet sentiment*
> *It's to be a thriving, pulsating muscle*
> *Supplying life-giving oxygen to all parts of the enterprise."*
> – Adele Ryan Malley

You've taken your beginning steps. Perhaps you've got a mid-life store crisis brewing, and you desperately need a leap forward. How are you going to leap when you haven't got the energy? How are you going to get the ideas when you've already done everything you can think of? You need that shot of vital energy that will propel you forward. You need a Board of Advisors. However, if your company is very small or you just cannot bring yourself to give confidential information about your company to another, for your peace of mind consider joining a peer networking group. It takes less work; you are not committed to anyone and you can simply leave at any time. If you are a very small company, it is also an opportunity to meet new friends who are living somewhat the same lifestyle you are.

Getting a Board of Advisors together may be something you have thought about but never "got around" to doing. Your Council of Smaller Enterprises or different business associations will help you, if you inquire. I'm sure you have mused how nice it would be to speak to someone about your hopes and vision and what to do about "Tom" who is giving you all kinds of problems. You are now in a position to *want and need* help to discuss your challenges growing or continuing to grow your business. You realize there must be a better way! You are anxious to more quickly get to your vision. You have gained confidence. You are ready for professional help. You can use a Board of Advisors. If you cannot afford a Board right now, and you like the idea, start by choosing one individual, meet regularly at agreed upon times. If you make progress and work well together, and when you are financially ready, decide how and when and who you will ask to be a second trustworthy individual.

What is a Board of Advisors?

A Board of Advisors is a small informal group of business (usually Owners or persons of rank) individuals chosen for their experience, size, or compatibility of their processes to yours. They hold no power. You will meet periodically at assigned times, usually every quarter or more often; it is up to you and their availability. Together they will offer you advice and direction for your business. Usually three to five members create a Board for a beginning or small business. They are given remuneration for their expertise and time. For a small business usually $500 will be adequate for each meeting. As the Board matures, more remuneration is usually added to acknowledge their good faith and help. However, if you are quite strapped, suggest $250 until you get on your feet. People like helping people. Just don't take advantage of their time or expertise. If this idea is still out of the question, read again in Chapter 8 about the Creative Thinking Process.

Always start with each member knowing they will be on the Board for a specified amount of time. Start with one or two years, so you can acquire another Board member. It keeps the thinking fresh and offering perhaps a different paradigm. Also, you can let go someone whose advice does not fit your needs. You can always ask a person to rejoin you.

What exactly can a Board of Advisors do and not do?

Can do:
- They will give you support, ideas for improvement, and help you sort out the direction of your thinking and concerns.
- They can remove the loneliness at the top!
- A Board can give you a leg up against your competition. Most American businesses do not have a Board.
- A Board can and will be available for telephone discussions if you need them.
- They can encourage you to discipline yourself to act on certain issues.
- They see the light at the end of the tunnel.

How Can a Board of Advisors help you?

a) Nothing on the Internet can replace one-on-one advice from someone who knows more or who has the experience first-hand giving you face-to-face advice.

b) They should help you to get a good view of where your company is today.

c) They will discuss your Profits and Losses, and offer ideas on how to improve your margins, and other numbers, to improve the level of your Profits and Losses.

d) An experienced and well-connected Board of Advisors can offer you
- Non-binding advice to help your business grow
- Will be connected to other people and will connect you
- Can bring more experience or knowledge concerning business growth
- Assistance so you avoid making costly mistakes both financially and emotionally

- Advice on how to use family members in right ways (Family Business) and help all of you achieve prosperity
- A clear view of family or others in your business, suggesting certain education or better positioning
- Discipline enhancements rounding out your business skills
- Increase your own accountability
- A sense of belonging that you may not have now
- Fresh ideas, offering unbiased and different perspectives, like opening windows in your mind and letting in fresh air
- A sounding board for new idea development
- Help with your strategic plan
- Ideas with work deployment within your management team
- Assistance of conferring of titles if they are necessary
- Their support through the transition if a death occurs or any crisis or even if leadership must be changed

Cannot do:
- They have no informal or formal power
- They have no legal authority
- They will have no power over your business
- They also will not discuss your business with anyone without your permission

How to get started acquiring a Board of Advisors

Tip: Keep good notes and date them. Make careful deliberations on your selection.

Investigate

Read about a Board of Advisors on the Internet. Talk with other businesses that have them, ask questions. Call your Chamber and ask if they could arrange a meeting for you with a businessperson who has an Advisory Board because you are interested in beginning an Advisory Board for your business.

Create a list of where you want to improve your company, not lofty ideas but actual things that concern you: internal challenges, what you find most difficult to do or how to begin a project, anything you find yourself not moving or even not moving fast enough to be following your business plan. Or, even to write one or make your present plan more realistic. Perhaps its how a very small company can best use technology or assistance in being able to inspire your Advocates to work better, together. Look back on the section about working with a SWOT which will include instructions to make a list of your company's Strengths. Weaknesses, and where the most Opportunities lie to make the business more efficient and effective. Ask your spouse what you worry about the most to get yourself thinking again about your Threats. Study your list and write your top three or four concerns. Now, approach trusted advisors: your banker, attorney, your CPA or another business person you admire.

Make sure you are on board with your Bank
- Call and make an appointment with your banker. Issue an invitation to come to your place of business for a chat.
- Show your Profit and Loss Statement
- Show your efforts to reduce your operating costs
- Show the individual responsibility of each of your helpers. Perhaps let them explain what they do and how they are helping. Tell how you are furthering their education/experiences. Show your Organizational Chart, Job Descriptions and Communication Conversations.
- Discuss your accounting firm and tell how you are working with their advice. Discuss how they have assisted you in better methods which should save you dollars. Does your banker have any ideas on how you can work smarter with your accounting firm?
- Does your banker think you should be working with a larger firm to be better covered with various kinds of assistance, or will banker tell you when it's time to use a larger accounting firm?
- Is there more that you should be doing? Could be doing?
- Can your banker suggest an active good business organization for you to belong to?
- Can your banker suggest another person who is working with a different product but doing essentially the same mechanics you are? Is your banker familiar with someone who has recently gone through what you hope to do?
- Tell your banker you are considering beginning a Board of Advisors, and you would appreciate any names that might make a good fit with your concerns. The person's company should be larger than your business to help you move forward. Tell your banker that you have discussed where you think you need the most help and have decided to narrow your focus for a short

time on (for an example) Internet growth, better accounting for inventory used, or assistance in writing a strategic plan.

Do the same as above with your accounting firm
- Ask them to interview your Bookkeeper and maybe Manager to make sure you are getting the support you should be receiving from them.
- Ask them if your Group can work more efficiently or effectively to cut down on billable hours.
- Suggest they meet for lunch or breakfast with you and your Bookkeeper because you want to make your company's Bookkeeper more familiar with them.

<u>Who should be on your Board?</u>
- Create a list of qualifications that matches your needs. Usually three to five members are enough to offer diverse strengths to bring different perspectives into play and can reach consensus quickly.
- Each potential member can be from various businesses—retail, Leaders of smaller corporations, mid-size but not smaller than you and not too much larger than you.
- Look for someone who has built a business unless you want someone who can operate a business. Remember, they should be just that much larger than yourself, so they have recently gone through what you hope to approach in size and/or dollars.
- Make certain they will be able to help you grow your business. Do not look for the most obvious person because sometimes their position in their company calls for skills not needed for your business at this stage. Ask discreetly from other professionals (Your banker, accounting firm, lawyer, member of a club you know who is familiar with several people) what their thoughts are about what kind of business experiences the person has. Have they started expanding or have they added stores? Are they interested in machinery like you might use? Do they pack for delivery? Do they have a call center? Do they ship a great deal of merchandise? Do they handle internal and/or outside sales forces? Does this person have the experience to ask me critical questions? Will this person be able to challenge my ideas because I truly believe they know more than I do about growth for my size business?

- Remember, it's your Board, and you should shape it as your needs require.

Who should not be on your Board?
- Your attorney
- Your banker
- Anyone from your accounting firm
- Anyone from your family. (This is a time for you to discuss freely.)
- Anyone who is making a living from your business
- Friends or relatives who have emotional ties to the business.

The first three listed can be on your board if you are certain their advice is not self-serving in any way. Also, you may already be guided by their information. However, you may be so impressed with their guidance you will want them on your Board. Still, putting any of the above on your Board is generally a mistake. They will usually have a lack of objectivity. If friends or family, they may hesitate to do the entirely right thing due to family relationships. If they are experts in their field, when information is needed, and you want their input, they can be invited to a Board meeting.

However, there are always exceptions, and we (Malley's) were. My husband Bill and I worked hand in glove, and I had been voted in as the next president when my husband retired. One of us was always stronger in certain subjects. People who worked with us commented on it. I figured it was Bill's business when I joined it, so on it. I always bowed to him in social/public business conversations. After all, he asked me to join him. It was just a very smart move ☺.

All that said, remember this is your Board, and you have the perfect right to assemble it as you please and how you please. What is right for you may not be right for your neighbor, but that does not make it any less right for you.

As an example, we placed an Industrial Psychologist on our Board because we wanted professional opinion available for anyone who wanted assistance with a matter.

Create a list of possible members
Ask for help from experienced businesspeople or call your Chamber of Commerce or Dean of Business at a University or College. After you juggle all that was discussed and suggested you will decide on whom to ask. Sometimes a candidate can point you in the direction

of another good candidate! Before you ask anyone make sure they are successful in their own fields. If and when they appear interested, ask your choices why they would like to serve on your Board. You want to find those persons interested in the challenge of helping you succeed. Gathering such a group together should take time. Don't rush it.

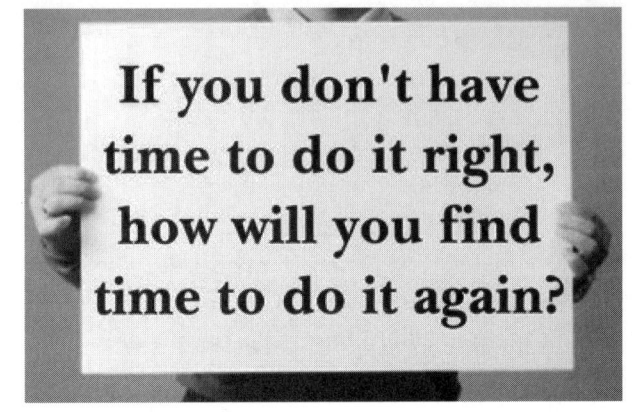

> If you don't have time to do it right, how will you find time to do it again?
> –John Wooden

Proceed with confidence

If you are hesitant—as most of us were—at starting a Board, after you create your Board, you see what an error it was not to create one earlier. You soon will come to believe it was an error, thinking you had to show a rosy bottom line with all your p's and q's lined up before you could invite someone in to view your business! Well, continue thinking—your customers are viewing your business every day or trying to work with your web site. It is said over 80 percent of businesses in the United States do not have a Board of Advisors. In my opinion, if you haven't put a Board in place, your company is passing up on some big strides forward. This is an important leg up on your competitor. Just think of the joy of having people you respect come into your business and take a very personal interest in it and help you develop the type of business you crave. Try for some oomph. Triumph! (Try-oomph).

What Can You Do Besides Have a Board?

Decide what you want to work on. Contact your person of choice, introduce yourself, tell how you came to place the call, and ask for a few minutes of their time. State what you are doing, what you want to do right now because this is an important project for your business. Tell them you know with their advice you will work wiser and get finished with this project in a better time frame. Be very direct that you know how busy they are, that you won't bother them constantly but would appreciate their help. If they are interested, suggest lunch to meet one-on-one, and give them a chance to meet you. It's like having a mentor but with a stop and a finish. This person may be your first Board member. If you can handle it, you may work with another professional in an unrelated part of your business at the same time. Be sure to show your gratitude. Remember, while working one-on-one with someone is helpful, having a Board of Advisors will be able to grasp your whole picture, and if you choose, be with you for years.

How Did We Decide on Our Board Members?

Bill had great respect for a gentleman he met (while working with a certain Board) who had a great amount of experience in starting businesses, owning and operating businesses, complemented by various other Board experiences. On the other hand, I had taken a strategic planning course from Dr. Jeffery Susbauer, chairman of the department of management and labor relations at Cleveland State University and the Owner, author, director and educator of Growth Strategies Inc., for The Council of Smaller Enterprises. I asked for his opinion. He suggested a gentleman who had retail experience who was also mentoring his own son in a startup company. Finally, the Industrial Psychologist we asked to be on the Board presented a seminar at our Council of Smaller Enterprises. We were impressed and invited him to lunch.

Tip: As you may have found as we did in getting loans and being involved in various other endeavors, manufacturing/retailing businesses are in short supply. Most likely you won't find your members if you look for them under that heading.

Send a letter or call the person(s) you are interested in having help you on a Board of Advisors. Invite them out for lunch/dinner. Become, hopefully, more than acquaintances. Meeting face-to-face will tell you so much as to the important fit between just the two of you. Tell them what you are thinking of forming, and would they have any suggestions as what to do? Tell them what you are expecting from a Board, and what do they think of your ideas? If they ask you interesting questions about your Board, perhaps their remarks might signal to you that here is a possible fit. However, ponder the following:
- Do they act above you?
- Do they share anything about what they have gone through?
- Do they try to maintain "the floor" instead of listening and asking

you interesting questions about what you are asking?
- Are they trying to impress you with their importance?
- Let your gut guide you but not make the final decision.

At the meal's end, thank them for their time. Explain you are meeting with others and trying to make a good fit. Give a time frame when you will call them. Give them a token remembrance—a box of Malley's Chocolates or tickets to the theatre.

If you must call with a negative remark for them, say something like the following, but tailored for your personality and comfort: "I enjoyed meeting you. Your knowledge and expertise really impressed me, and it was tough for me to decide not to ask you to help me. I have put together a good fit for a beginning Board. I am so grateful for your interest, and wonder if I may call you when I get a little experience as my Board matures?"

You can decide to send a note, again expressing your gratefulness. Or, enclose your sentiments with a box of Malley's Chocolates. You have possibly met a person whose guidance and friendship you certainly want in the future.

Allow your subconscious mind to work on the information from the meeting. Remember your subconscious can only work with the information you give it, so ponder it all—pros and cons. Make your decision after checking on anything the meeting brought to mind or puzzled you. Wait for your subconscious to give you its answer and be sure you consider it on all fronts the decision will touch. You now have your answer.

Advantages for Starting One- or Two-Year Membership on Your Board

By inviting them for one year, it gives you the opportunity to ask yourself if you've been able to make the progress you hoped for and perhaps you will ask all the members to stay on another year or let them all go. Invite the individuals back who were able to give you the advice you felt you needed. Setting this time limit is good to get different kinds of perspectives, being able to move a Board member whom you find is not a great fit and gives you the opportunity to perhaps add a new member whom you have met who you know can give you great advice. (Of course, you can always add a new member—size of membership is up to you, but so will the larger enumeration fees). For your first years with a Board, you may want to say, "I plan to ask each of you to stay with me for two years. At the end of that time, I will ask one member to excuse him or herself, and after the third year, I plan to excuse another and then the next year another to expand my thinking. I think after two years of meetings together; we will have made some significant strides." It's your Board. You call the shots.

How We Managed the Meetings

We always had provided breakfast: coffee, sweet rolls with juice, then deli sandwiches for lunch, as we met in the morning. After everyone has finished eating, remove the food and any plates, etc. Leave only the drink of choice and napkin and be ready for your business discussion. Our members usually came early for chat time.

We had our Board meetings either at the office, in our Conference Room or at home where we had total quiet. Sometimes we used a hotel area making sure the hotel did not set up a bedroom as a meeting room. Those areas can be smothering.

Approach this first meeting as if you were seeing a banker; be prepared! Five days to a week before the meeting, send to each Board Members' place of business a binder full of information.

> 1. The top sheet can be a thank you letter for offering to help you better your business. Tell them you look forward to your meetings and getting to know them and hearing their thoughts on what you will be telling them.
> 2. Tell what your goals are.
> 3. State why you chose each member and how you think they will be able to help you. Let them know you are interested in them because you feel they are a person who will challenge your present thinking, that they will provide advice and counsel.
> 4. In separate sections include information about each Board of Advisor member. I enclosed a biography from each Board member (which they supplied previously) and added both Bill's and mine. Adding these biographies, we all had a better understanding of the experiences and strengths of each other.
> 5. Then again with their permission, I wrote their full name, where they worked, cell number and email address. The Board members also gave permission for me to enclose their home address, phone numbers, and spouse's name. This information will enable them to discuss opinions with each other after hours if they choose to do so.
> 6. Include all your business and home information. Send direc-

tions to where your meetings will be held.

7. Write out your mission statement if your business has one. Include information about your present ideas on how to grow your business. Proactively seek their advice on issues that can help you take your company to the next level. Keep this sheet short and snappy.

8. If you have an operational plan and/or a strategic plan include it/them here.

9. Discuss your SWOT and what you think you should do about your Strengths, Weaknesses, Opportunities and Threats. Keep this sheet also short and snappy.

10. Explain that your helpers are the integral, most important, and fundamental part of your plan because they are representing you with your customers.

11. Possibly a picture of your business place or anything interesting about it.

12. Include a year calendar, so it will be easy when making the next appointment. You might mark on the calendars special days honored by your company and any seasonal busy times.

13. Create and provide an agenda for your first meeting. Make extra copies in case one member did not have time to read the binder. Give them a timeline for your first meeting. Most meetings are three hours in length.

14. Gathering this information for the Board members ahead of time will make your first meeting more fruitful because so much will have already been introduced to them.

First meeting with your Board
- Be sure to send agendas to each of the Board members well before the meeting; make sure you state how the first meeting will operate.
- You might begin this meeting, following this imagined agenda.
- Remind the Board you think it a good idea to speak of questions about the agenda information for ½ hour. One hour to discuss #1 Concern and 1 hr. to discuss #2 Concern then close. Is this agreeable with everybody?
- Ask if they have any questions concerning the preview.
- Tell them where you envision your business to be in five more years; don't be hesitant here, lay-out your thinking in all its glory. Include your vision of your busy store where people want to

come in because some one of their friends said it was the place to shop for what you are selling. Your numbers increase and increase. This is your vision talking.
- Go over your latest Profit and Loss Statement (P & L) and note that while it is important, you want them to look forward and tackle those spots for improvement that will change the P & L.
- What work should be accomplished before the next meeting concerning the P & L?
- Remember it's your vision, your plan. Listen to your Board; that is why you are paying them, for their good advice. Use it.
- For future reference, it would be helpful for you to write quick notes on the meeting just completed.
- Once a year you should write a paper telling what occurred and what was gained during the past year. It could also state what is, hopefully, going to be attended to during the next 12 months. At the end of the twelfth month, it will be a breeze to write the report because you have the notes you've made after every meeting. It might also show where your group needs shoring up to get more accomplished. Write what was completed and what drifted out of the meetings' conversations and what simply did not have the groups' support.
- If you did not accomplish what you set out to do the previous month with your Board, this lack tells you that you are not working on your business but rather in it. Stop this downward spiral, and get the work done. You will never achieve your goals if you don't drive your business. If you let someone else at the wheel (a person who lacks organization or follow-through, the whiner, the worrier) you have given up driving; you're just trying to please the new driver. This thought includes the perpetual complainer who has taken over the wheel and is the one driving because you are giving up time and energy, attending to their needs, while your whole company may be in stress because of that one individual. You simply cannot afford to give up the wheel.
- If you have more on your plate than you can or are willing to manage, talk it over with your Board. By saying it aloud with trusted people, you will see what needs to be adjusted or adapted to your circumstances but keep driving your vision. You will be surprised where you can find the assistance, the extra hours you wished you could have, the discipline not to

give in to what seems important but to keep your eye on what needs to be done now. Keep your eye on tomorrow and what must be done today to get there!
- Finally, ask if they choose to have you call concerning the work assigned for you to do. Keep them up to date.
- Remind them that they gave you the OK to call them at least once a month to discuss a challenge. Is this still OK with you?

TIP: Remember your Board may be the first one your invitee has been invited to participate on and is just as concerned they do everything right as you are. It's best to get all your thoughts out on the table when everyone is new. Also, they may want to ask questions on procedure.

Pitfalls of Having a Board of Advisors
- Board members who miss meetings and do nothing to make up for it. This person should be reconsidered.
- If they are always too busy to speak between meetings, you still have a right to call them at least once a month to discuss a challenge. (You discussed this requirement at your first meeting.)
- Having to complete the year with a member whose advice does not seem to fit with your concerns. If the situation is more stressful than it should be, make your move. Thank the member for accepting your invitation, but, currently, you believe you need to make a change. Would it be all right if I call you later when I can use your input?
- If it turns out members cannot get along, some change will have to be made.
- Make certain no one member monopolizes conversation.

Tip: Do not be so busy that you don't work on what the members tell you to do. Even at your meetings remember to work on your business not just in it. Make use of what you started. You are paying for it with your reputation, added stress from not being prepared, and hard-won bucks!

Chapter 13
Adjustments/Achievements: Consequences

Imagine you are a businessperson who was so anxious to get to work on your wonderful idea that you did not even plan. You just assumed you'd make it. You may be one of the businesses that didn't make it to the proverbial 3-5-year maturity date, and if you did make it, you're continuing to work very hard and wonder why you are not moving ahead. You may be playing the game of maxing out credit cards to finance the operation, thinking tomorrow will be different. In your mind, do you hear yourself starting to think about how to get out of this business and go for something that looks like a slam dunk? In your mind, are you saying to yourself, "There should be more to it than this!" You have lost the fire in your belly and start to think maybe you weren't cut out for what seemed like a great idea. Are you still sleeping in your brother's basement?

If so, there is a reason why you are not moving forward. If you are chastising yourself or find that you are the kind who jumps from start-up to startup, I'm going to tell you why this is happening. Everything is happening very fast for you. You might be starting to think you have to get some sort of control and "get a handle on things." Get to be "a real businessperson." You don't want to be known as someone who is always "flying by the seat of your pants." The stress of wondering if your bubble is going to break any minute or is going to get bigger tells you your business needs corralling. You can hire professionals to guide you through a business and strategic plan. Ask for help from your Small Business Association, a person you respect in business, your banker for instance, to find you a person who is willing to guide you or set up an appointment for you so you develop a list or calendar of goals with deadlines that they will develop and discuss, and have an interested party to give your reports on advancements. You will feel in control and be a great deal more knowledgeable about this great business you created.

Every Owner wants to be more successful, no matter where you are on the ladder of achievement. It may seem like an overwhelming task, but to grow and prosper, you must get the basics of simply being in business accomplished. Otherwise, you may someday see your beloved business collapse like you are visualizing as you sit on the side of your bed.

The work you put into your request for a bank loan to start your business is what should be guiding you now. How closely do you match, from where you started, to where you said you would be, at this time? Have you even looked at your business plan? It's full of the right kind of thought that you presented at the bank to professional people versed in business startups. You stated why you wanted to borrow startup funds, what you planned to do with the funds and laid out how you were going to go about being in business. Your chosen bank believed in you and gave you the funds. Then success didn't come fast enough, and you've spent all your time trying to sell, ignoring your plan.

This situation means it's been work, work, work for you and not much energy spent on a tactical approach to your challenge. Fear, nerves, and loss of belief in yourself has created a status quo or downward spiral of success. If you find yourself in this position, immediately reread what you presented to the bank when you were flushed with desire and psychological "can do" flowing through your veins. You need to read why you wanted to be in business and what else you wrote.

Arrange a chat with your banker and ask for assistance in meeting someone who can help you.

Knowing that your business is set up properly is going to be a big confidence boost and you will feel renewed and stronger. It begins with writing down and honing why you are in business, and its not to make money, its to know why you need to make money. What is the picture in your mind of what you want to be? That's the beginning of your Mission Statement. Take your time and make it be a true reflection of your mind's picture. Become very familiar with your decision. Know it, say it, write it down, think about it because all your future actions will be directed because of it.

Next, you will need a strategy, a set of directions on how you are going to get there. It will tell you how and when, such as where you should be every six months to a year. Organize your company to follow its mandate. Begin with what you know right now or get help figuring it out. You are never too small to not know what you are doing and why. Your Strategic Plan will be your guide. It will tell you

Your Strategic Plan will reveal:
    a) What you have to do to get going straight to your dream.
    b) It will show incremental achievement dates for each plan
    c) It will show knowledge of what's trending and competitors movements
    d) With good reason it will show adjustments to your plan.

Organizing your Strategic Plan into the actual steps in how you are going to get there will be your Business Plan. There is lots of mental and physical action here. It will show "what" is going to be done and "who" is going to do it.

If changes must be made because it will be impossible to meet a goal, the business plan should be adjusted, and changes made in the Strategic Plan. You must be able to look at your business plan and know how you are performing at any time during your fiscal year. It will show what you are capable of doing, what changes (education, machinery, job duties, cost estimates) are necessary to perform each step.

The Business Plan will show:
    a) Sharp attention to finances, the actual strategy, finance possibilities
    b) The over-all plan and individual first (second, third-) goal being developed
    c) How to attack what is to be done - check that Advocates are in

right seats on the "bus", check that all machinery and Advocate jobs, product in-put and out-put have checkers on each system
d) Who will be responsible - Consider giving this person the clout of penalty.
e) Consider using a white board or a bulletin board and list acceptance and due dates of all projects undertaken by individuals. Use a red X if work is not completed and a green check for completed work. Decide ahead of time how uncompleted work will be addressed.

> *"Mile by Mile, it's a trial;*
> *Yard by Yard, it's hard; but*
> *Inch by Inch, it's a cinch."*
> *- Gabrielle Giffords*

The following illustrates a quick trip to establishing your Vision or corralling it!
- Stated Vision (see above).
- Stated Mission (see above).
- Goals: How much do you want to accomplish, and how soon you want to accomplish it? (Example: increase sales to $00 million by so many chosen years.)
- Strategies: What approaches you must take to achieve objectives and goals (Examples: control of finances, continuously nurture marketing, infrastructure maintenance, machinery upgrades, educational needs, track employees' customer service techniques, source unique products or create a time-study for a manufacturing line).
- Tactics. What specific actions you must take to implement your strategies (Examples: attend trade and buying shows semiannually. Work with Retention Reviews to understand competences of all Advocates). Converse with Advocates your tactics to attain your strategies, ask for their input, get all on board with final plans. Together decide your return on coaching investment (ROCI.) How will you know it?
- Keep focused. Learn what other companies are doing; be aware of new businesses and what their thrust will be.

If following these steps is not excitement enough to reignite that fire in your belly, then maybe you are right; you are not meant to lead and build but perhaps to follow and execute for success.

Both positions are important functions as one cannot be successful without the other. Announce your choice early so as not to hold the company from going forward, and you can start doing the kind of work you really enjoy.

Another situation that may arise is when you are in that three-to-five-year-old stage. You may wonder when the butterfly stage comes, and you stop feeling like your business is a perpetual chrysalis stuck in the middle of a transformation from early stage to mature business. You're in tight times—work and work some more mode. The reality is that most everyone goes through it, so do not despair.

Are you reviewing every detail of your company, going over them and going over them while thinking (praying) things will straighten out in a few weeks? No matter how many times you do this, things are not going to straighten out until you do something different. Then, you can continue to grow and finally break from your chrysalis and spread your wings. One thing you should definitely do is ask for help. If you see your sales figures beginning to slip, put yourself in emergency mode and seek help. Don't speak openly about your situation or it will become general conversation, such as "Did you see that little store on South Avenue is not making it?"

That doesn't sound attractive to potential customers. And if your vendors get a whiff of you having problems, they will all begin asking for cash up front. There are three things to check up on right away when you're still in this early stage.

First, will you admit you are overwhelmed and get help?

If the answer is yes, seek council from your accountant, banker, attorney or other close advisor. Ask any of them if you could be directed to a successful businessperson who might become your mentor. Having a sounding board is always a good thing.

Next, in your panic have you become pushy with your customers?

If you're trying too hard to close a sale or consummate a deal, being pushy will scare them away. Think about how much you like it when Salespeople push you for the close. And, if your panic has rubbed off on your sales team, have you spent ample time teaching them how to let customers know they're in good hands with your company? Assuming you're not being pushy, or have caught yourself and corrected the behavior, have your employees listen to how you talk with your customers. Tell them how things should happen in your store. Talk a lot about customer care and make sure they know your products features and benefits backwards and forwards. Right there, your future will be told.

Outside of product, the fate of your business is often in the hands of your helpers. This is where you are going to make it or suffer an agonizing death until you close your doors in bankruptcy. This education takes dedication, work, and know-how. You want your customers to come back and also tell their friends about your products and your store. You want to make sure they meet you and learn a little about your enterprise. It all begins customer after customer, one at a time.

Finally, did you fail to generously calculate your expenses?

If you're short on cash, this may be the case. It's common when good plans and a strategy are not firmly thought out. But don't wait until you can't meet your payroll or pay your invoices... or even yourself. Figure out immediately what you should do if you notice a cash flow problem. Talk it over with your spouse. What can they do to help out? Try not to touch your home equity; this is your insurance if something drastic happens in your life and you need cash. As much as you want to protect your business, it's more important to protect your family. Between your spouse or significant other and yourself, decide how much you will need for living and work expenses. A business rule of thumb is to have enough cash reserves to carry you through the first six months or so until your business starts making money. If you're beyond the first six months and find yourself in trouble, you have two choices before you run out of cash: start thinking and working smarter or get out before your debts become too much.

If you opt for the first choice, it will require humility, more knowledge and work, and a lot of sacrifice. If you consider the second, don't make this final decision without the thoughtful care of your banker, mentor, or CPA. Any of your advisors may be able to help you get back on track again. Listen to what they say.

Here's a little story about a cherished endeavor that never quite got off the ground. During my Malley School of Merchandising, I discovered that many small businesses did not price their wares sufficiently. Many business Owners were also short-changing themselves—they neglected to charge for their own work. As an example, they felt they could make a basket of their products up for no charge because "gosh, they are buying all my products to put in the basket. I can arrange it because I'm good at it, and I always have stuffing grass or cello around because I buy it in a great quantity and popping a bow on it doesn't cost me much. Besides I feel I have a happy customer."

In another shop, this scene happened right before my eyes. It occurred in a dressmaking shop. I watched one lady enter the store and immediately sit down at a table and take out her work. The Owner approached her and began fixing a problem she was having. She waited on me while doing this and invited me to sit and she wanted to show me how to figure "the grain".

I stayed for about an hour.

Before leaving, I asked for the amount I owed her. She rang up on her register the items I bought, but that was all. I asked the price for the lesson she'd given me. She replied, "Oh I don't charge for helping you. I appreciate your business."

I told her how surprised I was and explained how I took various lessons, and that one store was very near her store. I told her what they charged for lessons and suggested she ought to charge as well. I gently told her that I helped folks in business keep that bottom line very black and thick. That opened the floodgates and we had a very revealing conversation.

It turned out to be another small store crisis. She and her husband were retired, and she had always wanted to have a little store. She had no help problem because it was either she or her husband managing the store. This left a huge gap in their retirement fun and that probably also meant retirement fund.

This also meant the husband had little knowledge of how to use the products she chose for her store. When I previously visited, I found that he was a great clerk. He greeted me with a smile, and we enjoyed some small talk. He asked what he might do for me and I told him why I came in the store. He was sorry he couldn't find the tape his wife had told me to come in and get. He called her at home and still could not find it. "She will be here tomorrow and I'm sure she will be able to help you," he said. I then left the store—empty handed and disappointed. No matter how charismatic he was he was a clerk—he sincerely tried to help me with what I asked for and certainly was polite—but he did not ask me any questions about what I was working on and possibly direct me to another part that I could work on until I could return. This gentleman did not connect with me. A simple sentence to start a conversation and show some interest in my interest he most probably would have made a sale and see me leaving happy (of course, use one or at the most two of these suggestions):

1. Asking if I had any buttons on the dress I was making because some new ones came in and I might like them (and take me to the buttons to point them out).

Adjustments/Achievements: Consequences

2. "While you are here why not take a look at our mark-down table? There are some interesting new items added."
3. "Have you seen our books on dressmaking? There are step by step directions the sewers seem to like . . . let me show them to you."
4. "So as not to leave disappointed, have you considered making some earrings or a necklace to go with your dress? I'll get the material you bought to make it and you can have some fun with them."
5. "Our new sewing magazines arrived and there is one about ways to make quick, useful dresses, for as they say, 'running around' (said with a smile.) They are right here on the upper shelf. Take a look." After a minute or two, ask if they would like to take a magazine home to read?
6. Suggest, "Would you like to take advantage of our specials?"

During my next visit, the Owner and I had a heart-to-heart. Finally, she charged me a decent amount for the help she'd given. It was at least a start.

The next year, when I visited her shop to show her my quandary about whatever I was working on and get her advice, her lesson fee had doubled. I smiled to myself that it hadn't taken long for the idea to catch on. But I thought she might be charging too much. I was worried about her and spoke generally about the challenges of being a retail shop Owner.

The next time we visited the area, I went to her shop and found another company in that space, selling a completely different product. I immediately felt sorrow for the woman I'd met and her husband. They were both such nice people. She had a very good location. She was very close in proximity to the people who would buy her product. And I'm sure she asked herself where she could get the help she needed—the knowledge to better operate her business. But alas, it appeared she had not done those things. And, as a result, found herself in challenging times without any help to assist her.

Adjustments/Achievements: Consequences

Chapter 14
Retention Review Practices

Dear Advocate:

The purpose of this yearly Retention Review is to assure us of your recall and reliable use of your Malley's Manners. Our valued customers deserve the very best care we can offer. The treatment we extend to each other is vitally important in preparing us to meet our customers and other Advocates.

*Signature of Retail Leader:*_____

Name:_____
Date:_____
Store/Address: _____

The above example is a potential cover sheet for an annual review. I highly recommend every member of your team write of their knowledge in this Retention Review. The following are sample questions.

As you gain some maturity, you have prepared perhaps three or four Reviews to be given to those Advocates that have some history with you. Group information that you think all newcomers should know, then what Skillshops everyone should understand and be practicing. Arrange your questions in this manner then it will be easy for you to know if the Advocate should know the answer. The idea and goals remain the same. This can be a useful tool in ensuring your team members are engaged. Suggested responses follow sample questions. If they can tell you the spirit of the answer, that's fine; in other answers, they need to know the correct answer. Be sure they don't generalize but express their answers in the Malley words' and spirit they were taught.

- What does culture mean? Belief, feelings, behavior. How we take care of and speak to one another and our customers or browsers. For us, it's how we care for everything Malley's. It's the unification of our ethics, integrity (honesty), attitude, refinements, our shared knowledge and values. [Sets the environment and instructs about what culture means and their part in its development.]
- What should everyone do before reporting for their shift? Check the condition of the outside of the store, including the parking lot and landscaping. Upon entering the store, report to your Leader and tell what you saw outside. [Teaches the importance of being aware and being responsible.]
- What does merchandising mean? Enticing a customer to want to buy. [To understand what it means to "merchandise" their store.]
- Why should the register and surrounding be kept immaculate? Customers, in line at the registers have time to notice displays and general presentation of cleanliness. It's one of our last opportunities to impress a customer.
- What do the words "being alert" and "being responsible" mean in the context of [your company]? Being alert means seeing how to help a customer, watching children for their safety, notice a person who might like a chair and suggest one. Being responsible means checking the lights at night that they are on and none are missing, watching for fingerprints that need removing, checking restrooms are spotless, keeping an "eye" on customers, etc.
- Why did you choose [your company] when you decided to get a job?

- Where does merchandising start in a company? Store merchandising starts in your parking lot and ends when they drive away. [Explains why everything a customer sees, touches, or experiences is a part of their experience while visiting us.]
- Why should you get to work ten minutes earlier than your shift time? To hang up your coat, use the restroom, say hello to everyone. Start work on time. (Teaches professionalism)
- Do you know how to use all the features on your store telephone? Putting someone on hold? _____Transferring a call? _____Making an announcement or query over the PA system using the phone? _____ How to make a connection with another store or department? ___
- What is one thing [your company] needs to do? (Asking for their valued opinion)
- What do you want to say to the telephone customer when it is necessary to put them on hold? May I have your permission to place you on hold while I check on your request? [Professionalism]
- If [your company] needs to make more of a product a customer requested, what do you say? I apologize to you that we need to make more of that (product). We do have some of what you requested in another piece with lots of flavor that is a very good substitute. May I show it to you? [Well versed in your product and customer care.]
- If a customer asks you your opinion about something and you do not care for it, how do you answer? "Oh, you are asking about a very popular chocolate. We make it in dark and in milk chocolate. I keep hearing about how delicious the flavors are, but, personally, I like something with caramel in it. Let me show you where we display [the ones the customer is asking for]. I can get you just as many as you desire since they are not boxed. The favorite among the folks who like creams is raspberry. Would you like some of those?"
- What is "Small Talk"? Idle chatter or unimportant conversation often used to fill an awkward void such as waiting for an elevator, a doctor's office, a reception. It is also used to let another person know you are interested in them. It gives the other person a sense of security or well-being.
- When is "small talk" especially important? When first meeting a customer. Small talk gives them an opportunity to speak with you

and realize you are nice and will probably take good care of them.
- What is the one thing that will determine the success or failure in or at your store? The environment created by the Manager and helped to develop by everyone in the store.
- Name four incidents (of many) when you should apologize to a customer, give three examples: Not being able to fill a request, keeping them on hold; telling them the person they wished to speak with is not available; when they are unhappy about something; they are having trouble placing an order on the Internet; UPS or FedEX has not delivered their order; whenever you think it's important, etc. [Shows you know how to handle yourself; Professionalism.]
- Why is it important to properly bag a customer's purchases? To be certain the products arrive at their destination as perfectly as they left our store. The bags also become little billboards for Malley's Chocolates.
- What does your company's training and education program do for you? It gives me more knowledge for the care of our customers and each other.
- What is your company's Mission Statement?
- What Mission Statement has your Manager and all of you devised? Malley's Managers decided on "Dear Customers, with combined efforts, quality, and service to you will always be our number one priority."
- What are the names of the Leaders of [your company] and what are their responsibilities?
- This is how we prepare and properly sample our chocolates: Use Manager or Assistant Manager's chosen dish, tray, or basket and make certain it is immaculate. Put on gloves used for food handling. Cut large pieces of chocolate in half, on a separate plate to catch bits and pieces, and then transfer the cut halves and arrange on chosen plate, etc. When you notice a customer or browser looking at the display of the sample you are giving out, approach the customer or browser, smile at them with your lips and heart and unhurriedly say, "I notice you looking at our display of Pecan BillyBobs. They are one of our customer's top choices. May I offer you a sample? Notice how delicious the caramel is with the pecan. [Smile] I'll be back to check on you." Then return the dish to a safe place. Never just leave a sample dish out unattended. These are expensive, delicious offerings, and, natu-

rally, they will be eaten up by customers. Be sure to return to the customer who seemed interested in the Pecan BillyBobs. Ask how they liked the BillyBob. Would they like a box? I can gift wrap one or two free of charge, and it will be all ready when they want to check-out. There are many other ways to sample: to a group, introducing a new item, helping to make a product more known etc.
- Name something we do that surprises some people: Sending chocolate to warm climates; that we even ship chocolate; they can call and order over the phone, they can also talk whenever they feel it necessary with any of the Malleys.
- [Your store name] Manager has the important duties of:
    1. Hiring right
    2. Setting the store atmosphere
    3. Customer Care
    4. Teaching and educating Advocates in Malley Manners
    5. Hearing Skillshop information and seeing it being used during the care of customers
    6. A Manager is a store's greatest strength
- Why do we keep you employed? [Makes the employee think.]
- How long has [your company] been in business? [Knowledge; Bonding]
- What is one thing we could do right now to make it easier for you to work with us? [Shows we care about them.]

End this review with a short note that says something in your own words like, "Thank you for being a Malley's Advocate. We appreciate your efforts in delighting your customers." And then, add the signatures of the Manager and Assistant Manager.

Chapter 15
Hierarchy of Responsibilities for a Beginning Business

The President; the Manager; the Assistant Manager(s); and the Advocate

We are all different and naturally have different thoughts. When you are just beginning in business or have some experience, and you want to get a handle on the division of responsibilities, think of your project as if a friend wanted to put together a basketball team. Tell your friend a basketball team needs five players—a center, two forwards, and two point guards, a coach, and an assistant coach. That's it. So, step one is to set a system in place so those working in your business will understand what you want their role to be and how you think they should develop it.

To start, consider who needs to be informed about your business structure and profit. Does a silent partner want to know these facts? Do you have a partner? If you are flying solo, think about who else needs to be in the loop. Written systems save countless expensive work hours and stress. Accurate work can be expected if there is follow-up that checks for adherence and instills discipline for not creating a bottleneck.

The President
Role of President

The president impresses with vision, sets the tone, spreads enthusiasm, follows through on his or her word, and if not considered as a friend, has made the acquaintance of everyone hired and usually is quick to smile.

As president, understand that hiring is one of your most important functions as president, deciding on your Manager is so important because their personalities will be the happy or bland atmosphere in your store. They will have an influence on all you hire. They will build relationships with your customers, and train and educate all the other Advocates. Their choice of words will soon be part of the general conversation. You might decide to offer a position of Supervisor to the person you are considering with a time frame of 90 days, and then discuss the position after some actual experience has taken place. Supervisors do not merit as much pay as a Manager. They cannot hire or fire. This knowledge should give you some wiggle room to increase the person's pay after the 90-day term is complete—if you choose to offer the Manager's position. If you decide to hire a Manager, consider not approaching any other hires as a done deal. Before an actual hire, get your Manager's approval of the selection. Perhaps you will want to consider giving your Manager (or Supervisor) a more prominent role in the selection. He or she may want to have a chat or take that person on a store tour to determine if the hire is a good match for him/her, and easily accepted.

Also, keep in mind that first workdays are very important. Getting them acclimated to your other Advocates and the store is necessary because first impressions linger. Ask your Manager to prepare other Advocates to be very welcoming and help the new hire to feel comfortable.

As for you as president, be down-to-earth, friendly, and business-like in your approach. Prepare. And save your notes to be used each time you consider a hire. Here are a few recommendations on what to convey to a new hire:

1. Offer a few sentences about why you started in this business.
2. Explain your mission statement and their part in its performance. This doesn't need to be too expansive. Make it simple. You can add to it or revise, as necessary. Here's an example: "Our customer is our honored guest. Their experience will be one of personal care, best value, finest service all given with

knowledge and a smile."

3. Describe the culture you want developed. Since your company may be newer, explain how they are able to play a large part in its establishment.

4. Provide an overview of your personal Skillshop system for knowledge transfer and training. If there will be additional work or responsibilities for them to consider name them now. If, for instance, you will be making your chocolates in-store explain how you see them fitting into the work. Will they assist in making, packing, wrapping or other duties? Explain your yearly Retention Review. This will help identify transfer of information success to the new hire. It may also help define possible enhancements to your system.

5. Tell the new hire what's in it for them as a new Advocate with the company. Position their role as mutually beneficial.

6. Explain important papers. Include your guide sheets that explain company policies and rules.

7. Review inventory times when their assistance would be required. If the work occurs after-hours, be clear about that.

8. Explain Communication Conversations and your company's policy around them.

9. If you have regular, bi-annual (every six months) meetings for everyone to discuss company performance, provide details about what the meeting is and what it covers.

10. Let the new Advocate know that after they become familiar with the company you welcome their ideas for improvements and other thoughts.

11. Explain the company hierarchy and make it clear to whom they should respond for direction or questions in different areas.

12. Describe your Open-Door Policy, if you have one. When I led Malley's I would tell Advocates that any time they felt they needed to discuss something that they didn't care to discuss with their Manager, to tell me. I explained that I was there for them and wanted them to feel comfortable and happy that they chose to work with us.

13. Finally, stand to signal the meeting is over; as you stand, extend your hand and say, "Welcome (use their name), thank you for choosing to help us."

Development of Role: For a Beginning Company for a Retail Store

The following are in no particular order based on level of importance.

1. Create business card sized cards and give them a catchy-yet-descriptive name. For example, "Head's up". These can be used to applaud an Advocate or Manager's actions, disapprove of something that disturbs you, to write yourself a note to act on, or leave a quick note for your Manager or assistants. Be careful of developing the thought of you having enough meetings with your Manager because of various communications quickly and easily accomplished. There is nothing to compare with sitting quietly with a Manager and discuss all the things roaming around in your head and you know they know… well they don't know. These thoughts are in your head and you are assuming that somehow, they just know. They don't know. No one can read your mind. Take the time to sit down and discuss the entire scheme of responsibility that carried the name of Manager in your thoughts. Tell them thank you for doing such a good job on such and so. "I noticed you are improving . . . "

Meet every two weeks or once a month for ½ hour to an hour. Talk about plans for the next "special" or troublesome area the store is experiencing. Speak about your program for training and education. Do they have any thoughts to improve it, what are it's sticking points, are the Advocates receptive? How can you make it better? Talk about your first reactions when you enter your store, are there boxes on the floor, is the open stockroom door spoiling the atmosphere? What is something they might like to discuss? Make definite plans and do follow-up on them in a given time frame. This is very important, and few Leaders of small business actually take the time to do this important function. You will most likely be reminded why you hired this individual, know more about your company, and have renewed energy to keep on track with your Business Plan.

2. Jot down ideas of what you will want to say to a new hire. Keep your points short and focused.
3. Regularly express interest in and inspire efforts of Advocates.
4. Set up an agenda of what should occur and when it should take place.
5. Check Managers' reports and react to them.
6. Create a store checklist that is available in the store or other

operations for Managers to use. Explain how you want the list used, and when and how to follow up on the reports. Ask each Manager to provide you each report.

7. Create an all-store cleaning schedule which includes the restroom, stockroom, lunch area, and any vehicle.

Thoughts for the President

1. Always be the epitome of friendliness for customer and Advocate care. When you say hello to others, do it with a smile on your face. And, smile as you speak. It's up to you to reach out to others. You're the Leader! Smile with your eyes, face, and voice tone. There are few times when a person will respond to a serious face. Wear a pleasant, relaxed look when possible.

2. Watch customer foot-traffic on sidewalks, in driveways, or on the street for ideas that might smooth out the efficiency of your customers' visit.

3. Look at how customers want to enter and leave your store. Watch how they flow through the store. Notice the ease—or difficulty—they have selecting products. What are your prime in-store locations?

4. Watch how the register money is handled and controlled. Also, if you have more than one register, are they all always open at the same time? Consider locking the one(s) not in regular use but have it fully operational to be used at any time someone is waiting to be checked out. Keep in mind that sometimes, depending on store or operation traffic, Advocates do not want to open a second register because there is a "counting out" factor involved. Another excuse is that if there are two or more Advocates in the store, one can ring customers up and the other can bag. The idea they may espouse is that it is faster. Psychologically, the closer a customer is to a register, the quicker they feel they're being checked out. Make a customer's experience delightful: start with a pleasant greeting, knowledgeable service, a sample, and speedy check-out with a pleasant invitation to return.

5. Decide when you should lesson amounts in the till for safety reasons; decide if you should make periodic drops at the bank during busy times—likely holidays or special events. We employ off duty police to direct traffic and another to have their presence in the store.

6. Watch how samples and shopping baskets are given to customers. Are shopping baskets convenient for guests to get one? Do not allow them to be stored directly on the floor. If using baskets not made of plastic, price-tag them in a very obvious place so customers can see they are buyable. At the check-out the cashier should inquire if they would like the basket for home.

7. Watch how displays are replenished.

8. Listen to Advocates' conversations with customers. Note their tone, their "want to help" factor, suggested selling of monthly specials or other offerings, and the combination of a pleasant greeting with an invitation later to return.

9. Make it mandatory that the restroom is refreshed every two hours.

10. Make notes or change immediately how you can be of greater service for efficiencies, comfort, and effective new ideas to present to customers.

11. Consider the atmosphere of your store. Are there smiles or pleasant expressions on the faces of those people representing you?

12. Check that lighting outside the operation or store is ample.

13. Be of service to your Advocates.

14. At holiday or event occasions, perhaps supply holiday cookies, fruit, an interesting drink, or something else from your imagination, in the lunch or dinner area. Choose something tasty, honoring the season or unusual. Everyone is expending extra energy, so offer them a little something extra!

15. In advance of a holiday or event, meet six weeks before it happens to discuss last minute plans.

16. Develop seasonal reports on pluses and negatives several times each year after a major holiday or event. Study them for improvement for the next go-around. Use new figures against last year's figures to understand whether today's circumstances have made an impact. Be sure to keep detailed notes about weather and other considerations.

17. Monitor Assistant Managers use of your company's Malley Manners program, focused specifically on store standards.

18. Review and approve Advocates' schedules with extra attention at the very busy times: consider the number of Advocates per shift. Be sure the Manager is on duty at your busiest times.

19. Each day, check displays, inventories, greeting areas, the

restrooms, and the cleanliness of your register areas. Pay attention to uniforms, if appropriate.

20. Each week: Remember hiring and also creating a friendly atmosphere in the store and among all your helpers, thus assuring the environment of friendliness and good will before your first customer arrives and your last customer and Advocate leaves. Your helpers are your customers, you want them to "buy" into your instructions, directions, and your ideas. Start with the "benefits' and then add the "features". Remember, they should know why you are asking this of them. Be conversational. Look them in the eye, make them comfortable but get your job done!

    a. Choose a company guidebook statement or Skillshop lesson to inform and remind. (For the first year have each day's selection noted in a tablet. Use that prepared list, adding, subtracting, exchanging the information every year.)

    b. Ask to see your Advocates' folders accounting for their accomplishments.

    c. Assess whether Advocates are aware of their part in the store's culture.

    d. Develop responsibility lists to cover the following:

        i. The Manager's first responsibilities are hiring and customer care, then working in and on their day-to-day plans to reach monthly goals. Next should be store upkeep, Skillshop education or review. The Manager should post a daily list of tasks to be completed. He or she should construct them and check for completeness.

        ii. Assistant Managers Activity are customer care, then their day-to-day jobs for supervision, attention to Advocates practicing their Skillshops, addressing store goals, and "encouraging Advocates' to practice Skillshops."

21. See that your technology is up-to-date or a step above
22. Create with your accountant, store financial goals and the education of your Manager to become more familiar with the organization's infrastructure.
23. List what presentations or ads create the greatest revenue for you, and the reasons for their success.
24. Keep notes about needed improvements and new ideas for the next holiday.
25. Create a team sense of unity among all Advocates.
26. Keep Advocates' files up to date.

27. Educate the Manager and Assistants about your responsibilities as the Leader. Describe the duties that are your responsibilities and help them understand your directions and requests.
28. Develop and follow a personal job description so you are certain you've covered everything necessary. Have it checked for accuracy by your attorney, accountant, or other professional advisors.
29. Smile—a lot!
30. Place ads, as needed, for enthusiastic Advocates.
31. Conduct Retention Reviews at least twice each year or more often, if needed.
32. Create a framework for feedback: Advocate to Assistants, Assistants to Manager and Manager to CEO. Reacting to comments is very important to show them you value their thoughts and ideas.
33. Discuss often with your Manager the culture you want continually expressed in every thought and communication with anyone and everyone.
34. Get your vendors lined up. Tap into their experience and knowledge—such as knowing when it is the best time to order ingredients, or wrapping paper, boxes, or other supplies.
35. Attend association meetings, conventions, exhibitions, and other gatherings where you can secure all-around knowledge. Develop a network of friends to whom you can call throughout the year to discuss ideas, problems, or challenges.
36. Create a marketing schedule:
    a. Decide when production should be ready with a product.
    b. Prepare store personal about the product and explain why it will be popular. Explain the features and benefits—verbally and in writing.
    c. Prepare any fliers or advertising at least eight weeks in advance.
    d. Decide on display assists that will be used.
    e. Ensure that price display cards are in place at the proper time: six weeks ahead for seasonal work and placement in store; six to seven weeks in advance for seasonal decorative merchandising support.

All the above tasks are in addition to traditional bookkeeping, decision making, business, banking, and other association needs. As soon as possible, assign your Manager responsibilities that address as many of the above elements as possible. Set a schedule for the discussion of every responsibility you have entrusted to them for implementation.

The Store Manager
Role of Manager

First, if you are told to do the hiring, understand it's one of your most important functions. Remember, customer care is the foundation for all other activities, and it starts right here. If you have not been instructed in company hiring procedures, ask for details. Here are a few of the items that should fall under the role of the Manager. He or she:

1. Listens and answers to the President.
2. Is responsible for correct hiring, coaching, bring imagination and friendly motivation for store culture; supervision; and meeting goals.
3. Schedules and teaches your company's unique Manners or Skillshops programs. He or she must know how to meet challenges and the correct method of firing, if necessary.
4. Must learn how to give store instructions rather than follow them if he or she previously served in a subordinate role. If not given, request instructions.
5. Understands how to lead a meeting. Ask for guidelines.
6. Develops Assistant Manager(s) in Manager's responsibilities.
7. Holds monthly meetings with the President to discuss progress.
8. Invites Assistant(s) to be present for two meetings with the President to make them familiar with the meetings.
9. Develops an agreed-upon personal job description.
10. Uses "Head's Up" or other personalized cards.
11. Give the personalized Retention Review with each Advocate as far as their proficiencies are noted in their folder. This is designed to ensure they have retained—and continue to learn—what is expected of them.
12. Attend any and all meetings outside the company that relate to the location of the operations. He or she should be prepared to participate.
13. Explain to Advocates what your plan is for the day or shift, and why the plan is important. This is so others can understand why they are doing what you have asked them to do. It's better

to have the whole story than to keep giving information out piecemeal. It's also easier to work knowing what the plan is and what you are expecting.

    a. Perhaps to make your planning smoother write on a white, black or green board or a large sheet of paper the following:
Today is: _____
Plan for day is: _____
Work to be caught up from yesterday: _____
Special note: _____
(Ex.: If it's winter, keep the walkways treated. If it's raining, watch out for water on floor that might cause slipping. If it's someone's birthday, is there a special order that must be prepared by a certain time).
Prepare for: _____
Manager's Note: _____
(Remark about some good thing that happened in the store yesterday. For example, call attention to an Advocate who finished all the introductory Skillshops. Or, you may want to mention if you need another Advocate. It's your very own space, so have fun with it.)

14. If entertaining guests or tours for customers, instead of Advocates smiling and being friendly, keep them smiling and friendly and give them something to say, short and simple and just about what the person is seeing; no personnel remarks.

    Finally, Ken Blanchard, one of the most influential leadership experts in the world, says, "Day to day coaching is one of the most important qualities of a great Manager." That means incorporating these three skills — flexibility, diagnosis, and partnering. They are three of the most important skills Managers can use to motivate team members and achieve better performance on the part of the people with whom they work.

Development of Role: Manager

The following are offered in no particular order or based on the specific level of importance. In fact, all are important. He or she:

    1. Listens and answers to the President.
    2. Is responsible for customer care, store culture, supervision, meeting goals, schedules and teaching or the education of your company's Skillshops.

3. Teaches your Assistants the responsibilities of a Manager's position.
4. Listens or sits in on some of your Assistants' guidance and feedback to a store Advocate:
    a. After the meeting is a good time to speak about how the meeting progressed
    b. Never be overbearing or call attention to your Assistants when a mistake occurs. It is never a good idea to undermine the authority of a teacher in front of a student.
5. Participates in and dispenses to your Advocates once a year your company's Retention Review. All positions of Advocates should engage in this review because it:
    a. Helps identify the transfer of information success
    b. Defines possible needed Skillshop enhancements
    c. Identifies necessities for system improvements
    d. Illustrates teacher or coaching improvement needs
    e. Points out the need for individual tutoring to assure learning retention
    f. Administers refreshers to returning holiday helpers
    g. Allows Advocate wishes to be made known, as well as shows the consistent demonstration of what is an appropriate performance level
    h. Establishes the value of your company's Malley Manners program

Thoughts for the Manager
Here are 26 steps for making yourself an exceptional Store Manager:
1. I know I help make my store what it is.
2. My goal is to give our customers an experience that turns them into enthusiastic fans.
3. I will make notes to be able to discuss issues with our President.
4. My store will have an atmosphere of friendliness if I am friendly. I must be upbeat no matter how I feel. That's my job.
5. My store will be always ready for customers and properly merchandised.
6. My Advocates will know what I expect from them and how I think they are performing.
7. Every person who enters my store will be valued.
8. All of us will see to it that each person is treated just the same

with a friendly smile, attention, and listening to their wants and needs...and then supplying those to the best of our ability.

9. We will always notice what is happening around us. We will help each other and help create every customer's experience through respect, listening, care, and knowledge of our products and history.

10. I will value my Advocates' wishes when scheduling, be fair when giving out work assignments, and give smiles and recognition for work tried or done well.

11. I want to earn the same from them: respect, listening, care, and fairness to what I ask and expect.

12. My Advocates will know that I value trying because it becomes knowing. Ken Blanchard, who wrote the informative book, "The One Minute Manager," tells us the way to develop a person's knowledge is to remember that "in the beginning approximately right is just fine." Note what was right and then gently show them how to make it better!

13. I will remember that my Advocates are people just like me. They too want to work in a peaceful, fun environment. It is up to me to make it that way.

14. I will respond to my Advocates in the same way whether the customers arrive at a smooth pace or if it gets hectic. By being consistent, my Advocates will know that I am steady and unfailingly ready to listen to them and what they have to say.

15. No one can be afraid to tell "the bad news" to a person who is reliable and in control. If I truly treat others as I really wanted to be treated "when I was in their shoes," then a helpful attitude will prevail.

16. If a problem arises, I will take the challenge, decide, and react without blame. I will take steps to correct why it happened later.

17. Everyone will be in my inner circle if I make sure they are invited in.

18. I will acknowledge the work performed regularly by my "Stars" as much as those Advocates who are trying.

19. My store will be full of customers if I develop my responsibilities. I will work not only in the store but also on my business of being an A+ Manager.

20. We will create my store's mission statement with the approval of my President, and then my Advocates and I will consistently work toward achieving it. This statement will be

short and to the point. An example might be what our Managers decided they wanted to work under: "Dear Customers: With combined effort, quality and service to you will always be our number one priority."

21. If something bothers me, I will have the courage to speak up.
22. I will not take home a work problem; I will discuss it before I leave and come to an understanding.
23. I will leave home problems at home when I check into the company's time, so I can be thoroughly prepared to give my customers and Advocates my best self.
24. If I do these things the best I can daily, then I will have done what I need to do.
25. I will know that I have safeguarded the trust put in me by the company President.
26. I dedicate myself to be all these things so that my store shows we are Advocates for our Customers and our President.

Role of the Assistant Manager(s)

The No. 1 job of the Assistant Manager is the care of customers. This position introduces your Advocate to more accountabilities for which he or she will be responsible. But make sure to let them know to never forget their most important job is customer care:

- Customer Care supersedes all other functions.
- Answers to Manager. Be alert and responsive to Manager's instruction.
- Through coaching and guiding I am accountable for Advocates' successes.
- Responsible for being proactive in learning as much as possible from Manager.
- Participate in a monthly meeting with the Manager to discuss progress report.
- Can assist with training if necessary.
- Holiday teaching and coaching will by the Manager/Assistant Manager.
- Every Advocate who has completed the [your company name] Malley Manners program will complete according to their signed proficiencies a Retention Review.
- In late August, or other chosen month, participate in a Retention Review of (Your Company name) Malley Manners.

Development of the role of the Assistant Manager

The Number One job of the Assistant Manager is the care of Customers. Thoughts on developing this role:

- It's imperative to understand the different kinds of work to do. You will be expected to perform, to be an understudy of your Manager.
- Leadership is the time to be extra pleasant, be the first to call out "Hello" to your co-workers and customers. Smile a lot from your eyes, your lips, your heart, and your mind to everyone.
- Ask your Manager to discuss what was explained to you before you accepted the position. No one can remember all the nuances of a job they hear the first time. Take notes.
- Ask the Manager how they envision you working with them. Go over your job description.
- Ask how you can help attain his/her store's sales targets. Discuss plans for success. Be sure to thoroughly understand the plan, or you won't be helpful reaching target.
- Never forget if you were engaged to be an Assistant Manager, it is the Manager's store and his/her systems in it.
- Every Advocate who has completed the "[your company name] Malley Manners" program will complete the semi-annual Retention Review, (according to their acknowledged abilities,) to confirm retention of learning and consistent demonstration of appropriate performance, each day choose a skill. Discuss its meaning and how to practice it.
- Use "Head's Up" (or "Reaction Flashes") cards.

Whatever you opt to do, make it fun to learn practicing new ways. It's a great deal more enjoyable to be creative in how you teach than just a sober run down of what the Skillshop teaches. It's up to you what kind of teacher you want to be.

Always be the first to notice what your Advocates are doing and compliment on the spot when you see something being accomplished well. As one famous motivator has said, "First time almost good with congratulations is a lot better than a negative remark because it wasn't all good. Always look for the good. Always comment in a happy way."

The first time an Advocate tries something, and it isn't perfect or even good, congratulate them on what they did right and remember to have "congratulations" in your eyes and a smile on your face. Have them try it again. This time work backwards of the instructions until you hear them say, "Oh yes, I forgot about that!" So, tell them they did very well right up to that point and go on from there. Have them speak aloud what they are doing. Be sure to congratulate them, later, see if they can duplicate their success!

Thoughts for Assistant Managers

The following are some thoughts to help give you some direction on what the CEO expects.

1. Discuss how you might help the other Advocates accomplish their share in the plan.

2. When the Manager is not present you assume his or her duties. Be prepared.

3. To make it easier on yourself, try not to have the same lunch periods or break times that you enjoyed with Advocates, before you were offered the position of Assistant Manager. But sometimes be sure to be there to celebrate an occasion. You can slip out so as not to hinder conversation. (They may want to talk about you and might resent your intrusion on "their" time.)

4. Ask for all the information you need to have to do the jobs placed on your shoulders. This inquiry will show your grit and ability to do the job. This head up attitude will demonstrate exactly why you were chosen for more responsibility. Believe this.

5. Let it be known you are not a placid person. "Whatever happens, happens" is not going to occur in your store or to the responsibilities your Manager has assigned you.

6. Never ever forget to treat every single person just as you would like to be treated and try to improve on it!

7. Get comfortable assigning work fairly no matter what age your Advocates are. You certainly want to be seen as being fair. Also practice kindness and charity and be in on some fun too! Whenever possible, share the job with them.

8. Learn to easily give orders for things needing to be done. Keep trying to give more and more work of what you are responsible for to your Advocates. Complete instructions and rechecking the progress will develop a strong team. You will be developing their self-esteem, and reaching your targets will bring credit to you.

9. Regularly check with your Manager that you are setting an example of an outstanding Assistant.

10. If you must give a reprimand to an Advocate, always, always do it in a place where no one will see or hear you speaking to

the person. Keep it short. Say something like, "I see you have gotten off track, and I need you to get back on". Explain what is wrong and how to do it correctly. Ask if they have anything to add or ask. "This is how I want your behavior to be. I want a store of happy and co-operative Advocates." Check back with me in private on Friday (or a certain number of days) and tell me how it is going. Thank you." Short and sweet said in tones of friendship.

11. If you ever hear an Advocate say something negative about a customer or hang up the telephone and make a remark about their conversation with a customer on the telephone, immediately step in and take the offender to your office or quiet place and tell them that customers "make [your company name] a success. Some customers just need a little more help or understanding from us. When you think about it, can you understand what I am pointing out to you? Don't let it happen again, or I will have to write the circumstances into your file. Now, smile, let's get back to our customers!"

12. Know your Advocate handbook and our Skillshops forward and backward. You set the standard to the expected specification. A Leader that arouses motivation does so by careful example. If your standards aren't high, why should anyone else reach for high benchmarks?

13. Learn to lead and, most importantly, learn to delegate. Never hover but be ready to give a helping hand when it's needed. Learn to have faith in whom you have given a responsibility. Ask them how things are coming along. If help is needed, discuss the difficulty and together decide on an answer while agreeing together to stay flexible as the two of you work out different patterns to success.

14. Are you following up on your Manager's instruction to an Advocate? What kind of a personal check list have you devised to be certain the training and education is taking hold in an Advocate?

15. Keep your Manager apprised of everything important to his/her requests of you and anything else that developed in their absence.

16. Put extra time in developing a strong relationship that gives confidence to new Advocates.

17. Do everything in your power to develop the heart of our business—the care of our Customers.

18. Manage your time. Aim above being simply sufficient, but be an inspiration, to what being a conscientious Advocate means to self-esteem and personal character.

Role of the Advocate
When you're an Advocate, you are significant in the support of our business. You should:

1. Know how we plan to stay business (the Mission Statement.) Malley's Chocolates is committed to making and selling the finest chocolates, roasted nutmeats, and ice cream. We generate profit for growth by providing the finest of services to the delight of our customers.
2. Recognize Customer Care is your prime concern.
3. Answer to the Manager or Assistant Managers.
4. Listen and respond to directions.
5. Understand success depends on your self-reliance.
6. Accept responsibility to become proficient in your company's Malley Manners program.
7. Follow and develop our job description.

Every Advocate will complete the annual Retention Review to assure they are practicing what they have learned and are noted for consistent demonstration of appropriate performance.

It helps to:
- Identify transfer of information success
- Define possible needed Skillshop enhancements
- Point out necessary system improvements
- Illustrates teaching or coaching needs for improvements
- Identify the need for individual tutoring to assure the understanding of the Skillshops and how to practice them (resulting in higher retention of information)
- Allow the Advocates' wishes and feedback to be known
- Establish the value of your company's Malley Manners' program

Development of the Advocate's role
Here are some ideas to become an outstanding Advocate:
- Put a smile on your face that came from your eyes and heart.
- Be a real team player. Help customers and other Advocates enjoy their time in your presence.
- Know the company's mission statement. What does it mean to you?

- Be the first to offer a greeting and acknowledge when one is given to you.
- Memorize every Advocates' names. Casually find out what they like to do, when they celebrate their birthday, what is their favorite chocolate or pizza, just fun things to let them know you are interested in them.
- Put all tip monies if a fountain store in the tip jar.
- Know that friends deter you from your appointed tasks. They are not to loiter or wait in the store for you at dismissal time.
- Discuss Skillshops with other Advocates; practice with them to become proficient.
- Give your Leader a warm smile. They work hard on their feet, and they are responsible for all of you.
- Always report to work at least 10 minutes early.
- When you arrive for work, notice the outside condition of your store's property. Are all the lights working; are there any papers lying around? Is the door clean of fingermarks? Report the condition to your Leader.
- With your Manager's permission, skirt the store to see what is new, condition of displays, floor, the entrance door, and restrooms.
- Always ask for the day's instructions. Perhaps take notes to remind yourself of requests or questions to ask.
- Do not have another person call in sick for you. Before calling in, do your best to get a replacement.
- If something is coming up you wish to attend, check your social and/or study schedules ahead of time, so the Manager can hopefully make an arrangement on the schedule, so you will not be expected during that time. Remember schedules are made up three weeks in advance. Know that our customers are expecting good service, and you were engaged to give it to them.
- If you are a new holiday helper, make your wishes known if you are interested in helping throughout the year and/or next year. Do you have your goal set on being an Assistant Manager, possibly leading to a Manager position afterwards? Tell your Manager!

Thoughts for the Customer Advocate

The following are some final thoughts about Advocates, and what they should consider:

- Do you see something needing attention and could possibly be

another Skill everyone should learn? Tell your Leader.
- Put extra effort into listening when customers or your Leaders speak to you. Listen with your mind, eyes and body language, meaning giving the speaker your full attention.
- Be careful to complete all tasks so your job will be finished. That's the goal.
- Remember you are responsible for your own success. When you feel you can use Skillshops recently taught to you, ask your Manager for more instruction.
- Never handle any other Advocate's money at the registers or tip monies. Be responsible for your own actions. If a customer leaves an amount that pays for example, a chocolate bar and walks away, never put it in your pocket to ring up next. To an unknowing person it will look like you are pocketing the money or other Advocates won't see you ringing up the sum. Remember you only have one reputation, safeguard it!
- If you think of another way to do something that might be more efficient be sure to tell your Leader about it. If not speaking to the Manager, ask that the Assistant tell you what the Manager thought of your idea.
- Write a personal mission statement. Give to your Assistant Manager or Manager. If approved, write it on your job description.

Chapter 16
The Power of Skillshops

Be the best you can be. Knowledge is clout.
    As mentioned throughout the book, a Skillshop is a brief (10-15 minute) structured opportunity during which a specific skill is taught to a new hire.

    The Leader, Chosen Representative, or Manager will explain a Skillshop and ensure their new hire understands it. Malley's Chocolates recognizes that it is vital to educate a new hire to understand the importance of what we want and why. Knowing "why" is fair, and once they know the whole picture, they may choose to conduct themselves and think about their effort in a different, more accurate manner. Next, we train our helpers so that everything is accomplished by doing the right thing at the right time.

    The Assistant Manager follows by guiding and encouraging the learner and signing in their folder the lesson is now their customary asset. Some Skillshop's are very simple to learn, and others can be not as easy, such as learning to be comfortable operating a cash register or another device or asking a customer to purchase a product.

There is a high probability that their jobs will all be well done when all the Skillshop's have been learned and performed correctly and consistently. 16 Skillshops in our Orientation Program will qualify them to meet customers. Altogether, we have 52 Skillshops in our complete program. Each Skillshop has four parts:
- Purpose – what needs to be done
- Education – Why it should be completed according to instructions
- Training (Skill) – How it should be performed
- Retention – Completed Skillshop's periodically reviewed to maintain consistency.

Role Players:
- The CEO, assigned representative, or Manager will teach the Skillshops.
- The Assistant Manager (Skillshops "graduate"), by demonstrating interest and enthusiasm, will monitor that their protégé's skill is consistently called upon to show their knowledge when with customers. When both believe the task is performed correctly and at each opportunity, the Assistant Manager signs in their folder that this is a completed Skillshop.
- The Advocate must know that the success of this developmental journey depends on their demonstrated responsibility for self-improvement.

The Leader, Representative, or Manager must understand that we all learn in various ways, for instance, by watching, hearing, and doing. Learning (especially knowledge retention) can be impeded by many factors, including inattention, distractions, or even lack of the instructor's appropriate preparation. It is constructive to use props or interesting fun poster-type reinforcements to what is taught. Skillshops directions should be made available so an Advocate can re-read them whenever they care to review them.

The Leader/Representative/Manager and the Assistant Managers need to teach and guide because it allows for working closely with various temperaments while getting the job done. It also instills co-operation and how to encourage while showing the formation of a hopefully new habit. These functions are essential to assume other positions later if wanted or called upon.

Following is an example of a Skillshop, which you can copy the formation of if you choose to write your own to cover what is essential for your helpers to give the kind of service your customers will enjoy and you want to see and hear in your store.

Purpose of Education: Safely Bagging Customer's Purchases

Purpose of lesson: (Why) Ensure that the customer's purchases are bagged correctly at the register or other cash-out device, so they arrive at their destination as perfectly as they left the store.

What (the How): The Advocate will be able to:

Demonstrate knowledge of:
- How to be a customer's friend: Smile, be alert, and if appropriate, start some Small Talk and be a part of what is going on.
- If a customer has numerous packages, help get them on the counter next to the register or other cash-out.
- Be careful (according to space available) not to mix products ready for bagging and those that need to be "rung" by the cashier.

Assistant Manager's Responsibilities:

Props to get ready: (At Malley's) Vinyl or large paper tote bags, novelty, boxed and bagged items, graduated sizes of company paper bags, and cartons. Consult Manager and add any additional items requested.

Manager's Responsibilities

Prepare an explanation for the new hire. (Example of Malley's Chocolates)

- Malley's Chocolates is a particular confectionary store. Our chocolates are a first-class luxury taste treat that has won many awards. We like our paper bags to show that something quite delicious is in them, so the bag or carrier must be made to look appealing. Every bag should be turned down at least 1 ½ - two inches and then creased along the fold. It makes no difference which side of the bag to place the folded top on if each side is identical; otherwise, put the folded part on the backside. Besides giving the Chocolates their due, the bags also become little billboards as the customer carries them.
- If appropriate, and you become alert to a possible need, offer a complimentary gift card. ("If you like, you could fill it out right here and I can scotch tape it to your package, and you will be all set!")
- Always be sure the customer receives their receipt.

How to Bag Customer Purchases:
- Person "bagging" should stand where it's convenient for the cashier. Stay there until there are no more customers in line. Go back to your usual work, keep an eye on the cashier and the number of customers, and return if a line forms.
  - Look customers in the eye and smile into their eyes.
  - Bag items once your cashier has registered them.
  - Place larger packages at the bottom of the bag or tote, centered on the seam.
  - Boxes filled with chocolates should always, if possible, face up.
  - Stack items upwards.
  - Smaller novelty items, place into your best fitting paper bag for the article first, then place on top of the other packages.
  - Bowed items should be placed in the bag last or placed in a separate bag.

Paper Bags:
- No more than two items – you should be able to place the item(s) into one of three sizes of your paper bags.

Company outer cartons:
- Larger items or many purchased items may be placed in your company's outer cartons. Be specific; cartons are in perfect shape. All items placed within still receive proper wrap or bagging.
- If possible, offer to help the customer take their many bags or cartons to their vehicle, then say an interesting farewell: "I enjoyed helping you. (With your bedazzling smile, say,) I'm Sally, and please come back to Malley's Chocolates soon!"

Assistant Manager:

Practice with your Learner bagging various items in different bags until they are proficient in this task. Tell them to enjoy some Small Talk to engage a customer if appropriate. At all costs, smile into the customer's eyes and say a few words, such as, "I notice you chose a Noah's Ark. Kids love getting them, and they are used for other reasons too. One lady used them as party favors during a rainy season!" Provide lesson feedback with lots of encouragement and smiles!

As Ken Blanchard says in his book The One Minute Manager, a winning tip for those managing others is, *"Compliment immediately when you see something good."* I agree with him. If it's not feasible to do it face to face, disarm your employees with a compliment written on your business card or the same size card but with just your name printed on it to be used for such occasions. Carry this card with you as you do your business cards, so it's always handy and gets the job done! Trust me that it will lighten an employee's heart to know they are appreciated and came from you. Wouldn't you like to be noticed when you have just done something "Head's Up?"

If necessary, slip a 'Heads Up" card or your business card to a manager or Assistant if another kind of store attention is needed. Order the job to be done and follow up that it is.

The following is taken from Ken Blanchard's book, <u>The One Minute Manager</u>. One-minute praising of goals achieved or any part of the goal (is the thing to do.) Praise the behavior (with true feelings,) do it soon, be specific, tell the person what they did right and how you feel about it, encourage the person (with true feelings) and shake hands. Success! If a goal is not achieved, go back to the relating Skillshop and review, clarify and agree on the process. Reprimand the behavior, do it at once, be specific, and tell the person how you feel about it. Shake hands. And SMILE!

Chapter 17
Why bother with Small Talk?
More Ways to say Hello and Get Friendly

"Small Talk" is characterized by lighthearted short conversations. "Small Talk" is needed because it is a form of communication which is critical to developing friendships that can lead to relationships.

For us to develop relationships, we must be able to draw from a vast repertoire of topics and feelings in order to communicate at various levels of familiarity. "Small Talk" helps to develop friendships and thereby represents at times the strongest and most important response to "getting started." You must know "Small Talk" at cocktail parties, family gatherings, and first encounters. Without the ability to engage another person in "Small Talk", you may never get onto relationship building. Potential friends and acquaintances are visually filtered; during "Small Talk" we apply a verbal filter. "Small Talk" is sort of an audition for friendship.

It's only after we are satisfied with the "Small Talk" that we venture into "Big Talk" which is characterized by greater focus and depth of personal disclosures. "Small Talk" provides a safe procedure for indicating who we are and how another person can come to know us better. We are playing for time, trying to display our best features. If we see they don't like who they see, we can bring out another of our many selves. "Small Talk" allows us to further reduce uncertainties about the other person while allowing others to focus more specifically on who we are. The fewer the uncertainties, the greater the chances of accurate predictions about the person—and the greater chances of moving from "Small Talk" to "Big Talk".

Another function of "Small Talk" is it can serve as a non-threatening time-killing activity with none of the pressures involved in more fact-finding or introspective processes. In short, it can be a release, an escape valve, or a diversion from other kinds of talk which require more conscious programming.

"Small Talk" provides a means for uncovering a combination of topics, or more simply, openings for more penetrating conversations and relationships.

Greetings can be powerful. Most obvious and seemingly incidental acts of initiating encounters comprise a good greeting. Greetings, however, are anything but incidental since they carry important connection information concerning formality, status, and friendliness; they also help to set the stage for the dialogue and relationship which will follow.

A facilitative thread found in all these processes—person perception, attraction, and "Small Talk"—is the significance of the two or those persons interacting finding commonalities between themselves.

More Ways to Say "Hello"
Non-verbal Greetings
- When you are very busy, tilt your head or give a waiting customer eye contact. This lets the person waiting know you are open to helping them and that you will be with them as soon as possible.
- Use a relaxed hand with your relaxed index finger pointing up. Your face giving a pleasant acknowledgment of the person's presence by making eye contact and a slight nod of your head.
- If crowded or any time you are held up from providing immediate assistance, always lift your head, give the line a smile, and go back to caring for your present customer. Now the "line" knows you are aware they are waiting to be served. If you do not acknowledge your customers, they will feel you are understaffed, work too slowly, or don't care that they are not getting good service. If you do not wish to help a person, do not give the

person any eye contact. This lack of action very definitely lets the other know you have no intention of waiting on him.
- This act may get you fired for being so rude and also not following instructions. Do not ever act put upon or complain about how hard you are working. You are a professional in a customer's eyes, and they expect to be treated by a professional—you.
- The best way to act is to be happy you are so busy and smile and talk with your customers. The others in line naturally listen, and time moves along more swiftly.

Helpful ways to initiate a greeting (any of the following can fall into several categories):
- Give a friendly "Hello" with your eyes and heart and pleasant voice.
- If you know them, call them by name.
- Personal inquiry: "How are you today?"
- If you recognize them: "Nice to see you again." or "Long time no see."
- Use compliments (If person is alone:) "That is a really nice-looking coat."
- Reference the here and now surroundings: "Is everyone at this table going to have Superman Ice Cream? It gives you energy to move really fast." "May I get you a larger bag?" "Here, let me help with that!"
- References to people or things outside of the immediate interaction setting: 'How do you like the weather we are having?" "Did you get to watch the game today?"
- References to the other person's behavior: "I notice you seem to be in a hurry."
- References to oneself: "Hello, I'm (your name)." or "Perfect timing, I'm all ready to take care of you."
- Apologies: "Excuse me, but..." Unexpected, humorous, or whimsical phrases designed to break the ice: "This is the best chocolate you will have ever eaten!" or "These are so good you'll have them for breakfast!"
- One way that is not recommended is immediate topic initiation which usually excludes any preliminary comments: "The reason I wanted to talk with you...."
- Another way to not start a conversation is using single words

Why bother with Small Talk? 253

or vocalizations which are essentially content-free: "Well!" or a muted grunting sound.
- Any given greeting may fall into several of the categories discussed. It is important for the greeter to know what kind of a relationship they want to build. To greet a regular customer as you might greet a new shopper will make the "regular" feel like their business is not appreciated—that you don't recognize them.

Here are more good opening lines for anyone to use:
- "Good morning."
- Direct references to the other person by name, nickname, or personal pronoun: "Hi Barb!" or "Greetings Luda!"
- Questions of personal inquiry: "What's new with you?" or "How are you doing?"
- Verbalizations expressing a desire to continue a past relationship "Long time no see." or "Nice seeing you again." "Hello. It's been a long time since we've seen you. Welcome!"
- Compliments: "I like those neat colors on your shirt." If person is alone you can make a direct compliment. If more than one - compliment so all can enjoy it. Say something about the concerns of a whole group. Let everyone be "in" the moment."
- References to here-and-now surroundings: "May I get you another drink?" or "May I help you find what you are looking for?"
- References to people or things outside the immediate interaction setting: "How do you like this weather we are having?" or" Did you watch the game?"
- References to another's behavior: "I noticed you were sitting all alone over here." or "I noticed you seem to be having a tough decision to make; perhaps I can help."
- References to oneself: "Hi, I'm here to help you!"
- Apologies "Excuse me, but ..."
- Unexpected, humorous, or whimsical phases designed to break the ice —or "This is the best cake I've had since breakfast!"
- Immediate topic initiation which usually excludes any preliminary comments: "The reason I wanted to talk with you...."
- Single words or vocalizations which are essentially content free: "Well!" or a muted murmuring sound.

Chapter 18
How to keep your Best Advocates

The Dish Ran Away with the Spoon - Mother Goose, 1626
*If you practice good leadership skills and give fair pay,
no one will ever want to leave you.*

What's the top way to keep your best Advocates with you? This question is important to ask yourself. Even if you have only a couple of helpers, a partner, or others. An Advocate will stay with you if they feel bonded to you, is doing fresh interesting work, and is receiving fair pay. Annually thinking about the happiness of our Advocates is the start of a practice that gets easier and easier.

Plan to plan. Ease into it. Start to prepare by thinking about it. Then, start approaching it in a more serious manner. Set aside a paper tablet and write yourself notes as you get prepared to spend quality time to think about how you are going to do your part to keep your best Advocates. Write anything that comes to mind; your ideas can be silly, out-of-this-world fabulous, serious, amazing, questioning, hopeful, helpful, educational, right, and good. Don't hold back; only you will be seeing your work. Your ideas are thoughts that with action can create directions that can lead you to where you want to be.

After a couple of days, set aside time on your calendar. Let nothing disturb you. When you meet your appointment time, start by getting your reserved tablet.

Carefully look at your notes. Possibly jot down some ideas next to individual notes. Again, ask yourself what are you doing to make your best Advocates want to stay with you?

Make a quick listing. Prioritize it. Answer these questions:
- How well do you know your Advocates?
- How well are they performing with the responsibilities you have given them?
- When was the last time you renewed the responsibilities you had given to an Advocate?
- If you had to replace someone, did you allow the new Advocate to slip in without training and education?
- Did you do a careful assessment of their strengths and where they believe they are weak?
- Do you know your own strengths and weaknesses?

As Manager you should play to your strengths and allow your Advocates to shore up your weaknesses. This strategy is not possible if you don't really know the competences and weaknesses of your helpers.

It is not possible to think of the best assignment for an individual's store activities without a little research; however, it does not take long. The best way to start is to identify the best business information you can know/learn. You have all the information right now; study your Advocate's application and other papers they wrote when applying for a position. Keep a journal on what they said about:

Name _____
Strengths_____
Hobbies _____
Experiences _____
What do they believe they are skilled at doing?
_____
What do people tell them they are good at doing?
_____
When do *they* feel they don't perform well?
_____

As you hire new Advocates, add their name to your list. Remove an Advocate's name who is not working with you.

Take your time on this short qualities' assessment. You want to give your Advocates what they think are very nice working conditions. Look at your jobs list and consider the best job choice to match your Advocates' competencies. Carefully choose how you want to organize your group. Do not be held back from making changes. *(Even though Agnes has always counted the order in.)* Do not be afraid of hurt feelings. *(Agnes may be afraid to tell you she would like to do something else. Maybe she is afraid she would be fired?)* First, remember this is your store, and you want it operated as you see best. Study your first thoughts. Think it through. And make your decisions. Plan to meet with everyone working with you even if it's your brother, spouse, partner, or whomever.

Explain the project. Tell of your research and planning and how you think they will find the most joy in their work. Shine on how important it is and how they can make "our" store better with their efforts. Ask for their opinion on your idea. Be ready to be flexible. They may surprise you with the direction they would like to work in and develop it to almost perfection! Discuss it and make your own decision. If you are not going to accept their hopes, tell them how much you appreciate them coming up with ideas and maybe different approaches. Tell them you will remember their thoughts, and you will try to work it into the store's responsibilities. Right now, you need them to do what you already have figured out.

The following thoughts are presented to you to give you an idea about making your store a rewarding place to work. Discuss new ideas with the Leader. It is up to you to exercise the privileges of your position. When you are finished preparing, practice what you will say. After you have practiced, you are now ready. Notice the calmness and added self-confidence that comes when you know you are thoroughly ready to make your presentations.

Retail store job responsibilities within the store are many. It is understood that customers always come first in thought and action. Yet, stores, like a home, need attending if they will be organized, clean, supplied, and ready to "face the day".

After studying the strengths and presumed weaknesses of your Advocates, decide how best they can enjoy their contribution, while throwing down the gauntlet to make a better system of it for a well-operated store. This method is how I believe you can challenge them with duties you need done. Again, ask yourself what you are doing to keep them interested and challenged? To have them feel your interest, spend a little time and work side-by-side with them, discuss what they are doing, encourage and show your interest in their work. To choose the right job to utilize each Advocate's strengths, review the accompanying Job or Duty List.

This list is itemized to possibly ease and quicken decision-making. Add to it or rearrange as you see fit. Of course, you will not have as many Advocates as opportunities written below. They are listed to help you in planning. You can certainly give an Advocate more than one responsibility. If you are lucky, you may be able to position them for a strength and possibly some work that will match the work of their passion or love for a chosen hobby. Such as if their hobby is making fishing lures, it tells you they have patience for detail work. Consider possible jobs listed if the Advocate stated this about themselves:

Highly organized?
1. Receiving the delivery
2. Putting the delivery away
3. Manager of the fountain
4. Keeping the store, cupboards and drawers well-organized

Very outgoing and friendly?
1. Being the Greeter and teaching others the joy and fun of it.
2. In charge of sampling and educating others of how and when to present (also teacher).
3. Being a "buddy Advocate" with a new Advocate/rookie (also

teacher). Give directions on how to do this responsibility.
4. Assists Assistant Manager(s) with an Advocate's Skillshop practice. Give directions on how to do this responsibility.

Strong Math Skills?
1. Pricing what is made in-store.
2. Figuring out Advocates' hours for you.
3. Leader for inventory.
4. Writing up next delivery order.
5. Counting out day's sales.
6. Counting supplies (Glassine papers, boxes, ribbons, printer papers, and so forth) and ordering as needed.

Creative?
1. Assist with decorating and preparing same for storing.
2. Builds and/or attends daily display sell-through and general repair.
3. Teaches other Advocates how to display and practices with them.
4. Can show and teach others how to make bows.
5. Create ideas for "what goes with what" to help with displays. Each time a new presentation is created, make the centerpiece of it interesting to view. A good and easy presentation for a display is to suggest what goes with what such as Sundae sauces, mints, and nuts as a dessert idea. Wool scarves, mittens, and warm hats if you are in that kind of business. You will see your display will appear interesting if you cluster items together in an odd number, such as three, five, or seven. Most always keep your "joinings" simple so as not to confuse your customer and allow them to "get" the idea quickly. Discuss with Advocates good "joinings." Make it fun and worthwhile to create.
Add to these suggestions, so your store is always ready with ideas.

   a. ***Valentine's Day***: Special Valentine's box, bag of Foiled Hearts, Truffles and Bordeaux for 'Him' (and wrapped in a masculine manner).

   b. ***Spring***: Nestle together a box of Carmallow eggs, a gift wrapped for Spring or Easter ½ pounder and foil wrapped eggs in a see-through container, Watermelon Slices in a see-through container.

c. ***Easter***: Three boxes of Luscious Eggs, Truffles, Carmallow Eggs

d. ***Passover***: Most always Rabbi blessed chocolates are consumed. Put together a pleasing grouping of items. Careful with packaging: no shiny bows, reserved wrapping paper—a high quality look. Be certain packages and signs state "Rabbi blessed".

e. ***Mother's Day***: Special Combination package for Mother's Day, Chocolate-covered Strawberry package, three Sample boxes to scatter in the "nestling," and Chocolate-covered Grape package sitting among a cluster of grapes.

f. ***Father's Day***: Bordeaux, boxes of Mixed Nuts, BillyBobs, Sea Salt Caramels.

g. ***Summer***: Chocolate-Covered Cherries, Peppermint Patties, Malley Mints.

h. ***Summer casual***: Taffy, Lollipops, Popcorn, Fudge (various flavors).

i. ***Fall***: Nuts, Malted Milk Balls, Buckeye's (Peanut Butter), Chocolate-Covered Pretzels, various Fudge flavors, Caramel Corn, and Cheese Corn.

j. ***Sweetest Day***: Strawberry Boxes, Grape Boxes, Gold Cup Assortment, Foil-wrapped Lips, another foiled chocolate for color.

k. ***Halloween***: Halloween Box; Pretzel Bars (in boxes, opened and displayed, contents wrapped in cello) enormous and smaller choices, Candy Corn.

l. ***Thanksgiving***: Hostess Package, Mixed Nuts, ½ lb. French Mints, Malley Mints. and Sandwich Mints.

m. ***St. Nicholas Day*** Usually small bagged items to fit in a shoe. "He" arrives the eve of Dec. 6th.

n. ***Hanukkah***: Only Kosher Chocolate: Gift boxes, Gelt and Kosher Dark Chocolates.

o. ***Christmas***: Show a couple of popular boxes that are not your top selling boxes. Foiled Santa's, Hot Fudge and Pecans (done up together for sundaes at home).

p. ***Kwanzaa***: Honors African heritage in African-American culture and lasts one week. It was established in 1966 as an alternative to Christmas and Hanukkah. Nestle together choices for a party. It's a pleasant happy time.

q. **_New Year Celebration_**: Groupings for party needs: Mints, Mixed Nuts, and chocolates.

r. **_Birthdays, Retirement, Anniversaries, New Job, Welcome, Hostess Gifts, New Baby_**: Group together at least three items to celebrate. Make it fun and upbeat.

Note: (Be sure to inform what kinds of products cannot be "nestled," such as a bowl of unwrapped chocolates or candies or any suggestion that what they are viewing can be taken as a sample dish.)

Photographer?

1. Ready to photograph celebrities in store, some great picture of customer with chocolate packages, displays etc. Making small posters showing an Advocate (or Advocates) smiling. Think up descriptive words to bring pictures to life: "Be Happy" or "Be the First to Give a Smile Today"

Loves to Clean?

1. Cleans glass doors.
2. Tidies Restroom during store hours.
3. Cleans all glass shelving.
4. Keeps drawers organized.
5. Keeps back counter free of packages and all unnecessary objects.
6. Checks condition of vacuum.
7. Checks mops, the area and hanging appropriateness.
8. Storeroom responsibilities.

Loves to Teach?

1. Assistant Manager's helper with practicing Skillshops.
2. How to wrap and make bows.
3. Caretaker of holiday helpers.
4. Adapt at machines? Help with register instruction or minor fixing.
5. In charge of sampling and educating others on how and when to present.
6. Being a "buddy Advocate" with a new Advocate/rookie.
7. In charge of email notifications and clarifications with every Advocate.
8. Keeps your Skillshop "Tools" in excellent condition and

prepared to be used. "Tools" are what you will need to teach and educate a Skillshop.

As an aside to show you how other companies use the threesome bundle, in my email today Frontier Communications also expressed a threesome:

Here is the actual email:

-Frontier Communications-
It's time to get cozy Adele!
Fall is here. Grab a blanket, some popcorn, and check out these new movies.

It is very important that you practice good and helpful management habits. The above is an excellent bonding mechanism if you make it fun and you get involved. Perhaps you might want to give the experience to an Advocate to get everyone thinking about what goes together and keep an up-to-date listing. You should develop how you will follow through on each Advocate and keep tabs on the progress so your effort and spontaneity can be seen and appreciated by your Advocates too. If you have more than one store, perhaps all the stores can do it, and then send all the ideas to one person in charge and that person can make up a complete list. This exercise will get your Advocates noticing, thinking and bonding and giving you ready-made ideas.

Follow these steps to learn how to be calm and confidant, and you will present your thoughts, efforts, and good will:

1. Think about what task you want Advocates to do. Let it be in your conscious thinking, and then tell your subconscious to work on it before sleeping. Then go on to other things.
2. A few days later, start by making lists of what you are thinking about or want to know more about. Find your answers to your questions.
3. Make an appointment on your calendar for project and needed quiet time.
4. Use your appointed time alone, so you can think properly, read your notes, and make your decision
5. As you decide, practice saying your idea aloud.
6. Meet with Advocates. Be prepared to be flexible.
7. Make final decision.

Work at and be creative in what you do to keep your best people. Remember what is said about the spoon; "A spoonful of sugar makes the medicine go down!"

Another fun idea is to use your iPhone and take quick pictures of each Advocate, and your holiday helpers, too. Make quick fun posters and place them in various places, such as the lunch area or stock room. Certain ones with big smiles will remind them of our special team and should be the last thing they see before going out to assist customers. Have the posters say something meaningful—perhaps what you are emphasizing, especially for a set group of days or a weekend. Change the wording and photos often—keep them fresh, fun and new. Use computer paper, have fun!

Chapter 19
Make it lively...Make it cheerful...
Make it exciting...Use LED lighting!

For 25 years in my Malley School of Merchandising, I taught attendees what they needed to know to make their stores and products inviting and enticing. Among its most important lessons for attendees was that if you are going to spend anything on your store, make it be lighting improvement! First, it's a smart investment because it offers the biggest returns. And lighting is crucial to understand because it affects not just your product, but everything that supports it—such as how you, your Advocates, and your store comes across to your customers.

Lackluster lighting affects your complexions, color of your clothes, and a dimmed twinkle in your eye, in general a flat-appearing store presentation. All this blandness because of tried and true lighting in your store and not understanding what you are missing. I know that lumens, diodes, mercury, and all sorts of numbers seem like another language, but you must work with a lighting specialist to be very cost effective and achieve a real thrill in your new or remodeled store. There is no way around it, you must check that your lighting decisions are founded on knowledge and expertise. Make sure the people you choose to work with have the knowledge you need. Everyone is so busy, and everything is improving so fast, it is hard to keep up, so check!

The most memorable comment made to me was from a company Owner who had taken my course, then gone home and changed out their store's lighting. He called me and said, "I can't believe it! My store looks great. We knocked ourselves out making nice-looking displays but were never satisfied with how the store looked—it always appeared flat. Now, with these new lights, the store looks terrific!" At the time, he switched to color improved fluorescent lights that made people and merchandise look more appealing, and he added halogen accent lighting which made the displays visually more interesting. Atmosphere blossomed in his store and transformed a flat discount store look into an upscale retail appearance. The correct kind of lighting for my attendee's store came alive for him! Lighting should be a major line item in your budget if you are building, renovating, or revamping, and various LEDs are the smartest choice you can assemble.

It was Thomas Edison and his invention of the first practical incandescent light bulb that gave rise to a new electric lighting industry—and the General Electric Company. Since that time, the lighting industry has transitioned itself over and over by offering exciting new products to an ever-hungry business and home audience. Retail stores and the various options for lighting them have also continued to evolve. By now, most of us have heard of LED lighting. For your own knowledge, read about how it can help you be business smart. What you do with the information may change the way you are planning your first store or next store because they are now mainstream, will always perform for you, and in three years or less recoup your investment.

LED stands for Light-Emitting-Diode. LED lighting is solid state lighting—no filaments, no tubes with mercury and fill gas similar to our television sets which no longer have picture tubes. When this diode or semiconductor device is energized, light is produced. High quality white light typically requires the addition of a chemical phosphor coating. Some kind of electronics (a power supply or driver) is needed to operate these LEDs. The result is a wide variety of durable, user-friendly lighting solutions for all kinds of applications with very high energy efficiency and very long life. Lucky us.

Why are LEDs taking over the lighting world? Here are some of the important performance features and benefits:

High-energy efficiency: At least five times more efficient than conventional filament lamps like incandescent or halogen; even more efficient than many fluorescent tubes. This increased energy efficiency is reflected in lower electric bills, and therefore, lower operating costs.

Very long life: How long? It depends on the type. Typically, 25,000 hours for screw-in replacement bulbs to 50,000 hours or more for LED fixtures. An LED fixture with a life of 50,000 hours operating 24/7 should be good for almost 6 years. For many typical retail hours of operations, life expectancy should be more like 10+ years. Longer life means reduced maintenance costs and reduced chance of unsightly burned out bulbs. (It should be noted that the life of LEDs is based on reduction in light output vs. actual failure.)

Less heat: Higher efficiency means lower power consumption (lower watts). And lower watts mean less heat that needs to be handled by air conditioning in a space which reduces the electric bill. LEDs have no radiated heat in the light output which is easier on displays that are more heat sensitive (go, show off the Easter Bunnies' whiskers) and on customers who won't feel the heat either!

No mercury: No strict need to recycle because of mercury content (e.g. in contrast to fluorescent tubes).

Very good to excellent color: Makes people and things look natural and normal. Warm to cool color tones are available depending on the application.

In summary, LED lighting should be a consideration whether you're looking for long-term savings and ROI, design pop, a move toward more green business practice, or a less-burdened maintenance staff. They provide more flexibility with color and creativity.

Historically, we've talked about the 3 A's of retail lighting: Attraction, Appraisal and Atmosphere. Lighting attracts customers to the store and guides them throughout the store. Lighting allows for effective evaluation of merchandise. Lighting enhances the store's brand and image and enhances the customer experience. It's through lighting design that these 3 A's are achieved - Lighting Design Strategies with LEDs.

One of the most useful starting points with lighting design in retail is to think in terms of "layers of light." In a typical store, general lighting establishes the basic light level and allows for navigation within the space. This layer can be provided by recessed downlights or "troffers" (square or rectangular fixtures), or suspended fixtures throughout the store area. Perimeter lighting along the walls can include recessed wall-washers or wall slots, or track fixtures that wash vertical surfaces with light to visually expand the space and create a pleasing ambience. A third layer is accent lighting—more focused beams of light that are recessed in the ceiling or hung from tracks that bring attention to displays and provide visual interest. Task lighting is an additional layer of light that can be added for more detailed visual tasks – e.g. for reading receipts or merchandise tags.

If your current general lighting is provided by troffers, they probably contain fluorescent lighting. There are LED tubes that will fit into these fixtures (please check with the requirements of the manufacturer). There is a wide variety of LED general lighting fixtures that will provide the best operating performance. If new LED lighting fixtures are not in the budget, an LED lighting retrofit kit will update the look of the fixture while providing the benefit of LEDs. Similarly, if general lighting is provided by downlights, they probably contain some kind of incandescent or halogen light. You can purchase LED replacement lamps that will fit right into that same fixture and reap the benefits of energy savings and longer life. But consider a retrofit kit that can be inserted right into the fixture, updating the trim and modernizing the look of the fixture. If budget permits, new LED downlights will open design options and optimize performance.

Existing stores may not have lighting fixtures in place to wash walls with light, so new LED wall-washers or LED flood light bulbs (note: bulb packaging will indicate PAR, BR or R which are the bulb shapes and "flood" indicates the spread of light) installed in track lighting can do the trick.

Accent lighting has traditionally featured various kinds of halogen reflectorized bulbs in narrow floods, spots, narrow spots, etc. A wide variety of LED replacements are available that will save more than 80 percent in electricity and last up to 10 times longer. The key to accent lighting is to provide at least three times more light on key merchandise than the surrounding general lighting level. The eye is attracted to the more brightly illuminated displays in the space. And don't forget store window displays that provide great marketing opportunities by attracting customers to the store right up front. Consider more dramatic accent lighting and perhaps even some creative use of colored light.

To set the right mood and atmosphere, decorative lighting fixtures are often added to the lighting scheme. Chandeliers, pendants, and wall sconces can make a real design statement. These fixtures can include integral LED sources, or be fitted with LED bulbs. There are traditional-style LED bulbs which give the aesthetic of a classic incandescent with the energy efficiency of modern LEDs.

One final lighting layer to consider is one we'll call architectural lighting. So think of coves, backlights, or the highlighting of interesting contours and edges within the space that will reveal the architectural details and add to the ambience.

What about lighting controls?

LEDs are very controllable. They can be dimmed and turned off and on without warm-up time. Why use lighting controls? They may be a requirement in building energy codes for new construction or remodels in your location. Aside from that, there are good reasons for lighting controls: shutting off or reducing lighting that's not needed saves energy. For example, separate switching of accent lighting and general lighting allows you to shut off unnecessary accent lighting during cleaning or maintenance activities. If you have a dimming system, you have the option of reducing light levels depending on the time of day. Note that the dimming system must be compatible with the LED solutions in place, so check with the lighting and dimming manufacturer to ensure compatibility.

Some general considerations:
- When considering LED lighting solutions, buy from valued sources. The lowest cost product probably isn't the best.
- Look for Energy Star® certified LED lighting solutions or DLC certification for fixtures – these products meeting strict quality and efficiency standard as tested by accredited labs.
- LEDs come in various color tones from warm tones to cooler tones, characterized by color temperature expressed as 3000 K, 3500 K, 4000 K, etc. The higher the number, the "cooler" the white light appears. Incandescent light bulbs, for example, are typically about 2700 K., Halogen is about 2900 K or 3000 K. The "right" color temperature depends on many factors, including location, application, and personal preference. 3500 K has often been called a "safe" choice when in doubt. Another metric, CRI – "Color Rendering Index" – is an indicator of how natural and normal people and things appear. It should be 80 or higher.

Make it lively...Make it cheerful...Make it exciting...Use LED lighting

- Don't change out a couple of lighting fixtures or bulbs at a time. To achieve a consistent, updated look right away, and to reap your energy saving benefits sooner, change out all the lighting layers to your selected LED solutions.
- Building codes are changing due to more stringent lighting controls and efficiency requirements. Be sure to check with City Hall.

Get busy – Decisions and Action Requirements

Here are three steps you can take today to address the lighting and ambiance of your operations:

Google it! Surf the Internet to see and learn about what you are about to invest in out of your new store or remodeling budget.

Go to stores, especially those known to be well maintained or new. Study their lighting. Sketch what you see. Notice their "layers of lighting" as mentioned above. If one display particularly catches your eye, be sure to sketch what you see as you may want to imitate the same set-up.

Hiring a lighting designer or lighting engineer. This will typically yield optimum results; they are experts in their field. This choice is especially recommended if you plan on multiple stores and your purchase will be substantial. For simpler plans, a manufacturer or lighting distributor may have trained personnel on staff who have experience with lighting layouts and can offer design assistance.

Tell them what your plans are (in a nutshell) and ask if they have a lighting designer or engineer in their group. If so, after discussing what you want to do:

    a. Ask if they have photos of some of the lighting responsibilities and other lighting functions, designs, choice of LEDs or situations they have photos of for their installations.
    b. What other types of help have they been able to assist customers with to keep in budget?
    c. Ask what kind of credentials they have. At the very least they should have credentials like LC (Lighting Certified) offered in the lighting industry, which establishes some baseline level of lighting knowledge.
    d. Show your collection of drawings and/or photos and tell why

you found them interesting.

e. Discuss the advantages of LEDs when working with foodstuffs, especially chocolate shops and bakeries (if this is your business interest).

f. Ask how they charge for this kind of help.

g. Before visiting with this lighting concern, speak to whomever is drawing your blueprints. Ask if it makes any difference to them if you buy your lighting needs from another source. If you're moving into a space already wired for light, ask if this person would check the wires and anything else you might need to know.

h. Will this person be available on site when the lighting is being installed?

i. Once complete will they come and maybe tweak it so it's perfect for your space?

j. Ask if you were to purchase all your lighting needs from them does this action warrant a special price break?

LED lighting is a silent steady worker. It's the greatest salesman around. It doesn't need to take a break or have lunch. It just wants to work. Vibration won't make it dance off its spot, but like a continuous tick tock of the clock, it performs every second of every day and night reducing cost while prompting colors to show their true strength. It shows off in a big way drawing out textures and highlighting items, energy, sparkle, and oomph. When it gets exhausted, it doesn't go to bed and leave a dark hole among all the other lights but only dims and stays with the party.

Don't base your lighting decisions strictly on energy and maintenance savings. There is no substitute for an atmosphere conducive to the retail selling presentation and buying process! Using more energy efficient and longer life LED lighting solutions will certainly reduce operating costs. But rather than only calculating return on investment or payback for better lighting (that may not even matter that much if you are renting a space and not paying directly for electricity), think about the possible impact on sales if your store has better lighting.

Let's say you have a 1500 square foot store in a moderately priced neighborhood. It's in a small Cleveland shopping mall with parking close to your front door. The typical sales for a well operated store in this area per square foot is about $350 each year That means total sales for the store would be $525,000 per year. What if better lighting could increase sales by 5 percent? That would mean a net sales

Make it lively...Make it cheerful...Make it exciting...Use LED lighting

increase of $26,250 and total sales of $551,250. Of course, this figure is before EBITDA and other responsibilities that must be paid. That $26,250.00 would more than pay for a good lighting upgrade, and it will continue to pay off year after year!

How about LED's new friend, Walmart? They chose GE to put in 1.5 million LED fixtures in 6,000 stores saving them $100 million dollars. Wow! Oh, wow! What an exciting technology! What an improvement for color, value, and clarity. What a savings magnet!

Make it lively...Make it cheerful...Make it exciting...Use LED lighting

Chapter 20
Plans and Opportunities: Thinking about the future

Do you have the guts and stamina to let go of the safety of the known and prepare for and embrace the new?

My husband Bill acquired his chocolate experience and knowledge from the time he was a child "helping" and then through all his years of education and war service, before entering full time employment at Malley's Chocolates and Ice Cream Concoctions. Since we both grew up in family businesses, the transition for Bill and me was uneventful. During the years our six children were quite young, I worked part-time with him and then together we worked full time as we continued to help build a business his parents created in 1935. Forty-five years later, I retired as Bill had six years earlier.

When Bill and I were young, the decision was made that we would retire when we came to our 66th birthday. We felt we were ready to lead when we were in our 40s and figured our children would feel the same. We knew if we did not make a pact to retire at our 66th birthday, we would probably never leave. Who wants to leave what they love? It is only right and fair for the company's success to give the reins to new, fresh, energetic minds that were raised with our values. Didn't you think you were ready to take the wheel of your family business when you were in your 40s? Did you start your own business? Don't you think your family's young adults are thinking about "driving" now?

As our children acquired their educations, they worked in most facets of our company from soda jerking to waiting tables to managing our soda fountains, cooking in our kitchen, double-checking our subcontractors to being the contact person for a new store, developing the web, IT, and manufacturing scheduling until we—and they—felt that they were in the best roles for their strengths and interests. We also hired an adult Malley sibling who had worked outside the company for 20 to 25 years. The four boys were all involved with membership on various Community Boards, giving speeches about the company or personal knowledge of interest, and were members of various business groups.

The fifth child, our daughter, was transferred to California by a large insurance company to set up offices to receive IT challenges from western states. She corrected problems of IT concerns in three states and in Hawaii. She had graduated cum laude from college and continued schooling in California. She returned to Cleveland and applied for the position of IT challenges and setting up new technical programs for the company. Our Controller said she far outclassed any other respondents and asked to hire her. While working at Malley's, she secured her Master of Business degree from Case Western Reserve University. Our oldest son and newest member was an editor of various professional magazines such as Crain's Business, was a founder of another specialized magazine, and was the only editor given a sales force and editorship of a business magazine. He received a letter from the New York chairman of the company calling him a "Renaissance man bringing both his magazine and sales force to the number one position in the company." He also was the advertising editor for a daily business newspaper. He had traveled overseas representing his company and had budget control amounting to well over many millions of dollars.

All the six children grew up enjoying the business. They had fun and the work of it too. When they were younger, they were often invited to go to one of the fountain stores with their friends while Bill checked out the registers. This arrangement was always fun because the fountain stores did not close until 11 or 12.

They helped open new stores; they were interested all the way. We never allowed them to get bored with what they were doing when very young and older. Their visits were short. As they grew older, they kept their interest in the business, and after "learning the ropes" they were assigned responsible positions such as fountain Manager which they performed to our liking, cut the grass, and generally anything we asked of them. During a 16th birthday celebration for Megan, the youngest, she excused herself and came back in the dining room dressed in the store uniform, and said, "Well, I'm ready!"

As they were growing up and through their college years, they all worked for other businesses. When they did join us, they experienced working or leading various departments such as store Manager or kitchen helper then Manager, outside sales, and marketing. One daughter was a summer intern beneath our store decorator, another worked in the administration offices. Both were waitresses, and held various positions in production, administration, outside sales, etc. Four of the six children attended my School of Merchandising.

What I learned as we traveled the roads to retirement, I offer for your review. Now, in 2022, our six children are in their 40's, 50's, and 60's. They had complete control 20 years earlier.

Depending on your company's size, type, and duration of young adults' tenure with your company:
- some of the following will apply;
- some will already have been accomplished; and
- some you will feel aren't necessary to think about or choose to do.

I advise anyone thinking about retirement or creating a Board of Advisors or even working on a project to think about football practice in the NFL that happens every summer. The professional football players practice over and over the basic paces and phases of the game. The coaches and Owners know it's all in the perfection of the details. Keep this idea in mind. Watch the details and never consider yourself too big to perform due diligence. Why wasn't that something Walt Disney believed – "It's all in the details"?

Just as sure as you are that night follows the day, anyone over 60 years of age should be just as sure your retirement is coming too. It's hard to think the time has arrived. Should you retire or not? Here are some thoughts to help you decide how effective a Leader you are.
- Is your company getting too big to get your arms around?
- Are you keeping up with what can help your company save labor, dollars and frustration? What are you doing about it?

- Do you have a budget for Technology advances that will be a godsend for your company?
- Are you aware of advancements of perhaps cost-cutting making a coveted machine less expensive? But do you need it? Look at your present consideration through a new paradigm. Some questions might be, when was the last time you coordinated your "must-have" with your Strategic Plan and your Business Plan? Are you aware that you can have identical or upgraded quality at a lower cost by outsourcing certain supplies? You can realize a lower (overall) cost in purchasing, labor, maintenance, less machinery, less banking "partnerships," finished product always available when needed, and less frustration? Give careful thought to your overall best use of funds. Customer care improvements? Remodeling and employee education to bring a lagging store to its former health? Give the people you hired because of expected possibilities customer care education to develop sales. If you haven't yet, change overall lighting in an "average" size store that guarantees a return on your investment in three years. Create your future, plan to step aside, give younger helpers the chance to prove themselves. Introduce a freshness or introduce a change that they need in your company. Be young in spirit and thought. Remember how you were at their age. Make what you have solid, bond with your people, give fair pay, initiate Casual Conversations with your employees, tell them what you are thinking and what are their concerns? Do this immediately before they plan to "run away with the spoon." (Mother Goose, 1648) Prepare your store(s) and business to be first-class in all ways, and retire with your head held high.
- Are you creating packaging in-house?
- Do you know today's business jargon?
- Are you telling your vendors what information you want them to supply to you? Are you making them work with you getting information from exhibitions, seminars, certain contacts, etc.?
- Are your people using Smartphones and tablets?
- Are you flexible in keeping your company in the foreground of sound business practices that meet today's opportunities?
- Are you holding your business back from remarkable advances due to your lack of knowledge of what modernity is available today?
- Do you understand cloud computing?

- How have you improved your method of taking inventory?
- Are you using Dashboards to help yourself and inspire your helpers?
- Are you continuing to educate your workforce so they can produce best results?
- Do you know the new government regulations concerning food labeling regulations, food inspection? And what about regulations being released by the Department of Labor?
- When was the last time you enrolled in a seminar? What did you do with the information afterwards?
- Are you working within the new "regulations" of your company?
- There are new food labeling regulations, health reforms, and insurance. The aforementioned Department of Labor uses reams of paper for their new ideas.
- If this applies: Are you keeping your adult children tethered to your way of guiding your business or are they free, after discussion with you, to introduce or change things they need in your company? Or for themselves?

Are you getting grouchy? You may look at this list and say to yourself, "I can hire out for all that information."

Wrong!

There is nothing to replace understanding the needs of today's marketplace, let alone the wants of your employees and their absolute needs to work more efficiently. Need flows through the company. Are you answering them?

Chapter 21
Retirement Preparation

Transition and the date of your retirement will be one of your biggest decisions. This plan must not be made on the corner of a napkin but slowly, thoroughly, and with professionals all along the route. It is a thought-provoking exercise. The considerations will sometimes be difficult and easily put off. However, now is the time to surround yourself with professional people who can guide you with their experience and knowledge of helping other families or to sell your company. It will be expensive, but nothing is more costly to you than not doing it right. You should work on the process at least five years ahead of when you'd like to retire. You will definitely need to make your retirement thoughts known to certain professionals and spouse. You will tell your family when your plans are more solidified. Other items you'll need to address include the following:

- **Audit your company.** Know its strengths and needs. Plan to correct what "needs" you are able and when your improvements are completed, then chart the increase in your company's value.
- If you are a corporation, **talk with your accountant/Controller**

about passing or selling the stock over a period of years in order to not get excessive taxes due in one year.
- Secure **an experienced transition attorney**.
- **Board of Advisors** (If you haven't created a Board, read a quick synopsis about how to set one up for your company at the end of this article. Do this promptly. See elsewhere in these pages "How to Acquire a Board of Advisors.")
- Discuss your children with your Board. Decide if anyone of them should get more education assuming they already have college degrees. If not, perhaps they need further education in mechanics, art, or computers. Decide if certain ones should join organizations dedicated to their strengths. Decide if working with community or philanthropic groups would be beneficial.
- Explain your retirement thoughts to your **accounting firm or your CPA consultants**.
- Consult a **financial planner** (We used two gentleman who had proven themselves to us and other valued people as our planners.)
  1. This advisor should be involved throughout every phase, working with only your interests in mind. Always look to safeguard your finances against any future surprising occurrences.
  2. Consult another **Advisor who should be working for the benefit of the next generation**.
- Make sure each professional knows of the others and what they will be doing. Write out your plan of action. Discuss it with your Board for confirmation. Perhaps the financial planner can wear two hats—one for you and one for the next generation.
- Remember to announce your plans as well as the anticipated date of retirement to your children. If not a family business, then to your company. If you have a spouse, you will have confided with him/her long before now.

To make a list, seek out professional guidance and then create your plan for retirement.
- Discuss amount of funds you and your spouse will need to meet your future needs and wants. You should both agree on its content for both of your future needs, wants, and security.
- Study any further available fund resources for you after you retire.

Remember, personal decisions are just as important as your business ideas. Your to-do list should include:
- Plan for your post-transfer and what you will do. Start making in-roads so when the time arrives, you do not feel as a ship without a rudder. Don't read this lightly. Start now deciding and getting involved with what you will do after you retire from your business. I did not say "life"; I said "business"!
- Remember throughout you are setting the example for how to transition from your business to a more private life. Keep notes to pass on.
- Long before you plan to meet your departure date your young educated adult[s] should be comfortable with leading and operating your business.

You can now, with the assistance of your advisors, decide how you are going to transition the next generation into the leadership role or roles in the case of more siblings. Here are some other things to consider:
- Discuss and agree how your Board of Advisors should go about interviewing the next generation. Direct your Board to develop meaningful work assignments that will highlight their strengths and weaknesses. This work will be answerable to your Board.
- Ask your Board for candid opinions of each of your children's readiness with no input from you. Is more education needed?
- Do you need to consider an interim company Leader until business maturity levels are reached?
- Discuss and agree on the timing of transitioning actual ownership of the company to the next generation. Should it be immediate or over a transition period? We discussed and agreed on the timing of our transitioning to the next generation. We also decided on a transition period of three years.
- If you haven't before this time, ask your Board for their opinions about how you operate your company and how you could better prepare the next generation to operate the company. Take copious notes, and act on their advice, or don't waste their and your time!
- Unless already addressed, to simply and quickly read the above bullet points, you are placing your business at great risk of failure. In your retirement, to see your once thriving company faltering, excellent workers leaving, and witness the final day of

bankruptcy is so humbling and sad, especially so because you did not leave your business in capable hands, and you know it was your responsibility. Don't allow this to happen to you. Practice "Tough Love" on yourself and your adult children or decide to sell it.

At this point, you start speaking to the rest of your family.
- Tell of your plans and desired departure date.
- Discuss your strategies that you have decided that need to be considered before you are able to retire.
- Tell them of the comfort and knowledge you have that they have your business (in our case, chocolate) flowing through their veins and perhaps love the business as much as you. For this reason alone, you are sure they want the best leadership possible.
- **To create new leadership with very capable hands and clear flexible minds:**

    You must be convinced that they understand the business and know how to lead, create the vision and understand the complete workings of your business and how to reach the vision goal.

    Each are comfortable with and understand the work needed for proper accounting.

    Ask them to write why they want to stay with the company, ideas on how it would be possible to improve and grow the part of the business they are involved with, and what they are willing to do to see that their ideas can happen. This point can include a more extensive range if there have been ongoing in-depth discussions, all have been party to, about the entire business. Each should have and be able to use basic financial statements in their repertoire. Include how you will interface and work with family members and what you are willing to do if difficulties arise. State how you will learn to be more beneficial to the company. State how you see yourself interfacing with each member of Administration and family members.

    Tell the next generation you will be asking the Board of Advisors to work with them. Tell them they may not agree with what the Board wants done, but they are to do everything the Board requests. The Board will want the metrics they set with the next generation met and your reports on time. How you handle the work given to you will tell the Board a great deal about you. It's up to you. As the young adults go through this process, they may decide that they prefer not to lead the whole company but to stay and work in a favorite part of the company. This revelation may come as this work progresses. Tell them this work may help them decide what they really want to do for their life's career. Include how you will interface and work with family members and what you are willing to do if difficulties arise. State how you will learn to be more useful to the company. State how you see yourself interfacing with each member of Administration and family members.

The young adults should be invited as guests to various Board meetings to see firsthand how your Board operates and decisions are made.

Have the young adult(s) meet with your Board without your presence at various times so they can have "down to earth" conversations without parent observation.

Realize if your children have married that their spouse may be coming to the table with completely different set of learned facts about what work is. They may have had parents who worked 9-to-5 jobs with set vacations and sick days. For family harmony, it is important that the spouse is brought in to a meeting to enlighten them on what will be the continued life style and only more so with more responsibility, the long hours, the emergency's, family meetings, the dedication, the hard decisions that will need to be made, what will be needed to continue for the business to grow and be successful. Mention perks they have now. Suggest the future is full of promise, but the decision is up to them. Absolutely do not make any promises or even hint at possibilities. You won't be there to fill them! Suggest they each discuss this opportunity with their spouse and decide for themselves to promise support. At our meeting, we spoke about the spouse being able to work in the business, what to do if a divorce occurred, should a child be able to work full time in the business, and other interesting decisions they would have to make. We had a facilitator head this meeting who was experienced helping other families make the transition. This professional could answer any question or tell someone they were not correct in their thinking. It was very helpful.

The next step is to meet with your Board of Advisors privately. Have the Board make up a list of comments about not only the business but their personal views of each family member and what goals the individuals have set for themselves. Find out if the next generation's values are the same as your core values. Direct your Board to give each individual, an obligation to fulfill with a set time to complete the work. Make it understood they will be answerable to the Board. Have your Board decide if the next generation will work well with each other and how best to use each strength. Make sure everyone gets all the financial data and has total access for a discussion with you or anyone on the Board. The Board can tell them they will be working in each department (if they haven't already) for an appropriate length of time to understand what work is accomplished there and how it is tackled. Make sure the next generation knows they are there to learn from each department Leader, that departments responsibilities; should there be any changes for efficiencies? What is their usual daily output? Their system of fulfilling requests; is supply and demand smooth? What are the difficulties? Are there any department needs? Is there good organization? Do they have the "tools" to do the job? What does the Leader think of their department, work, and happiness? How should the company address them? The young adult (s) are answerable to the Board. Have your Board decide if the next generation will work well with each other or what to do about it.

Discuss with your banker how best they can help in this transition process. Then make sure young adult(s) meet your banking people and become very acquainted with them. Have them discuss any loans and when they are due; explain what to have in order before they ask for a loan (and be able to defend their figures). Go over everything you do or keep in contact with at your bank(s). If they already have this experience, make sure they are very comfortable about speaking with them. See that they understand what financial covenants (goals) the company must meet each quarter and year to remain in compliance with any loan agreements.

In administration, be certain (if needed) they devote an appropriate amount of time to be shown the work of the department. Also spend fruitful time with your accounting firm. Make sure they can read a Profit and Loss (P&L) sheet and understand what the numbers are telling them. What should they do with the information gleaned from the P & L? Make sure the accounting Firm explains the importance of reducing fixed costs, trying to create new ways of business to cut variable driven numbers, and finding best margins and increasing them.

Have them attend all business meetings you deem worthwhile and make appropriate introductions. Have them choose a community organization of a subject or sport they are interested in. Perhaps get them or arrange for them to be on a Board.

If you have more than one young adult taking the responsibility to help operate the company, consider hiring a coach to teach family members how to "speak business."

Discuss with all professionals who the new or next president will be. Make sure your spouse (if not already agreeing with you) understands and hopefully can come to agree with your choice. This person is very important to be on board with the decision. If you don't agree, perhaps a meeting with your Board of professional people will convince the spouse why the chosen one is able to help the company best, so it can continue in good stead. List the qualifications met. Discuss thoroughly why the decision was made. Be prepared to answer any questions. Aim for understanding, co-operation, and peace in the family.

This is not the time to give up the driver's wheel. Remind yourself of Stephen Covey's Seven Habits. Especially address, "Begin with the end in mind." Do not allow emotion or the loudest "noise" take over driving your decision. Do not retire with battles yet to be fought. There is always a way to achieve your goal. It is your business and do what you must to keep it on a steady course for stability and growth. There are ways to achieve independence for your company. It must have a seat at the decision-making table. Keep yourself open-minded, fair to all and imaginative. Reread your plan and goals for retirement. Listen to ideas and suggestions from your Board, or trusted chosen others, and be flexible. Now is the time for proactive Tough Love. Change is difficult for everyone, especially at this time. Emotions can become the driver. Decide for yourself what you want.

1) A business that continues to thrive?
2) A business that continues to thrive with a family feeling atmosphere?
3) Give in to the loudest noise and hand that person or group your drivers wheel.

You have invested your adult life with your spouse, guiding a family in right ways. You have also driven your company to what it is today. Determine to keep both close to your vest with the help of professionals along the entire way. Your retirement may proceed quite smoothly and again it may not. It is good to have experienced professionals with you to be able to give right answers that all accept. Remember, there is always a way. You could set your company up now the way you want it after you leave so everyone will be in the right seats on the bus with experience and the transition will be like just another day at work... because you made it that way.

We had facilitators direct meetings that could possibly be stressful. Insurance and financial advisors worked with us who help family owned businesses and could help with family dynamics. Personal relationships within the family can sometimes outdo their desire for a well-run business or accept decisions made about their contributions and not be willing to change. Working with outside advisors with plenty of experience help immeasurably over the sometimes-rough road that you will have to traverse on the journey to a successful transition. All this transition only works if you do.

For various reasons you may decide to hire a person as an interim president (or give that person another title) but make sure this person has a background in operating a business at least slightly larger than your business. A main consideration should be that he/she understands how to transfer thought and information to others while getting compliance on directions given. This person should be on your payroll at least a year to go through all your business cycles. Be sure your young person is willing to work with him/her. You are looking for a person who doesn't impress you so much with what he has accomplished but a successful person who has transitioned others to new responsibility, not just appointed but helped in the transition and followed through. This move can take a load of pressure off you and give you assurances.

With the help of our professionals, Bill and I agreed to the melody of our swan song and retired completely. We were happy with our final decisions. We moved toward being completely retired, where we would have no say or decision-making opportunities, nor would we have the need. I have six bright, take-charge, thoughtful children operating Malley's Chocolates. It continues to grow and prosper. (That's because they have chocolate running in their veins.)

We decided how all the children would gain ownership in the company. We had felt it was very important that only those working in the business would have voting shares. At the time, we felt it was very important in our situation to have a transition ownership in place when we retired, one that fostered collaboration with those in the business to help them work as true partners.

Years before retirement, Bill and I met with our attorneys. It was decided that we would give our adult children stock in the company acting as placeholders until we both retired and then they would be given the actual stock. The meeting was being buttoned up and I asked who is going to get the certificates? I was told they would have some or we could get the certificates at any stationery store.

That did not sit well with me. I was excited about the idea and thought it meant too much to me to have anything to do with our beloved company to just "get something off the shelf". I immediately had a picture in my mind of the ceiling lighting fixtures, people trying out desk chairs, the rows of supplies and the commotion of customers. This just did not go well with the pictures I had in my mind of Malley's Chocolates. I asked if I could design them and was told certainly!

I immediately checked some of our stock certificates from various well-known companies and was left unimpressed. I went to work and decided to make the "placeholder" stock certificates cocoa colored because of us being in the chocolate business. The stock certificates signifying ownership would be in green because that was where the money was going to be. *(See certificate examples on pp 295-296)*

I had an artist draw the Irish braid to be the frame for both sides of the certificates. I was so busy getting them together I never thought about putting in some frames for future Leaders. Grandpa Malley never thought of himself as a Chairman and just referred to himself as a president, if at all. That is why the word president is beneath Dad and Bill's picture. Actually, Bill was referred to as Chairman when I was president. Then when I retired six years after Bill on our promised farewell date, we both became Chairman. I enjoyed doing it.

Here are some additional thoughts about retirement.

Professionals needed to get you to Retirement
- Board of Advisors or a gathering of experienced people with family business ownership
- An experienced transition attorney
- Accounting firm or CPA consultants
- A financial planner—one for yourself and one for the next generation
- Choose one from above list to be a facilitator for certain meetings

Preliminary Jobs to Complete: Remember to start doing this at least five years in advance of Retirement
- Create a Board of Advisors or create a "Special Project" group.
- Audit your company. Fix what you can and change your company's value.

- Measure your children or others like them working in your business for their actual contributions. Consider if they should be given more responsibility or a lateral change or other possibilities to develop their potential and see the company move forward. Don't leave the difficult decisions for the next Leaders.
- Decide when you want to retire and choose a date. Discuss with your spouse.
- Think about your future wants and needs. Discuss with your spouse.

If assembling a Board of Advisors, do it now. Learn how by following directions in this book, Internet information, or get to a Library. Talk to some of your friends who already have them. You will soon see how insignificant the worry over increasing your bottom line, getting better organized, or writing a mission statement are. These are nice wishes, but once you gather a Board of Advisors together you will see and understand how you have wasted valuable time and significant help. Discuss everything about it with your family who are working in your business or other very trusted administrative employees. (At no time should you use the words "we" or "us" giving them the idea they will be on the Board.)

In these conversations, explain why you are making the decisions in your selections. Hopefully, your young family adults will agree on your choices. Try to think out of the box on selections and make sure they have more experience than you do. These people should be expressive, direct, and knowledgeable. Unless you and your spouse work with roughly the same amount of responsibility and see eye to eye or if spouse is in another business setting do not invite the spouse to be on the Board.

This time is your time to "talk" the "talk" or the very basis of your doubts, worries/concerns. Perhaps meetings with your Board will give you that opportunity to instigate discussions you are not prepared to air. Remember it... However, remember you have gathered individuals together to help and support you operating your business. You have on your Board whomever you choose and organize it in whatever why you choose. Every individual has their own opinions, needs, and wants. It is your Board!

When you are ready, create an informative letter to the Board as to how you anticipate their assistance. Bring them up to date on your business and plans.

Among other things to address:
- List post retirement fund possibilities.
- Possible new avenues of interest or work post retirement.
- Write a Strength and Weakness Ben Franklin sheet about each of your children.
- Should an Interim Leader be hired?

From the beginning, keep notes so when it's time to invite your children to hear of your plans, notes will help you present the information with clarity and decisiveness. Decide best way and where to keep your spouse informed and included. The most important idea to remember is that communication is the crux and core of anything successful. You will need your best creative thinking to keep all involved content and, hopefully, happy and together. Involve your spouse, and if you don't agree on a point, ask your Board to discuss how you all came to the decision he/she is questioning. He/she might shed more light on the point which may change your position.

While you're doing these things, remember to protect your marriage by your faith and loyalty. Be the kind of mother or father your children can remember with ease and good feelings. Take some time and discuss just them and their interests and strengths. Make sure they know how much you love them and the aspirations you have for them for the future. Suggest schooling, travel, books you always found helpful or enjoyable and why. Ask them what they wish they could hear from you. Perhaps have them all meet together and you can tell them what you want them to know and to be. Tell them why you love your spouse. Tell them about your relationship with your in-laws and your own parents. Tell them . . . I'll appreciate your efforts at staying together, improving the company by investigating new directions, methods and acknowledging how important our Advocates are to the success of your company. We are all alike, we all want respect, kindness, loyalty and friendship. Each of us is different, as we all know, so always try to look for the good and negotiate your differences. Tell them you love them because . . . and that you trust them to be their best self always. To save problems later be sure to tell the same story to everyone about your history, your ideas for them and the company. Talk about being active in the community and its importance and to donate to favorite causes, after you have them checked out for efficient practices. Talk about how necessary it is for our new Leader to have an opportunity to decide on a different

Board, keep some of those on the Board now, or continue on with the present Board. Discuss being active in your industries association and why that is important. When problems develop, to agree with a sibling or siblings or trusted few that you will not air your grievance outside but to a person chosen by all to be fair to all and to use that person's suggestions. Shake on it because that is what they are sure to remember. Now, retire. Take a planned trip. Revisit your retirement plans. Now, you finally have what you have so desired; time. Use it well. Get involved with associations in your community and consider taking on enjoyable responsibilities. Bill and I became Snowbirds. He liked our Florida situation so much we started celebrating his birthdays at Siesta Key with all the children and grandchildren. We spent lots of enjoyable time at the beach. Bill and I started playing Gin Rummy every night. At first, he just couldn't get the idea in his head, I was going to win as often as he. We had a lot of laughs over that, then it became a highly entertaining and fun competition! What have you planned?

William Michael Malley
President 1967–1997

Albert Martin Malley
President 1935–1967

-19-
Shares

-9-
Number

MALLEY'S CANDIES, INC.

This Certifies that Michael Malley is the owner of Nineteen (19)——————————————————— non-voting fully paid and non-assessable shares without par value of Malley's Candies, Inc. transferable only on the books of the Corporation by the holder hereof in person or by duly authorized Attorney upon surrender of this Certificate properly endorsed.

Witness the seal of the Corporation and the signatures of its duly authorized officers.

Dated December 28, 1995

Adele Ryan Malley, SECRETARY

W. M. Malley, PRESIDENT

The following abbreviations, when used in the inscription on the face of this certificate, shall be construed as though they were written out in full according to applicable laws or regulations:

TEN COM — as tenants in common
TEN ENT — as tenants by the entireties
JT TEN — as joint tenants with right of survivorship and not as tenants in common
UNIF GIFT MIN ACT—_____ Custodian _____
(Cust) (Minor)
under Uniform Gifts to Minors
Act_____
(State)

For value Received_____ hereby sell, assign, and transfer unto

_____
_____

of the Shares represented by the within Certificate and do hereby irrevocably constitute and appoint _____ Attorney to transfer the said Shares on the Books of the within named Company with full power of substitution in the premises.

Dated_____ 19___

Malley's CHOCOLATES

Albert Martin "Mike" Malley founded Malley's Chocolates in 1935. Mike loved people and delighted in pleasing them with his wonderful chocolate and ice cream concoctions. His values and innovativeness built Malley's reputation.

William Michael Malley, Mike's son, is dedicated to preserving the Malley's values as he grows the company. With drive, vision and skill, Bill has expanded on his father's good works with new ideas, stores and marketing.

Surrounding the pictures of Mike and Bill are cacao pods. They represent Chocolate, called Theobroma, Food of the Gods. Fine chocolate is a Malley's hallmark.

The braided border is an ancient Celtic design. Its interlocking web is a symbol of life's rich interweaving of opportunities. The Malley's family is grateful to be able to serve customers, to contribute in the community, and provide a livelihood for those who work with us.

The shamrocks are an ancient symbol of Irish ancestry. St. Patrick used the three lobed leaves of the plant to teach the mystery of how three persons can be in one God.

Adele Ryan Malley

MALLEY'S CANDIES, INC.

William Michael Malley
President 1967-1997

Albert Martin Malley
President 1935-1967

Shares

Number

This Certifies that _____ is the owner of
_____ voting fully paid and non-assessable shares
without par value of
Malley's Candies, Inc.
transferable only on the books of the Corporation by the holder hereof in person or by duly authorized Attorney upon surrender of this Certificate properly endorsed.
Witness the seal of the Corporation and the signatures of its duly authorized officers.
Dated_____

SECRETARY   PRESIDENT

The following abbreviations, when used in the inscription on the face of this certificate, shall be construed as though they were written out in full according to applicable laws or regulations:

TEN COM — as tenants in common
TEN ENT — as tenants by the entireties
JT TEN — as joint tenants with right of survivorship and not as tenants in common
UNIF GIFT MIN ACT — _____ Custodian _____
                        (Cust)   (Minor)
            under Uniform Gifts to Minors
        Act _____
             (State)

For value Received, _____ hereby sell, assign, and transfer unto
PLEASE INSERT SOCIAL SECURITY OR OTHER
IDENTIFYING NUMBER OF ASSIGNEE

_____

of the Shares represented by the within Certificate and do hereby irrevocably constitute and appoint
_____ Attorney
to transfer the said Shares on the Books of the within named Company with full power of substitution in the premises.
Dated_____ 19___

Malley's
CHOCOLATES

Albert Martin "Mike" Malley founded Malley's Chocolates in 1935. Mike loved people and delighted in pleasing them with his wonderful chocolate and ice cream concoctions. His values and innovativeness built Malley's reputation.

William Michael Malley, Mike's son, is dedicated to preserving the Malley's values as he grows the company. With drive, vision and skill, Bill has expanded on his father's good works with new ideas, stores and marketing.

Surrounding the pictures of Mike and Bill are cacao pods. They represent Chocolate, called Theobroma, Food of the Gods. Fine chocolate is a Malley's hallmark.

The braided border is an ancient Celtic design. Its interlocking web is a symbol of life's rich interweaving of opportunities. The Malley's family is grateful to be able to serve customers, to contribute in the community, and provide a livelihood for those who work with us.

The shamrocks are an ancient symbol of Irish ancestry. St. Patrick used the three lobed leaves of the plant to teach the mystery of how three persons can be in one God.

Adele Ryan Malley

Chapter 22
Surprise, Surprise!

I want to give you a little surprise as we are parting company. The following are very important to develop as you choose your next move.

> #1 Check your finances as they stand today, and check them every day. Know your competition's strengths and weaknesses (opportunity?) Study Stephen Covey's Seven Habits; decide how they will influence your actions. Acquire a Mentor.

> #2. Educate and train your revenue producers. Develop them! Your Salespeople are not your Salesmen.

> #3. Stop talking negatively to yourself about yourself. Instead, remind yourself of this significant step you are taking. Remind yourself of all the things you are doing right. Decide on one thing you can do for someone: help with homework, help with the dishes, take a senior citizen for a ride, or donate to a worthy cause.

#4. Try never to say, "When you do this," or You always or Who did this? Instead, ask: What are we doing to do about this? Or "We need to discuss…, or "Joe usually has good reason for doing a thing, so let's wait until he is present to tell us, in the meantime let's fix . . . "?

#5. If you prefer not to follow schedules, take 30 seconds each weekday morning and write down one thing you want to accomplish before you go home. Save the daily notes. At the week's end, look at each of them and determine if you are satisfied with what you could get done or if you want to get more accomplished.

#6. You have approximately 7½ seconds to capture a passerby's attention. People's eyes travel from your sign to your windows. Make your Store sign and your windows do their work and bring customers in your door.

#7. If uncomfortable about a situation, rehearse what you need to or want to say. Speak it out loud. Then, with a pleasant expression upon your face, look the other person in the eye and speak your piece. If appropriate, smile.

#8. Teach Salespeople to say "our store," not "their store., and "what we are doing" rather than what "they are doing." Explain how much more professional they will come across if when referring to anything about the store, to say, "Sorry, "We" are out of caramels," instead of "I'm sorry, they " are out of caramels" or "We" have to make more of those, instead of "They" have to make more of those."

#9. When in your store, let your Salespeople know that you realize they (and you) make up a good group; everyone is trying their best to make the store a place customers want to come back to visit. If you must bring up a negative remark, think before speaking and ask yourself how you can do it diplomatically.

#10. Never go anywhere without your business cards. Print cards with your website and Email addresses in different colors to help the eye focus. Leave space on the front for notes.

Quick, any of the above you want to address? Circle it and do it (them) before you forget. Write the idea(s) on a business card and put it in your pocket. When you come upon it later and haven't acted on it yet, don't criticize yourself, you're trying. Reread the card and get busy. Success is in the doing!

God Bless You.

Adele

Get "Malley Manners" now!

Increase your Customer count today!

After completing "Conversations with Adele," I felt compelled to tell you about our System of educating and training employees to become Advocates to help us reach our goals. **Malley Manners** is the place to start for success.

Malley Manners is an Education and Training System that prepares a new hire to be an Advocate, grasp your company values, understand, and be motivated to give the finest of services for their customer's delight. It has been continually used for over 45 years,

Now, you can establish Malley Manners in your company. It works this way:

1. Detailed instructions are all enclosed with the System.

2. Each new hire will receive your company Orientation.

3. Preplanning, Planning, Presentation, and Follow-up is a 45-year-old proven system. Every new hire will receive the same information, and the Retention Review will spot any employee needing retail attention.

4. Acquire the information by tapping on your computer at **www.Malleys.com**. Then, Adele Malley, for further details.

I put the entire "Malley Manners System" in a PDF so information, posters, and more can be quickly and easily copied.

There is so much more to Retail than saying and doing: "Welcome, (smile), get what the person asks for, will there be anything else? (Smile) Good-bye (Smile)."

Increase your Retail awareness!
Find out all about it right now at
www.Malleys.com